Living Waters from Ancient Springs

Permissions

Scripture quotations marked (NIV) are taken from the Holy Bible, New International Version®, NIV®. Copyright © 1973, 1978, 1984 by Biblica, Inc.™ Used by permission of Zondervan. All rights reserved worldwide. www.zondervan.com

Scripture quotations marked (NASB) are taken from the New American Standard Bible®, Copyright © 1960, 1962, 1963, 1968, 1971, 1972, 1973, 1975, 1977, 1995 by The Lockman Foundation. Used by permission. www.lockman.org

Scripture quotations marked (ESV) are from The Holy Bible, English Standard Version® (ESV®), copyright © 2001 by Crossway, a publishing ministry of Good News Publishers. Used by permission. All rights reserved.

Scripture quotations marked (NRSV) are from the New Revised Standard Version Bible, copyright © 1989, Division of Christian Education of the National Council of the Churches of Christ in the United States of America. Used by permission. All rights reserved.

Scripture quotations marked (NKJV™) are taken from the New King James Version®. Copyright © 1982 by Thomas Nelson, Inc. Used by permission. All rights reserved.

Scripture quotations marked (NJPS) are from Tanakh: The Holy Scriptures: The New JPS Translation to the Traditional Hebrew Text, © 1985 by The Jewish Publication Society, with the permission of the publisher.

Contents

List of Contributors • ix
Preface • xi
Abbreviations • xviii

PART ONE: Old and New Testament

1. The Book of the Covenant and Elders
   —*R. Dean Anderson* • 1
2. How Will God Deal with Children of Parents Who Have Committed Idolatry?—*Wolter Rose* • 13
3. The Sinaitic Covenant in the Narrative of the Book of Exodus—*Gert Kwakkel* • 27
4. The Church Fathers' Spiritual Interpretation of the Psalms
   —*Hans Boersma* • 41
5. Social Injustice and the Existence of God: A Commentary on the Old Greek Text of Psalm 57—*Jannes Smith* • 57
6. Call Me Father! The Grief and Desire of a Loving Father
   —*S. Carl Van Dam* • 77
7. Wordplay and History in Daniel 5—*Al Wolters* • 90
8. The Epistle of James: Justification or Sanctification?
   —*Gerhard H. Visscher* • 102
9. The Lamb's Scroll of Life in Revelation 5
   —*Jakob Geertsema* • 117

PART TWO: Doctrine, Office, and Mission

10 Bavinck on Creation—*James Visscher* • 135

11 Specious Pacification and Pleasant Consensus: Calvin's Ecumenical Efforts in 1549—*Jason Van Vliet* • 152

12 Wellsprings of the Offices—*Roelf C. Janssen* • 169

13 The Old Testament, Ethics, and Preaching: Letting Confessional Light Dispel a Hermeneutical Shadow —*Nelson D. Kloosterman* • 185

14 Our Missional God: Redemptive-Historical Preaching and the *Missio Dei*—*Willem A. VanGemeren* • 198

15 Foreign Mission by the Local Church—*Arjan de Visser* • 220

Bibliography: Publications by Cornelis Van Dam • 235
Scripture Index • 253
Subject Index • 255

Contributors

R. Dean Anderson is Minister of the Word, Reformed Churches in the Netherlands, Katwijk, the Netherlands.

Hans Boersma is the James I. Packer Professor of Theology, Regent College, Vancouver, BC, Canada.

Arjan de Visser is Professor of Diaconiology and Church History, Canadian Reformed Theological Seminary, Hamilton, ON, Canada.

Jakob Geertsema is Professor Emeritus of New Testament, Canadian Reformed Theological Seminary, Hamilton, ON, Canada.

Roelf C. Janssen is Minister of the Word, Canadian Reformed Churches, Abbotsford, BC, Canada.

Nelson D. Kloosterman is Executive Director and Ethics Consultant, Worldview Resources International, St. John, IN, USA.

Gert Kwakkel is Professor of Old Testament, Theological University of the Reformed Churches in the Netherlands, Kampen, the Netherlands.

Wolter Rose is Senior Lecturer in Semitic Languages and Cultures, Theological University of the Reformed Churches in the Netherlands, Kampen, the Netherlands.

Jannes Smith is Professor of Old Testament, Canadian Reformed Theological Seminary, Hamilton, ON, Canada.

S. Carl Van Dam is Minister of the Word, Canadian Reformed Churches, Grassie, ON, Canada.

Willem A. Van Gemeren is Professor of Old Testament and Semitic Languages, Trinity Evangelical Divinity School, Deerfield, IL, USA.

Jason Van Vliet is Professor of Dogmatics, Canadian Reformed Theological Seminary, Hamilton, ON, Canada.

Gerhard H. Visscher is Professor of New Testament, Canadian Reformed Theological Seminary, Hamilton, ON, Canada.

James Visscher is Minister of the Word, Canadian Reformed Churches, Langley, BC, Canada.

Al Wolters is Professor Emeritus of Religion and Theology & of Classical Languages, Redeemer University College, Ancaster, ON, Canada.

Preface

On the seventh day of April 1946, Schalk and Jenny Van Dam were blessed with the birth of their second child, a son, whom they named Cornelis. Over time, the number of children in the family grew from two to seven. To be sure, there were many mouths to feed, but, looking at it from another angle, there were also many hands to do the work. And work they did! The Van Dam family had a vegetable farm near Burlington, Ontario, close to Toronto. The entire family pitched in, supplying local markets with fresh produce.

Soon enough the eldest son in the Van Dam family grew to be a young man, and his heavenly Father worked a desire in his heart to become a minister of God's Word, the gospel of salvation. After finishing high school, Cornelis, or Keith as he became known, went on to Wilfrid Laurier University in Waterloo, Ontario. In 1968, he graduated with a Bachelor of Arts degree. That degree, though, was only a stepping stone toward his goal of attending seminary. He began his theological training at Westminster Theological Seminary in Philadelphia, Pennsylvania. However, he soon switched to the newly founded Theological College of the Canadian Reformed Churches in Hamilton, Ontario. It was in this federation of churches that his family worshiped, and it was in this federation that he wanted to serve as pastor. As with any institution in its infancy, the Theological College started in humble facilities and with a small faculty. Still, the Lord blessed that education, and in 1971 he graduated with a Bachelor of Divinity and was prepared to enter the ministry. However, before taking the vow of ordination, he gladly made another vow, marrying his beloved, Johanna Buist, on August 21, 1971.

The call to serve as pastor first came from a congregation in Neerlandia, Alberta. Undoubtedly it was quite a change, moving from the well-populated Golden Horseshoe around Lake Ontario to a small, rural village in the northern part of Wild Rose Country, as Albertans love to call it. However, for the newlyweds, Keith and Joanne, there was little time to sit back and contemplate such matters. There was much work to be done in the congregation, and soon home life became busier, too, with the arrival of Stephen Carl, born on October 18, 1972. The family of three stayed in Neerlandia for a little less than three years before they moved on to Brampton, Ontario, to serve the Canadian Reformed congregation there. This move brought them back to more familiar territory and closer to extended family. However, it also opened up an opportunity for Cornelis to continue his studies. He entered the Master of Theology program at Knox College in Toronto, graduating in 1980. Shortly before this graduation, though, another call came from the Surrey "Maranatha" congregation, located just outside of Vancouver, British Columbia. So in the summer of 1979, the family once again packed their belongings, including all the books, and moved to the West Coast.

During this time in Surrey, Rev. C. Van Dam was introduced firsthand to another aspect of the ministry, namely, mission work. The congregation was active in sending missionaries to Brazil, and although, in God's providence, his stay in Surrey was not long, this involvement in mission work proved to have a lasting effect on his interests and activities. It was also during his family's time in Surrey that he took the next step in his ongoing studies and was accepted into the Doctor of Theology program at the Theological University of Kampen, the Netherlands. However, no sooner had he settled into the Surrey congregation and his doctoral studies, and a pressing need arose. The Theological College in Hamilton, where Van Dam had originally studied for the ministry, needed a new professor in the Old Testament department. Since this was the subject area in which he had been concentrating, he accepted the appointment and started teaching at the seminary in 1981.

Cornelis Van Dam's first years as professor were more than hectic. Not only were there many lectures to prepare and deliver, but his doctoral studies were still in process and would not be finished for another five years. However, with the work ethic cultivated in him while growing up on the family farm and, above all, under the Lord's indispensible blessing, he and his wife, along with their son, persevered through the challenges of those initial years of teaching. Indeed, the Lord provided sufficient stamina to allow him to complete three decades of fruitful teaching at the Theological College, recently renamed as the Canadian Reformed Theological Seminary.

This brings us to the occasion prompting the publication of this book. In September 2011, Dr. Cornelis Van Dam will officially retire from teaching at the seminary and join the honored ranks of the *emeriti*. Undoubtedly, his retirement years, just like the decades preceding them, will be chock full of activity. The agricultural work ethic still beats strongly in his heart. There are more intellectual fields to plow; there are more ecclesiastical harvests to reap. May the Lord provide Keith and Joanne with the requisite health to serve him and his church for many years to come.

The biographical sketch above already provides an impression of Cornelis Van Dam. However, a number of additional aspects are worth highlighting. First, although he has spent the last thirty years of his life as a professor in the seminary classroom, he has never lost his first love: preaching. Not only does he step up into the pulpit regularly, but it is also obvious that he enjoys being there. Whether preaching from the Old or New Testament, for him it is all about heralding the *gospel*, the glad tidings of salvation in the one Redeemer, Jesus Christ. Moreover, what is the main purpose of seminary training, if not to prepare ministers of the Holy Word? Van Dam not only taught that truth, he exemplified it.

Second, as a professor, he was as demanding on himself as he was on his students. Precision and thoroughness were qualities that pervaded his own lectures and were required of his students also. In class, while discussing the semantic range of certain Hebrew words, he would often say that this Semitic language has a "precise ambiguity." It sounds like an oxymoron, but it's true. Yet, when it came time to write a Hebrew exam for him, each student knew that his answers had better be heavy on the "precise" and light on the "ambiguity," lest his grades be swiftly pulled down by the gravity of insufficient preparation! Yet at the end of their seminary training, when all the exams were scribbled and scored, Van Dam's students graduated not only with a certain mark, but also with a clear methodology. All the rigor of academia could now be translated into carefully crafted sermons, well-prepared pastoral visits, and meticulously worded decisions in ecclesiastical assemblies. At the same time, precision does not mean having lost sight of the forest for the trees, and thoroughness need not entail wearisome wordiness. *Brevitas et claritas.* Brevity and clarity. Those are the goals that Van Dam set for himself and his students.

Third, even though a full schedule of preaching and teaching provided more than enough labor to occupy one man's hours and energy, Van Dam managed to gather up sufficient bits and blocks of time over the years to publish numerous books, essays, journal articles, and dictionary entries. Indeed, a quick scan of his bibliography in the back of this book ought to be proof positive that he has not hidden his knowledge under a bushel. On the contrary, it has consistently rolled off the presses, year after year. The impetus for his publishing program has not been literary fame or lucrative royalties. Far from it! Closer to truth are the words of the prophet Hosea: "My people are destroyed from lack of knowledge" (4:6 NIV). There are times in life when ignorance is bliss, but understanding God's Word and being well informed about the ecclesiastical scene do *not* fall into that category. Therefore, Van Dam did his part to instruct, not only in the classroom, but also through the printed word.

Fourth, this preacher, professor, and author has always been keenly aware and deeply appreciative of the bond he has with Christ's catholic church and, more specifically, with the federation to which he belongs, the Canadian Reformed Churches. In every sense of the word, Van Dam was, and remains, a churchman. He has been both a contributor for and an editor of the *Clarion*, a magazine widely read in Canadian Reformed circles. He was part of the steering committee that initiated the Burlington Reformed Study Centre, which sponsored a number of enlightening lecture series for the man and woman in the pew. Several of these lectures series were eventually published under Van Dam's editorial eye (again, see the bibliography at the end of this book). In addition to these efforts, when God's providential hand placed ecumenical opportunities along the ecclesiastical path, he was eager to do his part. For example, from the start, he was involved in the growing relationship between the United Reformed Church of North America and the Canadian Reformed Churches. Still, his eyes and his efforts were not restricted to the federation he served. His travels brought him to various places in South America, Asia, Africa, and Europe. His earlier exposure to mission work in Surrey and, more importantly, the prophetic vision of Psalm 87 spurred him on. From Babylon to Cush, from Mexico to the Middle East, the LORD is registering the citizens of his Zion from all nations, languages, and tribes. Van Dam has always been humbled and privileged to play a small part in the ongoing fulfillment of that psalm.

Fifth, it is not every professor who has a passion for politics, but this one does. Mind you, when most people hear the word politics, they immediately think of broken promises and questionable transactions. That is, most emphatically, not the kind of politics about which Van Dam is passionate. Rather, it is his conviction that Christian citizens should never take their freedoms for granted and, moreover, that governing officials should be made aware of their ultimate accountability to the King of kings and Lord of lords. For this reason, Van Dam not only wrote about political issues, but he also found occasion to personally address members of the Canadian parliament (see his booklet, *God and Government: A Biblical Perspective on the Role of the State*).

Last but certainly not least, Keith Van Dam is a faithful husband to his beloved wife, Joanne, a loving father to their son, Carl, and now also an exuberant grandfather to their grandchildren.

By now, after no less than six separate points, I have likely caused considerable discomfort on the part of the one who is being honored by this book. Never a man to seek praise for himself, I have a hunch that our professor will feel that far too much attention in this preface has been put on him as a person. In fact, on January 6, 2011, at the end of a conference organized in his honor, he spoke a few words, referring to Luke 17:10: "We are unworthy servants; we have only done our duty." That is true, and it applies to all of us. We are nothing more than unworthy servants of a most exalted Lord. Yet, it is exactly with this in mind that I am writing these few paragraphs. I describe the servant in order to ascribe greater praise to the Master. However, allow me to make my intention more explicit.

No faithful preacher can proclaim God's Word unless he is called by the Lord of the church and equipped by the Spirit of God. No theological professor has true wisdom to impart to his students, unless he mines the treasures, old and new, of God's holy and inspired Word. No author has the physical and mental stamina to write articles and books, unless that energy is provided from the hand of the Father in heaven. No churchman maintains zealous love and devotion for the bride of Christ, unless he sees the church as precisely that: the most beloved bride of the most gracious Bridegroom, the only-begotten Son of God. No Christian citizen of any country has the courage to stand before the power brokers of the political process, unless he is conscious that even lofty officials are but lowly creatures under the sovereign rule of the Almighty Creator.

Finally, no husband, father, or grandfather has the wherewithal to lovingly guide, support, and cherish his wife, children, and grandchildren, unless he confesses, "Whatever I have, whatever I do, it is all a gift from God, the overflowing fountain of all good." These truths apply generally, but they also apply specifically to Dr. Van Dam. I am sure that he will be the first to admit it. So it is true, we have written this book to honor a man, but not to praise him. All praise is reserved for the One who truly deserves it. *Soli deo gloria*.

A *Festschrift*, by its very nature, is a collaborative effort. The fifteen scholars who have each contributed an article to this book will have their say in the pages to follow. I do not intend to steal their thunder, as the saying goes. In addition, one more person, Joanne Van Dam, made a very significant contribution when she compiled an exhaustive bibliography of her husband's writings. As editor, let me express my heartfelt thankfulness to each of you. The various streams of your involvement have converged into a wide, flowing river of diverse reading. Yet, despite all the diversity, there is at least one common current running through all the articles: a desire to expound and apply the truth of Scripture. That inspired truth contains much more than interesting reading; it contains the living water that springs from ancient wells but flows forth into eternal glory (Isa 12:3; John 4:10–14; Rev 7:17).

At the same time, bringing together fifteen authors in one book poses certain challenges. Somehow these varied articles had to be collated into a cohesive whole. From the initial plans to the finishing details, John L. van Popta and S. Carl Van Dam provided invaluable assistance. From sending emails to offering advice to reading and rereading drafts, they did it all. Gentlemen, thank you! Equal gratitude is due to some ladies who competently devoted hours of their time and expertise to raise the level of literary polish in this document. In particular I am thinking of Rose Vermeulen, an administrative assistant at the Canadian Reformed Theological Seminary, who added some sparkle to the formatting side of things, as well as Julie Van Tol, a professional copyeditor, who meticulously rubbed away any lingering pieces of grammatical and syntactical tarnish that she could find. Both of them have gone above and beyond the call of duty; any remaining errors should certainly be attributed to me, not them.

Gratitude is also due to Pickwick Publications. They are to be commended for their prompt willingness to take on this publishing project.

Financial support for this book has been provided by the Publication Fund of the Canadian Reformed Theological Seminary, and all those involved in this book are indebted to them for their assistance.

Finally, in line with earlier comments made about reserving praise for the One to whom it is rightly due, let me end by expressing my sincere thanks to the heavenly Father for blessing this project thus far. What applies to houses applies equally to books: "Unless the Lord builds the house, its builders labor in vain" (Ps 127:1).

Jason Van Vliet
February 2011

Abbreviations

AB	Anchor Bible
ASOR	American Schools of Oriental Research
AUSS	*Andrews University Seminary Studies*
BAR	*Biblical Archaeology Review*
BBR	*Bulletin for Biblical Research*
BDAG	W. Bauer, F. W. Danker, W. F. Arndt, and F. W. Gingrich, *Greek-English Lexicon of the New Testament and Other Early Christian Literature*, 3rd ed., Chicago: University of Chicago Press, 1999
BDB	F. Brown, S. R. Driver, and C. A. Briggs, *A Hebrew and English Lexicon of the Old Testament*. Oxford: Clarendon, 1907
BETL	Bibliotheca ephemeridum theologicarum Lovaniensium
BHS	*Biblia Hebraica Stuttgartensia*, edited by K. Elliger and W. Rudolph, Stuttgart: Deutsche Bibelstiftung, 1983
Bib	*Biblica*
BKAT	Biblischer Kommentar. Altes Testament.
BSac	*Bibliotheca Sacra*
CahRB	*Cahiers de la Revue biblique*
CBQ	*Catholic Biblical Quarterly*
GKC	*Gesenius' Hebrew Grammar*, edited by E. Kautzsch, translated by A. E. Cowley, 2nd ed., Oxford: Clarendon, 1910
CO	John Calvin, *Corpus Reformatorum. Ioannis Calvini Opera Quae Supersunt Omnia*, 59 vols., edited by G. Baum, E. Cunitz, and E. Reuss, Braunschweig, 1863–1900

DCH	*Dictionary of Classical Hebrew*, edited by D. J. A. Clines, Sheffield: Sheffield Academic, 1993–2007
HALOT	Koehler, L., W. Baumgartner, and J. J. Stamm, *The Hebrew and Aramaic Lexicon of the Old Testament*, translated and edited under the supervision of M. E. J. Richardson, 4 vols., Leiden: Brill, 1994–1999
HTKAT	Herders Theologischer Kommentar zum Alten Testament
HUCA	*Hebrew Union College Annual*
ICC	International Critical Commentary
JBL	*Journal of Biblical Literature*
JETS	*Journal of the Evangelical Theological Society*
JNES	*Journal of Near Eastern Studies*
JSOT	*Journal for the Study of the Old Testament*
JSOTSup	Journal for the Study of the Old Testament, Supplement Series
KAT	Kommentar zum Alten Testament
LSJ	H. G. Liddell, R. Scott, and H. S. Jones, *A Greek-English Lexicon*, 9th ed. with revised supplement, Oxford: Clarendon, 1996
LXX	Septuagint
MM	J. H. Moulton and G. Milligan, *The Vocabulary of the Greek Testament*, 1930. Reprint, Peabody, MA: Hendrickson, 1997
MSS	manuscripts
MSU	Mitteilungen des Septuaginta-Unternehmens
MT	Masoretic Text
NETS	*A New English Translation of the Septuagint*
NICOT	New International Commentary on the Old Testament
NIDOTTE	*New International Dictionary of Old Testament Theology and Exegesis*, edited by W. A. VanGemeren, 5 vols., Grand Rapids: Eerdmans, 1997
NJPS	*Tanakh: The Holy Scriptures: The New JPS Translation according to the Traditional Hebrew Text*
OBO	Orbis biblicus et orientalis

OBT	Overtures to Biblical Theology	
OS	John Calvin, *Joannis Calvini Opera Selecta*, edited by P. Barth and G. Niesel, Monachii: Kaiser, 1952–1967	
OTL	Old Testament Library	
RB	*Revue biblique*	
SBB	Stuttgarter biblische Beiträge	
SBL	*Society of Biblical Literature*	
SBLSCS	*Society of Biblical Literature Septuagint and Cognate Studies*	
SJLA	*Studies in Judaism in Late Antiquity*	
SSN	*Studia semitica neerlandica*	
TCS	Texts from Cuneiform Sources	
TLG	*Thesaurus linguae graecae: Canon of Greek Authors and Works*	
TOTC	Tyndale Old Testament Commentary	
Vg	Vulgate	
VT	*Vetus Testamentum*	
VTSup	Vetus Testamentum, Supplement Series	
WBC	Word Biblical Commentary	
WCF	Westminster Confession of Faith	
WTJ	*Westminster Theological Journal*	
WUNT	Wissenschaftliche Untersuchungen zum Neuen Testament	
ZABR	*Zeitschrift für altorientalische und biblische Rechtsgeschichte*	
ZAW	*Zeitschrift für die alttestamentliche Wissenschaft*	
ZNW	*Zeitschrift für die neutestamentliche Wissenschaft und die Kunde der älteren Kirche*	

1

The Book of the Covenant and Elders

R. Dean Anderson

"THE ELDERS WHO RULE well are to be considered worthy of double honor," says Paul in 1 Tim 5:17.[1] In what way, however, did he expect elders to rule a congregation? At least one important aspect of this "rule" is indicated in 1 Cor 6:1–8, where Paul indicates that judicial disputes between brothers and sisters are to be settled out of court and within the covenant community itself. The elders of the early church took this very seriously and held court for the congregation every week.[2] It goes without saying, however, that if elders are to take this part of their task seriously they need a basic understanding of the judicial principles by which God intended the Ten Commandments to be applied in society. This brings us to the book of the covenant.

What is the "book of the covenant"? The title is taken from Exodus 24:7[3] where reference is made back to verse 3, which speaks of "the words of the Lord and all the ordinances (*mishpatim*)." This in turn refers back to Exod 20:22—23:33 where we find the revelation that Moses received from the Lord when he ascended the mountain for the first time.[4] The

---

1. All Scripture quotations in this article are from the New American Standard Bible (NASB).

2. See further Anderson, *1 Korintiërs*, 78–84.

3. For ease of reference in this article, I will use the regular English versification and not the Hebrew, which is sometimes different.

4. I will not discuss various form critical theories of the makeup of the book of the covenant, its dating, and its place in the book of Exodus. That is a separate subject. For

book of the covenant itself is divided into three sections. The first section deals with the worship of God. The second section begins at 21:1 where the title "These are the *mishpatim*" introduces a lengthy section of judicial laws, beginning with a series of "judgments," or case laws, which most appropriately fall under the rubric *mishpatim*[5] but also incorporate other kinds of legal formulations. The book concludes with a paraenetic section, 23:20–33, on the angel that will accompany the Israelites to the promised land.

The middle, legal, section itself is easily divided into two halves. The first part, 21:1—22:20, concerns judgments and laws to which penalties are attached.[6] The second, 22:21—23:19, concerns various laws and admonitions without penalties. It is the first legal section that concerns us in this present study. Many liberal scholars argue that the whole legal section must postdate the Sinai encounter with God because, among other things, the laws (e.g., concerning ownership of fields or the festival calendar) presuppose a settled life in the promised land.[7] It is, however, not difficult to imagine that God, at Sinai, desired to give his people a law code that would be useful in the settled condition of the promised land. More difficult, on the surface, is the nature of the laws themselves. As J. P. Hyatt has correctly observed, the laws seem to be "fragmentary and incomplete, not including by any means all that one would expect to find in a genuine law code."[8] The "judgments" seem to be rather specific case studies with little or nothing to connect them. They give the appearance of arising from legal precedent; that is, specific cases that were decided in the past. Yet the biblical text asks us to understand that God gave *this legal code in this form* to Moses for the Israelites.

---

summaries see for example, Houtman, *Exodus*, 87–106 and Childs, *Exodus*, 452–61. I accept its *prima facie* place in the canon as the revelation that God gave to Moses on the mountain.

5. On *mišpat*, see further Johnson "*mišpāt*," 86–98, esp. 94–95.

6. The laws with penal sanctions are mostly case laws with a formal introduction using the Hebrew *ki*. The only other laws in this book that use this introduction are found in 23:4,5. This form occurs seventeen times in this section. There are also four exceptions: 21:12, 15, 16, and 17. The occurrence of this form enables us to discern where the different laws are separated from each other in this section. Distinguishing the various laws from each other in the section concerning laws without penal sanctions is more difficult and therefore open to different interpretations. For further distinguishing characteristics between the two legal sections see Houtman, *Exodus*, 90–91.

7. For example, Childs, *Exodus*, 458.

8. Hyatt, *Exodus*, 218.

by bringing his way on his own head and justifying the righteous by giving him according to his righteousness" (cf. 2 Chr 6:22–23).

A specific example of such an oath is provided in Num 5:11–31 where a fairly elaborate ritual is used in the case of a husband who suspects his wife of adultery. The wife is brought to the temple and made to undergo an oath of purgation. Standing before the officiating priest with a special grain offering, she accepts a very specific self-imprecating curse with a double "amen," and drinks a special curse drink.[15] It is unclear whether such a ritual was typical of all oaths of purgation. It would seem that normally such oaths involved nonspecific curses. In Exod 22:10 the phrase "if he has not laid his hand on the property of his neighbor" (literal translation) uses an *'im* ("if") clause, well-known in oath formulations. The apodosis of such an oath was sometimes vaguely expressed, for example, "May God do so to me, and more also, if . . ." (2 Sam 3:35; cf. 1 Sam 3:17), but most often not even expressed with so many words at all.[16]

The use of the oath in cases presenting insufficient evidence enables us to diagram the basic system of justice presupposed by the laws in the book of the covenant as follows:

---

15. This law does not, on the surface, seem very attractive. The most difficult verse is perhaps v. 31, "Moreover, the man shall be free from guilt, but that woman shall bear her guilt." It is clear that it cannot be the intention to say that men are allowed to commit adultery while women are not! If there was evidence for adultery, then both men and women had the right to appear before the elders at the gate to bring charges. The possible guilt of the man here is that of accusing his wife of adultery when she had, in fact, been faithful. If, after completion of this ritual, it becomes clear that the woman is not an adulteress, there is no punishment for the wrongful accusation. If the woman was guilty, there ensues a physical punishment from the LORD resulting in the inability to bear any more children. In practice, few guilty women would have dared to undergo the ritual. This law protects women from the social dangers of being wrongly accused by their husbands of unfaithfulness. For potential dangers see Exod 21:10. Also see further my article "The Jealous Husband" at: http://katwijk.gkv.nl/anderson/uk/.

16. See further HALOT, s.v. "*'im*," 4. The priestly ritual following an unsolved murder in the country also involves an abjuration of innocence (Deut 21:1–9). Although the text does not specifically use an oath formula, this is probably intended. No apodosis is indicated. This purgation, despite the priestly ritual, does not occur in the temple, but rather in the countryside where the murder was committed.

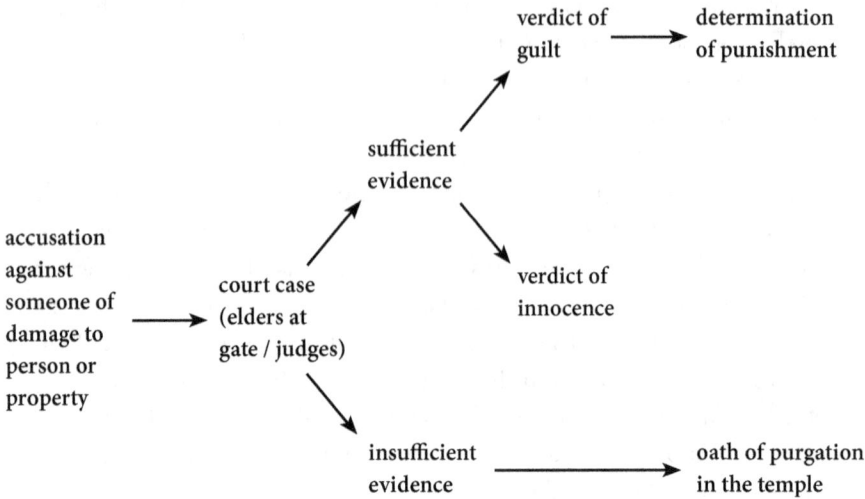

An accusation of one person against another inevitably involves damage to one's person or property. Slander is not a criminal offence unless it causes material damage.[17] If the judges determine that there is insufficient evidence, then an oath of purgation is applied (cf. Heb 6:16). This means that the accused must take an oath that he has not harmed his neighbor, or his neighbor's property, and asks God to punish him if he is lying. The matter is thus effectively given over into God's hands, and the accuser is bound to leave it there and take no further action, unless, we may suppose, more evidence should come to light. If there is sufficient evidence for a trial, the judges will pronounce a verdict. We learn in Deut 17:8–13 that cases too difficult for local courts could be handed over to a central court in the place where God had chosen to reside, which later became Jerusalem.

---

17. An exception is made in the case of a curse against one's parents (Exod 21:17; cf. Lev 20:9). However, we should bear two things in mind respecting this law. First, invoking a curse involves asking God (or gods) to injure one's parents. Second, the verb k-l-l (piel) denotes "treating with contempt and humiliating," an example of which is given in Deut 21:18–21 (see Sarna, *Exodus*, 123). It is interesting to note that cursing judges (*'elohim*) or a ruler (*nasi'*) of the people is only prohibited in the second section of laws and therefore does not incur a penal sanction (cf. Exod 22:28). The use of *'elohim* in this passage probably does not refer to "God," for that would be a capital offence (cf. Lev 24:11–15).

RESTITUTION

A third, and perhaps most significant, presupposition that these laws embody is a regulating set of principles for determining punishment. Such principles are nowhere enunciated in the laws of Moses that have been handed down to us, but may be discerned by a study of these case laws, which are surely intended to provide pedagogical examples of special circumstances and exceptions to general governing principles.

We should remember that it is not the intention of the book of the covenant to be a completely new legal system for Israel. It is not a "law book" in the modern sense of that word, wherein all possible situations and loopholes need to be covered. With these judgments, the Lord concerns himself with supplementing and correcting judicial practice and custom among the Israelites. We saw above that, already before the Sinai encounter, Moses could speak of the statutes and laws God had given for judging the people (Exod 18:16).

The principles upon which a punishment is determined may be summarized in a relatively simple way. All cases of damage may be placed into one of three categories as follows:

1. Damage inflicted with intent to harm requires restitution and the application of the *lex talionis* (eye for eye, etc.).
2. Damage inflicted through negligence requires restitution.
3. Damage inflicted by accident does not require restitution.

The principle of restitution is one that permeates the jurisprudence here. Time and again, the issue at stake is whether or not restitution should be granted. Medical expenses and compensation for lost work provide restitution for an injury (21:19). The owner of an uncovered pit is held responsible for domestic animals that fall into it, and must make restitution (21:34). A thief must make restitution (22:3). Likewise, restitution must be made by one whose animal grazed another's field (22:5), whose fire went out of control (22:6), and who borrowed another's animal and it became harmed (22:14). Many other case laws, which do not mention restitution specifically, may also be interpreted in this light. For example, a father, who is responsible for guarding his daughter's virginity, is recompensed with a heavy fine when his daughter's virginity is taken by another male (22:16–17).

The case laws show clearly that restitution is generally not required when the damage is caused by accident. If an animal is given to someone for safekeeping, and it dies or is hurt or is driven away, the guardian does not need to make restitution, unless it can be proven that the damage was caused by the guardian himself (22:10–11). It is likewise implied that inanimate property damaged while entrusted to someone for safekeeping does not have to be restored. The law in 22:7–8 is only interested in whether or not the guardian himself has laid his hands on the property. Other case laws provide nuances and exceptions to this general rule of thumb. When a person has borrowed an animal to use for himself, he remains responsible for it and must provide restitution even if it is hurt by accident (22:14). However, the responsibility remains with the owner if he was with the animal at the time (22:15). Another special case concerns an ox that is not known to be dangerous goring someone to death. The owner of the ox is not held responsible for the accident, but the dangerous ox must be killed (21:28).

The last example touches on a series of special cases involving the death of someone. A dead person cannot be restored to the family. It would appear that any thought of *restitution* by monetary recompense is excluded. The sanctions involved when a death has occurred should be viewed as punishment and not a form of restitution. Before we return to this point, however, it is necessary to discuss the general principle for punishment, or retribution, that governs the case laws; namely, the *lex talionis*.

The principle is expressed in Exod 21:23–25: "life for life, eye for eye, tooth for tooth," etc. A simple example of the application of this principle is the punishment normally accorded a thief. He is to pay double what he stole (22:4, 7, 9); that is, restitution and retribution equivalent to the amount he stole.[18] When applied to physical injuries, there is good reason to believe that, generally speaking, the principle was only applied literally in the case of death. This can be demonstrated in the following manner. The principle "eye for eye, tooth for tooth" was a legal one stating the need for a punishment equal to the crime. This principle is found in two other places in God's law, Lev 24:17–20 and Deut 19:21. Essentially, it requires that each sinful deed must receive an equally fitting punishment. In each case, it is a principle with a judicial context.

---

18. The case laws make an exception to this principle only in the case of stolen oxen or sheep that are not recovered.

For this reason, the Lord Jesus turned so sharply against the Pharisees when they abused this principle as an excuse to justify personal revenge (Matt 5:38–39).

This principle of a just retaliation means that when a victim loses a body part he may demand before the judges that the perpetrator's same body part be removed as a punishment. If your neighbor plucks out your right eye, then, according to God's law, you may demand from the judge that your neighbor's right eye also be removed. This is not restitution but retribution. The practice may sound somewhat cruel, but we should understand that in reality it seldom appears to have happened. Although the principle of applying this type of punishment remains, it is clear that the victim had the *alternative* of allowing the literal vengeance to be commuted into a fine (cf. Josephus, *Ant.* 4:280). In other words, instead of demanding the right eye of the perpetrator, the victim may demand payment of a financial penalty. Of course, the victim will benefit much more from a payment, which he rather than the court receives, than he will from the perpetrator's loss of an eye. Since it is the victim who gives permission for substitution and has the right to negotiate the extent of the fine, there is not so much scope for discrimination between rich and poor. The wealthier the perpetrator is, the more money could be extracted from him in lieu of a body part.

Although there is no direct legal text in the selection of Mosaic laws handed down to us that outlines the substitution of physical retaliation with a monetary fine, there are several examples of this practice. The law in Exod 21:29–30 provides for commuting a death penalty into a fine. From the book of Proverbs we learn that the same possibility of substitution existed for adultery. The prescribed punishment for adultery is the death penalty (Lev 20:10; Deut 22:22). However, concerning cases of adultery, Prov 6:32–35 warns us that the plaintiff, that is, the injured marriage partner, could become so angry that he would not even be prepared to consider a fine as substitute for the death penalty (cf. Prov 13:7–8). We see here that the right to insist on having the official sentence executed remains with the plaintiff.[19] "The one who commits adultery with a woman is lacking sense; He who would destroy himself does it. . . . For jealousy enrages a man, and he will not spare in the day

---

19. This also helps us to understand Joseph's initial reaction to the pregnancy of Mary. He was well within his rights to choose not to press for the death penalty, but to quietly arrange for a divorce instead; see Matt 1:19.

of vengeance [i.e., at court]. He will not accept any ransom, nor will he be content though you give many gifts [i.e., even if you offer him a fortune as redemption]."

That such substitution was standard legal practice is quite clear from the one case where the Lord forbids it. We read in Num 35:31–33, "Moreover, you shall not take ransom for the life of a murderer who is guilty of death, but he shall surely be put to death. And you shall not take ransom for him who has fled to his city of refuge, that he may return to live in the land before the death of the priest. So you shall not pollute the land in which you are; for blood pollutes the land and no expiation can be made for the land for the blood that is shed on it, except by the blood of him who shed it." The penalty for murder or manslaughter may not be commuted into a fine, implying that for most other penalties this was an acceptable solution.

At this point, we can return to the question of sanctions when a death has occurred. As stated above, this is always a special case in view of the fact that restitution is impossible. Exod 21:12–14 makes it clear that when death is the result of an action designed to harm the person, the death penalty applies according to the principle of *talio*. However, Num 35, as cited above, makes it clear that in this case the punishment is mandatory and not able to be substituted with a fine. The same passage also states the reason for this measure, namely, that blood pollutes the land and demands atonement by blood. The wording here recalls Gen 9:6, where the death penalty is also required for murder. In this text, one other important facet is added, namely, that man is created in the image of God. The honor of God himself is assaulted when a person is killed. His image is destroyed.

When death is the result of an accident the law differentiates between two distinct cases. The first instance concerns death that is the result of negligence by the owner, as in the case of an unprotected, dangerous ox (cf. Deut 22:8). The governing principles for punishment would demand restitution, but not punishment. However, in this case restitution is not possible. Therefore, the owner is made liable to the death penalty, but in this case it is commutable (Exod 21:29–30).

The second instance is death by accident without negligence. Here the law isolates two possibilities. If the death is an accident caused by the property of the owner, for example, an ox that unexpectedly gores someone to death, there is no penalty (21:28). However, when the accident is caused by the person himself, he is compelled to flee to a city of refuge until the death of the high priest (Num 35:9–11). Such provision of sanctuary is presupposed in Exod 21:14 when it is stated that one who intentionally commits murder may be removed from the sanctuary of the altar.

FINAL REFLECTIONS

When we further reflect upon the basic principles of punishment in the book of the covenant and the way in which the case laws apply them to difficult circumstances, at least two things may strike us. In the first place, nowhere do we find provisions for the cutting off of hands, or other body parts, as punishment. By way of comparison, many of the other ancient Near Eastern legal codes do stipulate the cutting off of hands as a punishment for theft. In the second place, there is no provision for confinement as a judicial sanction. In fact, the whole principle of rehabilitation, if it was considered a principle at all, remains secondary.[20] The judicial process seeks primarily to provide restitution and an appropriate retribution. The retribution in most cases serves to benefit the victim and satisfy his upright demand that the wrong perpetrated against him be avenged. In this way, the punishments are designed to promote harmony and peaceful relations in society.

There is much to be learned here by elders of the church, especially when their task of promoting the peace in the congregation is taken seriously. They are given a ruling function in Christ's congregations (Acts 20:28; Heb 13:17) and may be expected to function as judges in cases of civil disputes (1 Cor 6:1–11). In that respect, the book of the covenant, while not in every respect applicable today, does provide basic principles of justice from which we may learn. They are principles given to us by the revelation of our God, the same God who provides reconciliation with himself through the substitutionary punishment of his own Son, Jesus Christ.

---

20 Rehabilitation *may* be considered to be effected through observance of the principle of restitution, but this idea is not made specific in the law.

BIBLIOGRAPHY

Anderson, R. D. *1 Korintiërs: Orde op zaken in een jonge stadskerk*. Commentaar op het Nieuwe Testament. Kampen: Kok, 2008.

Childs, Brevard S. *The Book of Exodus*. OTL. Philadelphia: Westminster, 1974.

Houtman, C. *Exodus Deel 3*. Commentaar op het Oude Testament. Kampen: Kok, 1996.

Hyatt, J. P. *Exodus*. New Century Bible Commentary. Grand Rapids: Eerdmans, 1971.

Johnson, B. "*mišpāṭ*." In *Theological Dictionary of the Old Testament*, edited by G. J. Botterweck et al., translated by D. E. Green, 9:86–97. Grand Rapids: Eerdmans, 1998.

Kautzsch, E. *Gesenius' Hebrew Grammar*. Translated by A. E. Cowley. 2nd English ed. Oxford: Clarendon, 1985.

Sarna, Nahum M. *Exodus*. JPS Torah Commentary. Philadelphia: Jewish Publication Society, 1991.

Van der Merwe, C. et al. *A Biblical Hebrew Reference Grammar*. Electronic ed. Oak Harbor, WA: Logos Research Systems, 1997.

Vaux, Roland de. *Ancient Israel: Its Life and Institutions*. Translated by J. McHugh. 1961. Reprint, Grand Rapids: Eerdmans, 1997.

Waltke, Bruce K., and M. O'Connor. *An Introduction to Biblical Hebrew Syntax*. Winona Lake, IN: Eisenbrauns, 1990.

2

How Will God Deal with Children of Parents Who Have Committed Idolatry?

WOLTER ROSE

THE SECOND HALF OF the Second Word[1] of the Decalogue is usually translated in one of two ways. The first possibility is found in the English Standard Version: "I the Lord your God am a jealous God, visiting the iniquity of the fathers on the children to the third and the fourth generation of those who hate me." The other option is used by the New International Version: "I, the Lord your God, am a jealous God, punishing the children for the sin of the fathers to the third and fourth generation of those who hate me."[2]

This article is about the translation of the clause alternatively rendered as either "visiting the iniquity of the fathers on the children" or "punishing the children for the sin of the fathers." Particular attention will be paid to the first word in this clause. The difference in meaning between "visiting" and "punishing" is relatively small. Both renderings

---

1. Following biblical precedent ("ten words," Exod 34:28; Deut 4:13) and Jewish tradition, I use the phrase *the Second Word* for what is usually called the first and second commandment. Traditional terminology, "Ten Commandments," fails to do justice to the fact that the First Word is not a commandment but a word of grace in which the Lord presents himself as a God who sets people free. Also, with Vance, *Introduction*, I will use G for what traditionally has been called *qal*, N for *nifal*, D for *piel*, H for *hifil*, etc. I thank Ian Hamilton and James Horgan for comments on earlier drafts of this article.

2. Unless otherwise noted, Scripture quotations in this article are taken from the New International Version (NIV).

indicate inflicting punishment on someone. They translate the Hebrew verb √*pqd* (פקד).[3] In the rest of this article, I will call this clause, which the ESV translates as "visiting the iniquity of the fathers on the children," the PQD-clause.

THE VERB √*PQD* WITH WRONGDOING AS ITS OBJECT IS USED IN MORE THAN ONE WAY

The literature on √*pqd* is immense, and it is beyond the scope of this article to provide a survey.[4] To give an impression of the range of meanings in which the verb is used, I will simply list the meanings which some recent Hebrew dictionaries distinguish in their entries on √*pqd*. *HALOT* distinguishes five senses in which the verb √*pqd* in the G stem is used in biblical Hebrew: to make a careful inspection; to look at, see to something; to pass in review, muster; to instruct, command, urge, stipulate; and to call to account, avenge, afflict. *DCH* lists ten basic meanings for biblical Hebrew √*pqd* G:[5] visit; observe; count; assign a task or object; assign guilt or the punishment for guilt; harm; appoint; muster; deposit; and determine.

Cases Where √*pqd + Wrongdoing Does Not Mean "Punish"*

It is often thought, and sometimes stated explicitly,[6] that when it has wrongdoing as its direct object, √*pqd* is only used in one way and should be translated as "punish." This view needs to be challenged. I will point to three occurrences of such a collocation where a translation such as "punish" is problematic.

---

3. A √ sign preceding the transcription of a Hebrew word indicates the verbal root and not a specific verbal form.

4. For some useful surveys, see Spencer, "*PQD*"; and Creason, "*PQD* Revisited."

5. And a couple more for Qumran Hebrew: command, keep.

6. Levinson, *Legal Revision*, 56 n. 56: "The verb, when combined with a personal reference as definite direct object, may indeed mean 'to visit' in a neutral way: 'Samson came to visit his wife,' ויפקד שמשון את־אשתו (Judg 15:1). However, when the same verb takes a noun with the semantic range of wrongdoing or sin as its direct object, the meaning is quite different: יזכור עונם יפקוד חטאותם, 'He will remember their iniquity / He will punish their sins' (Hos 9:9; NJPS)."

Just Asking: 2 Samuel 3:8

The first case of this use is 2 Sam 3:8, where Saul has died and a war has erupted between the house of Saul and the house of David. In order to prepare his audience for what comes next, the narrator comments, "Abner had been strengthening his own position in the house of Saul," and then continues, "now Saul had a concubine named Rizpah daughter of Aiah" (2 Sam 3:6). The next thing we read is a question that Ish-bosheth, Saul's son, asks Abner, Saul's cousin and army commander: "Why did you sleep with my father's concubine?" (2 Sam 3:7).[7] Abner responds indignantly: "Yet now you accuse [פקד] me of an offense involving this woman!"

In this case, √pqd + wrongdoing (עָוֹן) refers to a question asked by Ish-bosheth. It seems premature to find a reference to punishment at this phase of the argument between Abner and Ish-bosheth. Here, in my opinion, those translations are correct that do not use "punish," but instead employ translation equivalents such as "charge with" (NRSV; ESV)[8] or "reproach over" (NJPS).[9]

Translating a Qatal with a Future (1): 1 Sam 15:2

Usually, the subject of √pqd + wrongdoing is God. 1 Sam 15:2 is one example where God is the subject and the collocation probably does not mean "punish."[10] Most English versions translate in the style of the NIV: "This is what the Lord Almighty says: 'I will punish the Amalekites for what they did to Israel when they waylaid them as they came up from Egypt.'" However, the translation found in the ESV provides an exception to this consensus: "Thus says the Lord of hosts, 'I have noted what Amalek did to Israel in opposing them on the way when they came up out of Egypt.'"

Not only is the meaning of the verb (פקד) taken differently (punish vs. note), but so is the tense (future vs. past). To begin with the latter,

---

7. Ish-bosheth would have considered sleeping with his father's concubine to be something close to a claim to the throne (compare 2 Sam 16:21 and 1 Kgs 2:17, 21–25).

8. See Hertzberg, *I and II Samuel*, 255, but I like the German better: "und dann machst du mir heute eine Szene wegen einer Weiberschuld?" Hertzberg, *Die Samuelbücher*, 208 (adopted by Stoebe, *Das erste Buch Samuelis*, 122); Firth, *1 & 2 Samuel*, 343 ("accuse of").

9. Also see Alter, *The David Story*, 210.

10. In most cases the wrongdoing is expressed by a noun; in this case the direct object is not a noun but a clause.

rendering a Qatal verbal form as an English future tense, as the NIV and others do, requires justification. Obviously, something like "I have punished Amalek" does not make sense in the context, where the next verse makes clear that punishment is something in the (near) future. If √*pqd* + wrongdoing can only mean "punish," then one has to assume that the Qatal is used in a special way,[11] a possibility that, of course, cannot be excluded. In this case, though, it seems more natural to take the Qatal as a past tense and translate √*pqd* differently. In recent English Bible translations this may be an exception, but, by contrast, in commentaries this seems to be a common way of interpreting √*pqd* in 1 Sam 15:2. To give just one example, Alter translates, "I have made reckoning of what Amalek did to Israel . . ."[12]

Translating a Qatal with a Future (2): Lam 4:22

The final example, from Lam 4:2, has some similarities with the one just discussed. Most modern translations render Lam 4:22 in a way similar to that of the NIV: "he will punish your sin and expose your wickedness." Looking at the Hebrew text, one discovers that both verbal forms are Qatal (פקד and גלה). Once more, the use of the future tense ("*will* punish . . . expose") requires attention. One can defend the translation of a Qatal with a future tense by pointing to what has been called the "prophetic perfect."[13] However, the category of prophetic perfect is not without its problems,[14] and should not be employed indiscriminately. In my view, Lam. 4:22 is one of those instances where one should question the interpretation of Qatal forms as cases of the prophetic perfect.

Lamentations 4:21–22 forms a literary unit, bracketed by the addressee of the words: "the Daughter of Edom." In these two verses, one finds both Yiqtol and Qatal forms (see Table 1). The Qatal forms are all found in v. 22. The first Qatal is rendered in most modern translations with a past tense. The last two verb forms of v. 22 are both Qatal, usually

---

11. Driver, *Notes*, 121–22, is one of the few commentators who addresses the issue. He takes the Qatal as "expressing determination," and points to GKC §106m (to represent future actions "as finished, or as equivalent to accomplished facts"). He admits that this is "unusual in prose." That is probably the reason that the proposal is rejected by Hertzberg, *Die Samuelbücher*, 92 (= Hertzberg, *I and II Samuel*, 120).

12. Alter, *David Story*, 87; see also, e.g., Stoebe, *1. Samuel*, 283; Firth, *1 & 2 Samuel*, 168.

13. E.g., Renkema, *Lamentations*, 569.

14. See Rogland, *Alleged Non-Past Uses*, ch. 3.

translated with a future tense, just like the only Yiqtol form in this verse. Unlike modern translations, both the Septuagint[15] and the Vulgate[16] translate the Qatal forms with a past tense.

Obviously, a translation like "he has punished your sin and exposed your wickedness" is problematic in this context, because v. 21 ("to you also the cup shall pass; you shall become drunk and strip yourself bare") suggests that the punishment is yet to come for Edom. This explains why the Qatal is taken here as a prophetic perfect. Given the distinct use of both Yiqtol and Qatal forms in these verses, this interpretation of two Qatal forms seems somewhat arbitrary.

TABLE 1: Qatal and Yiqtol Forms in Lam 4:21–22

verse	verbal form	NRSV
21b	Yiqtol	will be passed
21b	Yiqtol	shall become drunk
21b	Yiqtol	shall strip
22a	Qatal	is accomplished
22a	Yiqtol	will keep
22b	Qatal	will punish
22b	Qatal	will uncover

Another solution to the problem may be found when one reconsiders the meaning of √pqd in this verse. The New Jewish Publication Society translation renders the verb here with "note,"[17] which makes good sense. However, rather than a future tense, a past tense does more justice to the Qatal form: "He has noted your iniquity, Daughter of Edom; he has uncovered your sins."

Read in this way, the verse suggests that the Lord has finished dealing with the Daughter of Zion and now it is Edom's turn. The evidence is clear, expressed by the parallelism of "noted" and "uncovered."[18] Now

---

15. LXX: ἐπεσκέψατο ἀνομίας σου θύγατερ Εδωμ ἀπεκάλυψεν ἐπὶ τὰ ἀσεβήματά σου.

16. Vg.: visitavit iniquitatem tuam filia Edom discoperuit peccata tua.

17. NJPS: "Your iniquity, Fair Edom, He will note; He will uncover your sins." See also Renkema, *Lamentations*, 569: "It is worth noting that the idea of 'observing'/'seeing' is characteristic of the root פקד. Thus it can stand parallel with the *hiph'il* of √ גבט. . . ."

18. If "punish" were the sense intended here, one might perhaps have expected a different order in a case of synthetic parallellism: first גלה and then פקד.

is the time for the verdict and its execution concerning Edom's behavior (v. 21).[19]

Conclusion

Thus, against the claim that √*pqd* with wrongdoing as its direct object can only have one meaning, namely, "punish," I have discussed three cases where this meaning simply does not fit (2 Sam 3:8) or can only be maintained by translating a Qatal as a future tense (1 Sam 15:2; Lam 4:22), while such an unusual interpretation of the verbal form becomes unnecessary when one translates √*pqd* with a word like "note."

WHAT √PQD MEANS IN THE SECOND WORD

In the first part of this article I have argued that √*pqd* with wrongdoing as its direct object may have different meanings. It is usually taken to mean "punish." I have discussed cases where this interpretation is problematic. Having established that √*pqd* + wrongdoing may mean something other than "punish," I now want to address the following question: is "punish" an appropriate translation of √*pqd* in the PQD-clause, or is the PQD-clause one of those instances where √*pqd* is used with a different meaning?

For a number of reasons, it is not easy to answer this question. In the first place, there seems to be little in the immediate context that helps us decide whether one should translate as "punish" or look for a different meaning of √*pqd*. Second, this particular use of the √*pqd* + wrongdoing collocation is unusual due to the number of parties involved. Normally there are only two parties involved: on the one hand, there is the one who does √*pqd*, in many cases the Lord, and on the other hand, one or more potentially guilty persons. The PQD-clause is found four times in the Old Testament (Exod 20:5, 34:7; Num 14:18; Deut 5:9). In all these four occurrences, there are not just two but three parties involved in √*pqd* + wrongdoing: the Lord, the guilty person, and the descendants of the guilty person.

---

19. See Renkema, *Lamentations*, 570: "YHWH sees / examines the sins of Edom and He will effect the relevant punishment in a visible way."

Ways in Which the PQD-clause Has Been Interpreted

Collective Retribution

If "punish" is the correct translation, then the PQD-clause is an instance of what some scholars have called "collective retribution": an individual or group is punished for the wrong behavior of others, not of themselves.[20] Collective retribution[21] is found in the Old Testament in some specific circumstances. One well-known example is the "complete destruction" (חרם) judgment on the idolatrous inhabitants of Canaan at the time of the conquest (Deut 7). In a small number of cases such complete destruction is also executed, or to be executed, on communities within the people of God (e.g., Josh 7; Deut 17:12–18). The punishment of family members of high officials like kings is another example (2 Sam 21:1–14).

Personal Retribution

Others interpret the PQD-clause in the Second Word as an instance of personal retribution.[22] In that case, "punish" would not be an appropriate rendering of √*pqd*. Personal retribution means that an individual of a group is punished for his own wrong behavior.

The Wider Context

The Later Prophets

Some people want to settle the issues of the interpretation of the PQD-clause on the basis of the well-known words from Ezek 18:20: "The soul who sins is the one who will die. The son will not share the guilt of the father, nor will the father share the guilt of the son. The righteousness of the righteous man will be credited to him, and the wickedness of the wicked will be charged against him."

This passage leads them to favor a personal retribution interpretation of the PQD-clause. One may want to applaud this from the perspective of doing justice to the unity of Scripture as a whole, but there is a danger of bringing in related Scripture passages such as these too early.[23]

---

20. E.g., Levinson, *Legal Revision*, 54.

21. On collective and personal retribution, see Kaminsky, *Corporate Responsibility*; Schmid, "Kollektivschuld?"; and Mol, *Collective and Individual Responsibility*.

22. E.g., Houtman, *Exodus: Chapters 20–40*, 28–29.

23. One could also think of Deut 24:16: "Fathers shall not be put to death for their children, nor children put to death for their fathers; each is to die for his own sin." This

It seems fair to assume that people from the time of Moses must have been able to comprehend the meaning and significance of the PQD-clause without having to wait hundreds of years for Ezekiel to arrive and reveal what it really meant.

In addition, pointing to Ezek 18 may simply disclose one's preference for a personal retribution interpretation. Someone might legitimately ask, why not point to a passage that on the surface would suggest something very different? For example Jer 32:18 could be mentioned: "You show love to thousands but bring the punishment for the fathers' sins into the laps of their children after them."[24]

Dealing with Idolatry in the Laws of the Pentateuch

The best place to start an exploration that may enable us to decide what is the best translation of the PQD-clause is not Ezekiel or Jeremiah, but something closer to the Second Word, laws given that relate to the Second Word in the Pentateuch. There is a good reason for limiting this exploration to laws related to the Second Word. Three out of four times where the PQD-clause occurs, it is found in relationship to issues addressed in the Second Word, such as worshipping other gods and worshipping images. On those three occasions, the one who speaks the PQD-clause is God (Exod 20:5, 34:7; Deut 5:9). The fourth time (Num 14:18), the PQD-clause is spoken by Moses and prayed back to God, with something like a confessional status, in a context that no longer concerns issues relating to the Second Word.

Leviticus 20:1–5—A detailed procedure for dealing with disobedience to the Second Word is found in Lev 20:1–5. The passage deals with a case of giving one's child to Molech by burning the child as a sacrifice. The

---

verse shows that (unlike some other cultures in the Ancient Near East) *in the civil court* in Israel there was to be no space for vicarious punishment of one generation for the misbehavior or neglect of the other (cf. 2 Kgs 14:6). One cannot assume, however, that in the religious court things are regulated in exactly the same manner (see Greenberg, "Some Postulates"; Mol, *Collective and Individual Responsibility*, 221).

24. Jeremiah uses a different verb: שלם rather than פקד, complemented by the phrase אל־חיק. These two details create a strong impression of the element of real punishment in this verse. To answer the questions of (1) the exact nature of the relationship between Jer 18:32 and Exod 20:5 and (2) whether we are dealing here with collective rather than personal punishment, one needs to read at least one more verse (v. 18b): "Your eyes are open to all the ways of men; you reward [נתן] everyone according to his conduct and as his deeds deserve." See also Deut 7:9–10.

normal course of action (v. 2) would be for the people to stone the guilty person only. A second scenario (vv. 4–5) describes what will happen when the people look the other way. When the people fail to address disobedience to the Second Word, the Lord himself will step in. First, mention is made of those targeted by the intervention of the Lord. What makes this case interesting is that the family or kin group (משפחה) of the guilty person becomes part of the picture: "I will set my face against that man and his family. . . ." Next, mention is made of those who will receive punishment: ". . . and will cut off from their people both him and all who follow him in prostituting themselves to Molech."

So there is a distinction between the target of the scrutiny (שׂים פנים) of the Lord, the family of the guilty person, on the one hand, and the target of his punishment (כרת), those who share responsibility for the act of worship of Molech, on the other hand. The precise meaning of the terminology used in both cases is not entirely clear.

What can be said with confidence, though, is that the assumption that the whole family is punished together with the guilty person, irrespective of their own behavior, would make the presence of the phrase "all who follow him in prostituting themselves to Molech" superfluous. By contrast, the target of both scrutiny and punishment is the same in the first scenario in v. 3, and so a personal pronoun is sufficient: "I will set my face against that man and I will cut *him* off from his people."

Deuteronomy 13—In Deuteronomy 13, one finds three different cases all dealing with disobeying the Second Word. In the first two (vv. 1–5 and 6–11), the guilty person alone receives punishment (v. 5: "That prophet or dreamer must be put to death"; v. 10: "Stone him to death.") The second case is of special interest for our purposes, because it describes a situation in which the instigator is a family member, such as a brother or a wife, or an intimate friend. In either case, no mention is made of family members who should be executed together with the guilty person.

The third case (vv. 12–18) is more complex: there is a rumor that "scoundrels" (NJPS) have succeeded in making the fellow inhabitants of their city serve other gods. The course of action for dealing with this rumor starts with an investigation. No less than three separate verbs are used ("you must inquire, probe, and investigate it thoroughly," v. 14) to highlight the meticulous nature of this investigation. Another accumulation of clauses describes the situation of uncovering damning evidence during the investigation: "if it is true and it has been proved that this detestable thing has been done among you" (v. 14).

With this outcome of the investigation, the punishment targets the city as a whole. Both people and livestock have to be "destroyed completely" (חרם). When a city turns away from the LORD to serve other gods, the LORD tells his people to treat them as they once had been commanded to treat the idolatrous Canaanites. In such a case of large-scale disobedience to the Second Word, the punishment is collective. There will most likely be children among those destroyed. But the punishment comes only after a thorough investigation has established that the inhabitants of the city have turned away from the LORD to serve other gods.

Deuteronomy 17:2–5—A case in some respect related to the one in Deut 13:12–18 is found in Deut 17:2–5. Here we are not dealing with large-scale apostasy, but apostasy by an individual. The case specifies "a man or a woman" who has worshiped other gods. Once this has been reported, an investigation has to be made, as in Deut 13. This time, however, it is expressed with only one verb: "you must investigate it thoroughly." If the evidence is beyond questioning ("if it is true and it has been proved that this detestable thing has been done"[25]), the guilty person alone is to be punished ("take the man or woman who has done this evil deed to your city gate and stone that person to death").

Conclusion

I have surveyed how some laws in the Pentateuch deal with disobedience to the Second Word. The laws cover different forms of apostasy. The regulations may be summarized as follows:

1. The community of God's people is responsible for dealing with those within the covenant community who have committed idolatry.
2. The idolater is to be put to death by the community.

---

25. Exactly the same elaborate phrase is found in Deut 13:14.

3. When the community fails to take its responsibility, the Lord will act, and

   a. the kin group of the idolater is included in the investigation, and

   b. the idolater and his followers have to be put to death.

4. In case of large-scale apostasy of a complete city,

   a. a thorough investigation has to provide damnable evidence, and

   b. the city is to be "completely destroyed."

Next generations figure explicitly in the third item. A father has sacrificed a child to Molech and the community has turned a blind eye (Lev 20:4–5); the Lord will direct his attention to the guilty person and his kin group, and will punish him and his followers. Next generations figure implicitly in the fourth item as well, a scenario of large-scale apostasy in which a complete city is involved (Deut 13:12–18). If an investigation has established the idolatry beyond questioning, then that whole city is to be punished with complete destruction (חרם), which is the punishment reserved for the original inhabitants of the cities of Canaan at the time of the conquest.

Personal Retribution the Rule, Collective Retribution in Case of Large-Scale Apostasy

Turning back, now, to the question of the translation of $\sqrt{pqd}$ in the PQD-clause in the Second Word, I would draw the following conclusion from looking at the details of the laws in the Pentateuch with respect to the Second Word. Translating "punishing the children for the sin of the fathers" would cover only the one case of large-scale apostasy and suggest that this is the usual way of dealing with children of parents who have committed idolatry. To see this one case of collective retribution as the exception does more justice to the variety of cases prescribing how to deal with disobedience to the Second Word. The rule is more aptly summarized as personal retribution: only the guilty person is to be punished, and if the kin group becomes the target of attention, only those who have followed the guilty person in his wrong behavior receive the same punishment.

The *PQD*-clause: A New Translation

Finding the right translation equivalent for √*pqd* has proven to be a challenge. At the end of this article, we are now in a position to propose a new translation for the PQD-clause in the Second Word. It should account for what we have found in our exploration of the laws dealing with issues related to the Second Word. Personal retribution is the rule in cases dealing with disobedience to the Second Word, and when the Lord intervenes he will include the kin group in the investigation. Ideally, the translation should also reflect something of the use of the participle of √*pqd* in the PQD-clause. I would suggest the following translation: "I, the Lord your God, am a God who does not tolerate rivals. Where there is misbehavior of parents, I will be monitoring the children, and the third- and fourth-generation descendants, of those who reject me."

Only the Second and Third Word contain a clause announcing the Lord's action in the case of disobedience. The *PQD*-clause in the Second Word underlines the unique seriousness of the sins of worshipping other gods or using images for worship. God will deal with the parents—they are not passed over, just as parents who "love Me and keep My commandments" are not passed over when God shows his love (Exod 20:6). However, he will also keep an eye on how the children, and the third- and fourth-generation descendants, respond to the idolatrous worship of previous generations. Exodus 34:6–7 makes clear that, even when the sins of parents are forgiven, the Lord will continue monitoring the next generations. Forgiveness does not mean ignoring sin but dealing with it, in all its seriousness.[26]

Epilogue: The Christian Church and the Second Word

It is easy for Christians to think that idolatry is not our problem: *we* don't have images or statues in our homes to which we bow down. Jesus and the apostles show this to be very naive.[27] Jesus himself warns against

---

26. See Moberly, "How May We Speak of God?" 200: the words in the second half of Exod 34:7 "serve to clarify that YHWH's forgiveness is truly forgiveness, not leniency, still less moral indifference . . . This means that the unparalleled emphasis upon divine mercy and forgiveness is simultaneously accompanied by an implicit control to prevent the words from being misunderstood and misused."

27. Matt 6:24; Rom 1:18–32 (the words Paul uses to describe the human idol industry are taken from Old Testament passages which describe the idolatry of *God's people*, Israel: Deut 4:16–18; Ps 106:19–20); 1 John 5:21.

the impossibility of serving both God and Mammon and, in so doing, shows the spiritual dimension of idolatry. People who don't have images or statues in their homes had better take a good look at what goes on in their hearts. The Apostle Paul diagnoses the idol industry as a universal human problem, not just a problem among pagans. It is everyone's problem; it is *our* problem. The warning of the Apostle John still needs to be heard, and taken seriously: "Dear children, keep yourselves from idols" (1 John 5:21).

Frederick Buechner provides a helpful definition of idolatry when he writes, "Idolatry is the practice of ascribing absolute value to things of relative worth. Under certain circumstances money, patriotism, sexual freedom, moral principles, family loyalty, physical health, social or intellectual preeminence, and so on are fine things to have around; but to make them the standard by which all other values are measured, to make them your masters, to look to them to justify your life and save your soul is sheerest folly. They just aren't up to it."[28]

We are often very capable of judging what the idols are in the lives of other people. This also happens between different generations in the church. An older generation may look at a younger generation and worry about the things that are important in their lives. By the same token, a younger generation is often able to identify precisely what really matters in the lives of the generation(s) before them.

As Scripture makes abundantly clear, God takes idol worship very seriously, because it blinds people to the beauty of his unrivaled glory and because it destroys people's lives. The Second Word contains a serious warning for an older generation: the object of your worship will not only transform your own life—we become what we worship, for better or worse. It will also impact the life of the generation coming after you. That new generation will see what has captivated the heart of the generation before them and, consciously or uncritically, adopt their worship behavior.

The warning at the end of the Second Word challenges us to look farther than our own lives. What we worship will impact the next generation—they may become what we worship, for better or worse. That is why, whether we are of retirement age or still young, we all so greatly need the light of the knowledge of the glory of God in the face of Christ, which will make our joy in worship everlasting.

---

28. Buechner, *Wishful Thinking*, 49.

BIBLIOGRAPHY

Alter, Robert. *The David Story: A Translation with Commentary of 1 and 2 Samuel*. New York: Norton, 1999.

Buechner, Frederick. *Wishful Thinking: A Seeker's ABC*. San Francisco: HarperSanFrancisco, 1993.

Creason, Stuart. "*PQD* Revisited." In *Studies in Semitic and Afroasiatic Linguistics Presented to Gene B. Gragg*, edited by Cynthia L. Miller, 27–42. Studies in Ancient Oriental Civilization 60. Chicago: Oriental Institute of the University of Chicago, 2008.

Driver, Samuel Rolles. *Notes on the Hebrew Text and the Topography of the Books of Samuel: With an Introduction on Hebrew Palaeography and the Ancient Versions and Facsimiles of Inscriptions and Maps*. 1913. Reprinted, Eugene, OR: Wipf & Stock, 2004.

Firth, David. *1 & 2 Samuel*. Apollos Old Testament Commentary 8. Nottingham: Apollos, 2009.

Greenberg, Moshe. "Some Postulates of Biblical Criminal Law." In *Yehezkel Kaufmann Jubilee Volume: Studies in Bible and Jewish Religion Dedicated to Yehezkel Kaufmann on the Occasion of his Seventieth Birthday*, edited by Menahem Haran, 5–28. Jerusalem: Magnes, 1960. ["Some Postulates of Biblical Criminal Law." In *Essential Papers on Israel and the Ancient Near East*, edited by Frederick E. Greenspahn, 333–52. Essential Papers on Jewish Studies. New York: New York University Press, 1991.]

Hertzberg, Hans W. *Die Samuelbücher*. Das Alte Testament Deutsch 10. Göttingen: Vandenhoeck & Ruprecht, 1965.

———. *I and II Samuel: A Commentary*. OTL. London: SCM, 1964.

Houtman, Cornelis. *Exodus: Chapters 20–40*. Historical Commentary on the Old Testament. Leuven: Peeters, 2000.

Kaminsky, Joel S. *Corporate Responsibility in the Hebrew Bible*. JSOTSup 196. Sheffield: Sheffield Academic, 1995.

Levinson, Bernard M. *Legal Revision and Religious Renewal in Ancient Israel*. Cambridge: Cambridge University Press, 2008.

Moberly, R. W. L. "How May We Speak of God? A Reconsideration of the Nature of Biblical Theology." *Tyndale Bulletin* 53 (2002) 177–202.

Mol, Jurrien. *Collective and Individual Responsibility: A Description of Corporate Personality in Ezekiel 18 and 20*. SSN 53. Leiden: Brill, 2009.

Renkema, Johan. *Lamentations*. Historical Commentary on the Old Testament. Leuven: Peeters, 1998.

Rogland, Max F. *Alleged Non-Past Uses of Qatal in Classical Hebrew*. SSN 44. Assen: Van Gorcum, 2003.

Schmid, K. "Kollektivschuld? Der Gedanke übergreifender Schuldzusammenhänge im Alten Testament und im Alten Orient." *ZABR* 5 (1999) 193–222.

Spencer, John A. "*PQD*, the Levites, and Numbers 1–4." *ZAW* 110 (1998) 535–46.

Stoebe, Hans J. *Das erste Buch Samuelis*. KAT 8.1. Gütersloh: Mohn, 1973.

Vance, Donald R. *An Introduction to Classical Hebrew*. Boston: Brill, 2004.

3

The Sinaitic Covenant in the Narrative of the Book of Exodus

Gert Kwakkel

During their trek from Egypt to Canaan, the people of Israel camped at Mount Sinai for almost a whole year (cf. Exod 19:1 and Num 10:11). This year provides the setting for a large part of the Bible, namely, the section from Exod 18 to Num 10. No other period of similar duration in the history of salvation receives so much attention, except for the last year of the life of Jesus Christ.

Obviously, the Sinai events were fundamental to all that happened subsequently in the history of Israel. A major, if not the most important, element of these events was the covenant that God made with the people of Israel. The making of this covenant is at the heart of this study. More particularly, this study concentrates on Exodus 19, 24, and 34, for these chapters are the only ones in the Sinai narrative of Exodus 19–40 in which the Hebrew word translated as "covenant" (i.e., *berit*) refers to a covenant that God made at Mount Sinai (viz., 19:5; 24:7–8; 34:10, 27–28).[1]

In Exodus 19, God reveals the special status that he will give to Israel as his covenant people. In the analysis of this chapter, special attention will be paid to God's promise that Israel will be "a kingdom of

---

1. The Hebrew *berit* also occurs in Exod 23:32; 34:12, 15, but there it refers to the treaties that Israel was not allowed to make with the peoples of Canaan. In 31:16 it is used for describing the celebration of the Sabbath as "a lasting covenant."

priests"[2] (19:6). This expression does not recur in Exodus 24 and 34, but the exegesis will demonstrate that it still plays an important role. Exodus 24 describes a ritual related to the making of the covenant. Moses reads "the Book of the Covenant" (24:7). He sprinkles blood on the people and says, "This is the blood of the covenant that the LORD has made with you" (24:8). In the Sinai narrative, this is the first occurrence of the Hebrew idiom usually translated as "making a covenant"; that is, the verb *krt* ("to cut") and the noun *berit* ("covenant"). The idiom recurs in Exod 34:10 where God says, "I am making a covenant." Next, God says to Moses in 34:27, "Write down these words, for in accordance with these words I have made a covenant with you and with Israel." Apparently, Moses is the first recipient of this covenant. Furthermore, it seems that the expression "these words" refers to God's words found in 34:10–26 and not to the Ten Commandments of 20:1–17 or the Book of the Covenant mentioned in 24:7. Therefore, the question presents itself: what is the nature of the covenant of Exodus 34? Is it the Sinaitic covenant or a restoration of the Sinaitic covenant, which was necessary because Israel had made the golden calf (Exodus 32), or yet another covenant?

EXODUS 19

In Exod 19:5, God orders Moses to say to the Israelites, "Now if you obey me fully and keep my covenant, then out of all nations you will be my treasured possession." In the preceding chapters, all references to God's covenant related to his covenant with Abraham, Isaac, and Jacob (see Exod 2:24; 6:3–5). The same covenant might also be meant here, but it seems more probable that God is alluding to the covenant that he will make with Israel at Mount Sinai.

The parallel phrase "if you obey me fully" shows that keeping God's covenant is equal to doing what he prescribes. Accordingly, God's promise that Israel will be his treasured possession is conditional upon Israel's obedience. In this respect, the text differs from Exod 6:7, where God also said that he would take Israel as his own people but did not formulate any condition. How can this difference be accounted for? First, it should be realized that God's promises in Exod 19:5–6 surpass the promises of Exod 6:7. God now uses more splendid terms, namely, "my treasured

---

2. All Scripture quotations in this article are from the New International Version (NIV), unless stated otherwise.

possession," "a kingdom of priests," and "a holy nation." Second, in Gen 15:18–21, God made a covenant with Abraham in which he promised to give a large territory to his descendants. He did not formulate any condition in connection with this. However, God's relationship with Abraham had conditional aspects right from the beginning. God first ordered Abraham to leave his family and then promised to make him into a great nation and bless him (Gen 12:1–3).[3] Later on, in Gen 17:1–2, God's promise to make a covenant with Abraham and increase his numbers was preceded by his command, "walk before me and be blameless" (see also Gen 17:14). Subsequently, the conditional aspect was expressed very clearly in Gen 18:19 where God linked the fulfillment of his promises with the behavior of Abraham's descendants.

In view of this, it is not strange that Exod 19:5–6 has conditional elements while Exod 6:7 does not. God's relationship with people, which is sealed by covenants, is dynamic and develops over the course of time. New promises can be added to those given before. The reciprocal nature of the relationship can be made clearer by formulating conditions that were not previously there or were simply taken for granted.[4]

As for the new terms used in God's promises, a "treasured possession" (Hebrew *segullah*) is the private property of a person, as distinguished from the property of the family or the nation (cf. 1 Chr 29:3). Such property is very precious to the owner. In the last words of Exod 19:5, God presents himself as the owner of the whole earth. Thus, he underlines that it is a privilege for Israel to be his "treasured possession." After all, he also could have given that special status to another people.

The special status promised to Israel is further described as "a kingdom of priests." According to several authors, this implies that Israel was called to serve the other nations as priests. One of these authors, Christopher J. H. Wright, defines the task of priests as teaching the law, handling the sacrifices, and blessing the people in the name of the LORD. For Israel, to be priests meant that they "would have the historical task of bringing the knowledge of God to the nations, and bringing the nations

---

3. Gen 12:1–2 can be translated as follows: "Go from your country, your people, and your father's house to the land that I will show you; then I will make you into a great nation and I will bless you; I will make your name great, and you will be a blessing" (author's translation). Cf. Joüon and Muraoka, *A Grammar of Biblical Hebrew*, §116b, h.

4. Cf. Kwakkel, "Verplichting of relatie," 124, 130.

to the means of atonement with God."[5] Furthermore, they had to be a blessing to the nations, in accordance with Abraham's task described in Gen 12:3.

This is a very interesting point of view, for it implies that from the beginning God's special relationship with Israel, formalized in the Sinaitic covenant, was aimed at the salvation and blessing of all the peoples. Other texts, such as Deut 4:6–8 and Isa 43:21, show that Israel indeed had a mission towards the nations. Furthermore, 1 Pet 2:9 applies the titles "a royal priesthood," "a holy nation," and "a people belonging to God" to the New Testament church, and then immediately links them with the church's task to declare the praises of God. With hindsight, then, one can maintain that when God promised Israel that they would be a kingdom of priests, he may well have meant their priestly task to be for the benefit of all nations. However, it seems doubtful that the people of Israel standing at the foot of Mount Sinai were aware of this wide perspective. At that time, they had priests in their midst (see Exod 19:22, 24), but all regulations concerning the task of the priests still had to be given. So, how might they have understood God's words?

In those days, all nations in the Near East had priests. Abraham met the priest Melchizedek (Gen 14:18). Moses' father-in-law, Jethro, was the priest of Midian (Exod 18:1). In Egypt, the country the Israelites had just left, the priests were a privileged class. Since they received income from Pharaoh, they could keep their own land when all the other Egyptians had to sell it in order to be able to buy food (Gen 47:22, 26). Of course, the main privilege of priests was that they served at the temples. They had more direct access to the deity than their fellow countrymen. Moreover, it is precisely this capacity of the priests that is mentioned further on in Exod 19, as v. 22 characterizes the priests as those "who approach the LORD." Their special status is further expressed in the first word of this verse (Hebrew *gam*), which says that not only the common Israelites but "even" the priests must consecrate themselves.

When people or objects are consecrated, they acquire a holy status. According to Exod 19:10–11, Moses had to consecrate the people because the LORD would come down on Mount Sinai in their sight. Later on, the laws now found in Leviticus would teach the people what it meant to be a holy people. Yet the distinction between holy and profane was certainly familiar to them, since it was a pivotal concept in all reli-

---

5. Wright, *The Mission of God*, 330–31. Cf. also Riecker, *Ein Priestervolk*, 229–64.

gions. Holy people and holy objects had a special status and were ruled by distinct provisions, which made them appropriate for approaching the deity or for being used in worship (cf. also Exod 19:23). Accordingly, both expressions used in Exod 19:6—"a kingdom of priests" and "a holy nation"—revealed to the Israelites that God would give them a special status, which distinguished them from all other nations. They would have to observe special rules, but they would also enjoy the privilege of a very close relationship to God. They would be his intimates, who had direct access to him.[6]

If this is the primary meaning of God's promises in Exod 19:5–6, there is a tremendous tension in the chapter. When the LORD came down on the mountain, no one was allowed to approach him, except for Moses. Any of the other Israelites, including even the priests, who ventured to go up the mountain had to pay for it with his life (see Exod 19:11–12, 21–24). Evidently, the people who were called to serve God as priests were still far from being able to do so!

Israel's disobedience had already come to light in the previous chapters. In Exod 19:8, all the people declare that they will do everything the LORD has said. However, only a few days later they would rebel against God by making a golden calf. Apparently, God's promise that Israel would be his treasured possession, a kingdom of priests, and a holy nation might possibly lead to nothing because of their failure to keep the covenant. Yet, there was hope. It can be found in Exod 19:4. In the very first words that Moses had to speak to the people, God reminds them of what he had done in the recent past. He had saved them from the Egyptians, carried them as on eagles' wings, and brought them to himself. All this they had seen with their own eyes. Since he had done this for them, he would certainly be willing and able to make them come as near to him as priests.

EXODUS 24

The next verse in which *berit* refers to God's covenant with Israel is Exod 24:7: "Then he [Moses] took the Book of the Covenant and read it to the people." The Book of the Covenant is the document in which Moses had written down "all the words of the LORD" (Exod 24:4, NKJV). Obviously,

---

6. For a similar interpretation of Exod 19:5–6, see, e.g., Houtman, *Exodus: Chapters 7:14—19:25*, 445–46.

these words of the LORD correspond to "all the LORD's words and laws," which Moses had spoken to the people (v. 3). The present reader of the Bible finds them in Exod 20:22—23:33 (cf. 20:19, 22; 21:1). This part of Exodus mainly consists of precepts that regulate Israel's future life, but there are also some promises about God's acts on behalf of his people (cf. Exod 23:20–31).

After they had heard the words of the LORD, the people promptly responded that they would do everything the LORD had said, just as they did in Exod 19:8. They made this response unanimously, "with one voice" (24:3). Yet Moses thought it necessary to make them hear the words of the LORD once more the next day by reading his words from the Book of the Covenant (24:4, 7). Then the people repeated that they would do "everything the LORD has said," and they added, "we will obey" (v. 7b). After this repeated vow, Moses sprinkled blood on the people. The only explanation of this act is Moses' statement: "This is the blood of the covenant that the LORD has made with you in accordance with all these words" (v. 8). Evidently, the blood confirmed to the people that the LORD had made a covenant with them. The covenant was his initiative (cf. "my covenant" in Exod 19:5), but from now on there could be no doubt that they were really involved in it.

It should be noted that this confirmation was given only after the people had declared twice (or thrice, if Exod 19:8 is included) that they would do everything the LORD had said. Furthermore, in his explanation of the act of sprinkling blood, Moses said that the LORD had made the covenant "in accordance with all these words." Since the indefinite pronoun "all" is linked with the words of God in vv. 3, 4, and 7, "all these words" refers to the contents of the Book of the Covenant. Therefore, by this phrase, Moses reminded the people once again of the crucial importance of God's words. The covenant could only persist and reach its aim if God fulfilled his promises and if Israel obeyed his regulations.

However, one should also consider the origin of the blood that Moses sprinkled on the people. It was the blood of the animals that had been sacrificed as burnt offerings and fellowship offerings (24:5–6). Although the regulations of Leviticus 1, 3, 6, and 7 had not yet been given, the Israelites were already familiar with these types of offerings.[7] Accordingly, it can be safely assumed that they were also aware of their meaning. The burnt offering, which involved the burning of all parts of

---

7. See Exod 10:25; 18:12; 20:24.

the animal on the altar, gave expression to the intention of the sacrificer to dedicate his whole life to God. The fellowship offering was followed by a sacrificial meal in which the sacrificer and his relatives ate portions of the meat, in this way giving expression to the sacrificer's conviction that real life depended upon fellowship with God and his worshippers. Although burnt offerings could be used to make atonement (see Lev 1:4), the idea of forgiveness of sins was not central to these offerings or to the fellowship offerings. In this respect they differed from sin offerings and guilt offerings.

Why did Moses make burnt and fellowship offerings? Part of the answer may be found in the goal of the exodus as formulated in the first part of the book of Exodus. God ordered Pharaoh to let Israel go into the desert so that they could offer sacrifices to the Lord (Exod 5:3; 8:27 [MT 8:23]). In Exod 10:25, these offerings are specified as "sacrifices" (*zevahim*) and "burnt offerings" (*'olot*). Both words recur in Exod 24:5, the latter without any essential change and the former as the first of the two Hebrew words translated as "fellowship offerings." Another clue can be found in the instructions for making altars at the beginning of the Book of the Covenant (Exod 20:24–26). There the Lord speaks about burnt offerings and fellowship offerings. He does not mention sin offerings. At this moment, when Moses made offerings, which accomplished the goal of the exodus,[8] it was apparently not necessary to make sin offerings. The Lord had not ordered him to do so, and the people had just declared that they would do everything the Lord had said.

As for the sprinkling of the blood of the animals on the altar, this blood represented the life of the animal (see Gen 9:4; Lev 17:11, 14). When the blood was sprinkled on the altar, the life of the animal was given to God. This shows once more that Moses' offerings were a symbolic expression of the people's willingness to dedicate their lives to God. Viewed from this perspective, the ritual act of sprinkling the other half of the blood on the people is very meaningful. The fact that Israel's involvement in the covenant was confirmed by this blood showed that the covenant was forever bound up with their willingness to dedicate their lives to God.

It should be added, however, that the animals in some sense took the place of the people themselves. Of course, many aspects of the function of vicarious suffering in God's relationship with his people still had

---

8. Cf. Schenker, "Les sacrifices d'alliance," 489–91.

to be revealed. Nevertheless, the ritual act that confirmed the Sinaitic covenant connected Israel's life in the covenant with the altar and sacrifices. Further revelation could elaborate upon this.

The Old Testament presents no parallel to the act of sprinkling sacrificial blood on the altar *and* on people, except for the consecration of the priests in Exod 29:20–21 and Lev 8:30. In Exod 19:5–6, God had said that if the Israelites kept his covenant they would be a kingdom of priests and a holy nation. The combination of these facts suggests an additional interpretation of the sprinkling of the blood on the people, namely, that Moses consecrated them as priests or a holy nation.[9]

Although the parallel texts in Exodus 29 and Leviticus 8 differ from Exod 24:8 in some respects (such as using the Hebrew word *nzh* for "sprinkling" instead of *zrq*, and the inclusion of anointing oil in the ritual), the suggested connection is attractive. Perhaps Exod 24:9–11 provides further support for it. These verses relate that after the sprinkling of the blood, Moses, Aaron, Nadab and Abihu, and seventy elders of Israel went up the mountain and saw God. They could do so without losing their lives. In other words, God did not apply the sanctions of Exod 19:12–13, 21, and 24 to them. The other Israelites were still not allowed to go up, and Moses was the only one who could come near to the LORD (Exod 24:2). Nevertheless, these elders, who represented Israel, clearly enjoyed some of the privileges of people belonging to "a kingdom of priests."

A final comment must be made on the last words of Exod 24:11, which say that these men "ate and drank." This element of the story not only implies that they really stayed alive, but it may also relate to the making of a covenant (cf. Gen 26:30; 31:46, 54). Even if the meal was not a formal part of making the covenant, it clearly demonstrated that the purpose of God's covenant was that his people would have a blessed life.

In conclusion, several links connect Exodus 24 with Exodus 19. Both chapters emphasize the conditional nature of the Sinaitic covenant. Several elements in the chapters suggest that God has begun with the fulfillment of his promise that Israel would be a kingdom of priests and a holy nation. However, Exodus 24 also surpasses Exodus 19 in that it alludes to the function of sacrificial blood.

---

9. Thus, e.g., Ruprecht, "Exodus 24,9–11 als Beispiel," 165–7; Nicholson, *God and His People*, 172.

EXODUS 34

In Exodus 34 the situation has radically changed. In a flagrant contravention of the second commandment and the first instruction of the Book of the Covenant (Exod 20:23), the Israelites had made a golden calf and worshipped it as their god. Several elements in Exod 32 make it clear how serious this violation of the covenant was. The LORD no longer considered Israel his people, and he did not take responsibility for the exodus any more (32:7). He would even have destroyed them, if Moses had not intervened (32:10–14). Moses himself smashed the tablets of the Testimony to pieces, which probably means that in his view the covenant was broken (32:19).[10]

In Exod 33, the central issue is God's decision to send an angel with Israel instead of going with them himself. Moses pleaded for the people once again and God reversed his decision. Moses then asked the LORD to show him his glory (33:18). Apparently, this would demonstrate that the LORD was really willing to be personally present in the midst of his people.[11] The LORD granted this request, albeit in a modified form (33:19–23). Next, he ordered Moses to come up the mountain with two new stone tablets on which he would write the same words as the first tablets (34:1–2). No one else was allowed to be seen on the mountain (34:3), which implies that Israel had returned to the conditions of Exod 19, in contrast with those of Exod 24:9–11.

When Moses arrived on the mountain, the LORD passed in front of him and proclaimed his name (34:5–7). This name testified to his compassion, grace, love, faithfulness, and willingness to forgive sins, just like the name revealed in Exod 33:19. However, the name ended with an element that could be taken as ominous: "Yet he does not leave the guilty unpunished; he punishes the children and their children for the sin of the fathers to the third and fourth generation" (34:7b; cf. also 32:34).[12] In his reaction, Moses passed over this element (34:8–9), instead appealing to what God had said about his willingness to forgive. He repeated his request that the LORD might go with his people, and asked him to take them as his inheritance (34:9). In Exod 34:10, the LORD replies to this

---

10. Cf. Sarna, *Exodus*, 207; Dohmen, *Exodus 19–40*, 307.

11. Cf. Trimp, *Bevindingen*, 19.

12. For comments on this phrase and alternative translations see, e.g., Piper, "Prolegomena," 212 n. 35; Moberly, "How May We Speak of God?" 199–200; Dohmen, *Exodus 19–40*, 355; cf. also the article in this volume by Wolter H. Rose, p. 13.

request by stating that he is going to make a covenant.[13] At the end of the long speech that follows, he orders Moses to write down "these words, for in accordance with these words I have made a covenant with you and with Israel." Evidently, the expression "these words" refers to what God had said in vv. 10–26, and the substance of this covenant is defined by his words in those verses.

The words of God in Exod 34:10 open with an announcement of his future acts. The LORD will do unique wonders and an awesome work. All the Israelites shall see his deeds, but Moses particularly is the one for whom the LORD will act (cf. "for you," which is singular, at the end of the verse). The text does not specify whether the wonders will be advantageous or disadvantageous for the people,[14] yet it does make it clear that if God's relationship with Israel continues in a favorable way it will only be due to his marvelous deeds. Exodus 34:11–26 contain commandments (except for the promises of vv. 11b and 24). All these commandments were promulgated before, especially in the last part of the Book of the Covenant.[15] The only new element in the passage is v. 24b, where God says that when the Israelites go up to appear before him three times a year, no one will covet their land. Obviously, with this promise God intends to motivate them to leave their possessions behind and to trust in him confidently.

As an appeal to trust in God, this promise interacts with the people's wish to have a visible god, a wish which resulted in the fabrication of the golden calf. Their wish was clearly inspired by a loss of confidence (cf. Exod 32:1–4). A similar connection with the episode of the golden calf can be detected in most of the commandments found in 34:11–26. This clearly is true of vv. 12–16, where the LORD forbids worshipping other gods and everything that could lead to idolatry, and it applies particularly in the case of the ban on cast idols in v. 17. From v. 18 onward, the relationship with the cult of the golden calf is less obvious. Verse 18 itself, however, links the Feast of Unleavened Bread with Israel's exodus from Egypt, thereby alluding to Exod 32 where, in v. 4, the people ascribed the exodus to the golden calf. The Feast of Unleavened Bread

---

13. "With you" in the NIV is an interpretative addition.
14. For the former possibility, see Judg 6:13; for the latter, Exod 3:20.
15. See Exod 23:12, 15–19, 24, 28–33. Other texts that correspond (albeit less exactly) to elements of Exod 34:11–26 are Exod 13:12–13; 20:23; 22:28–29.

should, however, help them to honor the LORD as the God who gave them their national freedom.

In the following verses, the relationship with the cult of the calf can be found, if it is realized that a bull calf was a symbol of strength and fertility. The later history of the Northern Kingdom would demonstrate how the cult of the golden calves could be introduced for the sake of self-protection (cf. 1 Kgs 12:26–28). Participation in the cult could easily lead to the worship of Baal as the god who guaranteed the success of agriculture and reproduction (cf. 1 Kgs 16:31; Hos 2:5, 8, 12–13 [MT 2:7, 10, 14–15]). The meaning of several commandments in Exod 34:19–26 becomes clear when viewed from this perspective. The instructions of vv. 19–24 and 26a all relate to agriculture, animal husbandry, and reproduction. The same might be valid for vv. 25 and 26b, but it is less clear there. Be that as it may, the commandments clearly incite the people to demonstrate in several ways that they thank the LORD for their food and fertility and that they trust in him. As such, they are a meaningful reaction to the people's attitude in the events of the golden calf episode.

However, are all these commandments really addressed to the people of Israel? The only text that clearly addresses the Israelites is v. 13. This verse is in the second person plural, whereas all the other verses are in the second person singular. Admittedly, the singular is often used in commandments directed to all the Israelites.[16] However, in Exod 34:10 the second person singular refers only to Moses, since he is distinguished from the other Israelites, who are denoted as "your people" and "the people you live among." If, then, in the next verse God continues to use the second person singular by saying, "Obey what I command you today," the most logical interpretation is that he is addressing Moses in this and the following verses. Obviously, the commandments of Exod 34:11–26 had to be carried out by all the Israelites and not only by Moses. Otherwise, the second person plural in 34:13 would be inexplicable. All the Israelites had to obey, but the second person singular pronoun in this chapter shows that Moses bore primary responsibility for their obedience. That is why the LORD says in 34:27, "I have made a covenant *with you* and with Israel."

The details of Moses' plea in Exod 33:12–23 and 34:8–9 make his role as primary recipient of the covenant more clear to us. In his plea, Moses refers several times to the favor he has found in God's sight

16. See, e.g., Exod 20:2–17; 21:2; 22:26–30 (MT 22:25–29).

(33:12–13, 16; 34:9). In itself, this may be merely a polite phrase, but in this case it is certainly more than that, as it is paralleled by the claim that God knows Moses by name (33:12). Using these phrases, Moses appeals to his special relationship with the Lord as the reason that God should really go in the midst of his people and forgive their sins (33:15; 34:9). Moreover, in 33:17 the Lord himself endorses Moses' appeal. He says that he will grant Moses' request because Moses has found favor in his sight, and God knows him by name. God's continuing presence among Israel was a favor accorded to Moses because of his special relationship with the Lord. Accordingly, Moses was given a unique role in God's dealings with his people, a role which found expression in the covenant of Exodus 34 and in the phrase "I have made a covenant with you" in v. 27.

The special position of Moses distinguishes the covenant of Exodus 34 from the covenant in Exodus 24. Yet there is continuity between the covenants. All the commandments found in Exodus 34 have their counterparts in the covenant of Exodus 24. Moreover, the words of the covenant on the second set of tablets that Moses receives (Exod 34:28) are the same as those on the first tablets (Exod 34:1), that is, the Ten Commandments.[17] Accordingly, the covenant of Exodus 24 continues in that of Exodus 34. After this second covenant was made, the construction of the tabernacle, ordered in Exodus 25–31 but blocked by the cult of the golden calf, would be realized in Exodus 35–40. At the end of the book of Exodus, the Lord would show his personal presence among his people when his glory filled the tabernacle (40:34).

Thus, the covenant continued, but on a different basis. Moses had been given the unique position of mediator of the covenant. The covenant still had a conditional nature, as the commandments in Exod 34:11–26 reveal. God makes it clear, however, that since Israel had broken the earlier covenant, his future relationship with her can only be based on the wonders to which his name testifies; that is, his undeserved mercy, compassion, grace, love, faithfulness, and willingness to forgive (Exod 33:19; 34:6–7).

---

17. Cf. Nicholson, *God and His People*, 146–47; Houtman, *Exodus: Chapters 20–40*, 725–26.

CONCLUSION

According to the Hebrew text of Exodus, two covenants were made at Mount Sinai. If Israel kept the first covenant, they would be God's precious possession, a kingdom of priests, and a holy nation. They broke this covenant shortly after it was made. Consequently, God's intentions could only be realized by means of a second covenant, which was based on his compassion and the favor that Moses had found in his sight. Conditions, commandments, and obedience were at the heart of the Sinaitic covenant. Nevertheless, when Israel left Mount Sinai it was already crystal clear that grace was the ultimate basis of their future life with the LORD their God.

BIBLIOGRAPHY

Dohmen, Christoph. *Exodus 19–40*. HTKAT. Freiburg: Herder, 2004.
Houtman, Cornelis. *Exodus*. Vol. 2, *Chapters 7:14—19:25*. Translated by Sierd Woudstra. Historical Commentary on the Old Testament 2. Kampen: Kok, 1996.
———. *Exodus: Chapters 20–40*. Translated by Sierd Woudstra. Historical Commentary on the Old Testament 3. Leuven: Peeters, 2000.
Joüon, Paul, and T. Muraoka. *A Grammar of Biblical Hebrew*. Revised ed. Rome: Pontificio Istituto Biblico, 2006.
Kwakkel, Gert. "Verplichting of relatie: verbonden in Genesis." In *Verrassend vertrouwd: Een halve eeuw verkondiging en theologie van Henk de Jong*, edited by Jan Bouma et al., 117–30. Franeker: Van Wijnen, 2009.
Moberly, R. W. L. "How May We Speak of God? A Reconsideration of the Nature of Biblical Theology." *Tyndale Bulletin* 53 (2002) 177–202.
Nicholson, Ernest W. *God and His People: Covenant and Theology in the Old Testament*. Oxford: Clarendon, 1986.
Piper, John. "Prolegomena to Understanding Romans 9:14–15: An Interpretation of Exodus 33:19." *JETS* 22 (1979) 203–16.
Riecker, Siegbert. *Ein Priestervolk für alle Völker: Der Segensauftrag Israels für alle Nationen in der Tora und den vörderen Propheten*. SBB 59. Stuttgart: Katholisches Bibelwerk, 2007.
Ruprecht, Eberhard. "Exodus 24, 9–11 als Beispiel lebendiger Erzähltradition aus der Zeit des babylonischen Exils." In *Werden und Wirken des Alten Testaments: Festschrift für Claus Westermann zum 70. Geburtstag*, edited by Rainer Albertz et al., 138–73. Göttingen: Vandenhoeck & Ruprecht, 1980.
Sarna, Nahum M. *Exodus*. JPS Torah Commentary. Philadelphia: Jewish Publication Society, 1991.
Schenker, Adrian. "Les sacrifices d'alliance, Ex XXIV, 3–8, dans leur portée narrative et religieuse." *RB* 101 (1994) 481–94.
Trimp, C. *Bevindingen: Verzamelde opstellen*. Franeker: Van Wijnen, 1991.
Wright, Christopher J. H. *The Mission of God: Unlocking the Bible's Grand Narrative*. Downers Grove, IL: IVP Academic, 2006.

4

The Church Fathers' Spiritual Interpretation of the Psalms

Hans Boersma

THE WORLD OF THE church fathers may seem far removed from our everyday lives. In some respects, that is indeed the case. It would be foolish to try to appropriate their writings into our theological and cultural contexts without taking into account the many centuries that separate us from the Fathers. Despite the obvious developments and changes that have taken place since the patristic era, however, there is an underlying commonality that links faithful biblical interpretation today with the exegetical endeavors of the early church. Over the past number of years, there has been a growing recognition of the shortcomings of historical critical exegesis and, as a result, an increasing appreciation for the church fathers and their spiritual or theological interpretation of the Bible.[1] In this essay, I will focus on three theological concerns that we, along with the Fathers, may continue to bring to bear on our reading of the book of Psalms. In particular, I am thinking of (1) the Psalms' focus on the harmonious virtue of the person who sings them, (2) the Psalms' christological focus, and (3) the need to appropriate the Psalms in a personal manner.

I want to preface my analysis, however, by recognizing with gratitude that, long before I started reading the church fathers, I encountered

---

1. For helpful introductions to theological or spiritual interpretation, see Billings, *Word of God*; O'Keefe and Reno, *Sanctified Vision*; and Treier, *Introducing Theological Interpretation*.

each of these three elements in the teaching of Professor Cornelis Van Dam. His teaching radiated personal integrity (section 1: "Harmonious Virtue"); a focus on Jesus Christ (section 2: "The Voice of Christ"); and an obvious desire to appropriate the contents of the Scriptures into his own life (section 3: "The Personal Appropriation"). For each of these aspects of Professor Van Dam's teaching, I am truly grateful. In this essay, then, I will highlight these three characteristics of the Psalms, which the Fathers of the church were deeply conscious of and which we need to incorporate also in our exegetical work today.

This essay will focus on several fourth- and fifth-century church fathers and their approach to the interpretation of the Psalms. It would have been possible to focus on almost any other Old Testament book, and in each case, we would have been able to locate important underlying characteristics of the Fathers' spiritual or theological interpretation of Scripture. The Psalms nonetheless stand out as a particularly fruitful entry into our topic. Brian Daley, the well-known patristic scholar from the University of Notre Dame, has pointed out that the Psalms were hugely popular throughout the early church and the Middle Ages: "Early Christian commentaries on the Psalms easily exceed in number those on any other book of the Old or New Testament; we still possess partial or complete sets of homilies or scholarly commentaries on the Psalms—sometimes more than one set—by at least twenty-one Latin or Greek Patristic authors, and this interest did not abate in the medieval Church."[2] The popularity of the Psalms throughout the church's history means that we have a great deal of material from which we can infer how people used to read them theologically or spiritually. Moreover, we are fortunate to have two fairly lengthy fourth-century writings that explain *how* we are supposed to read the Psalms. I am thinking of the *Letter to Marcellinus* written by Athanasius (c. 296–373), the ardent defender of the doctrine of the Trinity against Arian heresy, and of the *Treatise on the Inscriptions of the Psalms* written by the mystical theologian Gregory of Nyssa (c. 335–c. 394).[3] There is also an introduction to the Psalms written by Basil of Caesarea (c. 329–379), Gregory's older brother, which reflects on principles of interpretation one should bring

---

2. Daley, "Is Patristic Exegesis Still Usable?" 204.

3. Athanasius, "Letter," 101–29, 144–47; Gregory, of Nyssa, *Gregory of Nyssa's Treatise on the Inscriptions*, 83–213.

to bear on a reading of the Psalms.[4] I will especially focus on these more general hermeneutical treatises, and also, as an example, look at how Basil of Caesarea, Hilary of Poitiers (c. 300–c. 368), Augustine of Hippo (354–430), and Theodoret of Cyrus (c. 393–c. 457) read Psalm 1.

HARMONIOUS VIRTUE

Psalms are for singing, not just for reading and preaching. That is to say, they fulfill a double function in the liturgy. This opens up an interesting avenue of reflection as here, more explicitly than elsewhere in Scripture, we enter the realm of aesthetics. Questions of beauty and its function come to the fore when we reflect on the role of music in the liturgy. Athanasius reflects explicitly on the role that music and singing play in the liturgy. "It is important," he writes in his *Letter to Marcellinus*, "not to pass over the question of why words of this kind are chanted with melodies and strains."[5] As he addresses this question, Athanasius explicitly rejects the notion that singing in church is simply for aesthetic pleasure. Some, he writes, imagine that "on account of the sweetness of the sound . . . the psalms are rendered musically for the sake of the ear's delight. But this is not so."[6] The purpose of liturgical music, we could also say, is not sensual or material; the purpose is spiritual. It is, says the Egyptian bishop, "for the benefit of the soul."[7]

Athanasius points to two benefits of singing in particular. First, he comments that in singing the voice "is richly broadened."[8] What he seems to mean, is that the sounds of the words are lengthened, dragged out as it were, while at the same time they span various tonal inflections of the human voice. This allows people, says Athanasius somewhat cryptically, "to love God with their whole strength and power."[9] Second, for Athanasius, the melody accompanying the words serves as "a symbol of the spiritual harmony of the soul."[10] Just as the soul has different faculties, so music combines various sounds into one. The harmony of the

---

4. Basil, of Caesarea, *Exegetic Homilies*, 151–54.
5. Athanasius, "Letter," no. 27, p. 123.
6. Ibid. A little later, he reiterates, "[T]he Psalms are not recited with melodies because of a desire for pleasant sounds" (no. 29, p. 125).
7. Athanasius, "Letter," no. 27, p. 123.
8. Ibid.
9. Ibid.
10. Athanasius, "Letter," no. 28, p. 125.

music, we could say, is analogous to the harmony of the soul. And the way in which the faculties of the soul are ordered is no less important than the way in which the various sounds of a song are ordered.

Following Plato, Athanasius holds that human beings have three faculties: reason (*logistikon*), affections (*thumētikon*), and passions or desires (*epithumētikon*).[11] For those three faculties to be in harmony, it is important that reason govern the passions. After all, says Athanasius, "the most excellent things derive from reasoning, while the most worthless derive from acting on the basis of desire."[12] However, there is more to it than just an external analogy between the harmony of the Psalms and the harmony of the soul's faculties. Athanasius appeals to typology to make clear that there is an intimate connection between the two. "The harmonious reading of the Psalms," he claims, "is a *figure and type* of such undisturbed and calm equanimity of our thoughts."[13] A little later, he again comments that the harmonious combination of cymbals, harp, and the ten-stringed instrument is a "*figure and sign* of the parts of the body coming into natural concord like harp strings, and of the thoughts of the soul becoming like cymbals."[14] The harmonious character of the melody of the Psalms and of musical instruments serves as a figure, a type, or a sign of the harmonious character of the body and of the faculties of the soul. For Athanasius, genuine aesthetics recognizes the need to move from outward (aesthetic) beauty to inner (spiritual) harmony.

This concern for harmony, along with the language of typology, pervades also Gregory's discussion. Gregory, much like Athanasius, makes reference to the narrative of David playing the harp and thereby soothing King Saul's troubled disposition, restoring harmony among his soul's faculties (1 Sam 16).[15] Gregory observes that people tend to sing the Psalms on all sorts of occasions, including "banquets and wedding festivities."[16] He then deals with the question of what it is that makes people take such pleasure in what the Psalms teach. It is not just the fact that we *sing* the words that causes this pleasure, insists Gregory, but

---

11. Cf. Smith, *Passion and Paradise*, 52–58.
12. Athanasius, "Letter," no. 27, p. 124.
13. Ibid.; emphasis added.
14. Athanasius, "Letter," no. 29, pp. 125–26; emphasis added.
15. Ibid., 125; Gregory of Nyssa, *Treatise on the Inscriptions*, I.3, p. 92.
16. Gregory, ibid., 88.

singing the Psalms puts us in line with the order of the universe.[17] The universe itself constitutes what the Cappadocian theologian calls a "diverse and variegated musical harmony," so that it sings a "polyphonic tune."[18] One can observe in creation a rhythmic oscillation between rest and motion. Together, rest and motion create a musical pattern in praise of God. Gregory calls this cosmic harmony "the primal, archetypal, true music."[19] Gregory then moves from the cosmos to humanity, insisting that human beings are a microcosmos, as human nature reflects the musical harmony of the cosmic archetype.[20] Even the human body, insists Gregory, shows this harmony: "Do you see the flute in the windpipe, the bridge of the lyre in the palate, the music of the lyre that comes from tongue, cheeks, and mouth, as though from strings and a plectrum?"[21] Gregory, while focusing on spiritual realities first and foremost, obviously does not disdain the human body; instead, he considers it an intricate work of divine art, reflecting the musical order of the cosmos.

The conclusion we need to draw, according to Gregory, is that music forms the very pattern both of the cosmos in general, the archetype, and of human beings in particular, the microcosm. This implies that musical expression fits well with the content of the Psalms, since the teaching of the Psalms is meant to harmonize the faculties of the soul. "In this singing," says Gregory, "nature reflects on itself in a certain manner, and heals itself."[22] The very fact that we *sing* the Psalms is a symbolic act, Gregory insists repeatedly, pointing to the "proper rhythm of life"; that is, a virtuous life in which the passions have been subdued. At this point, Gregory concludes that people take such pleasure in the teaching of the Psalms because harmonious singing puts us in harmony with the cosmos, with human nature, and therefore, ultimately, with the teaching about the virtues, which we find in the Psalms.[23] Harmony and virtue, beauty and goodness, go together for the Cappadocian Father.

---

17. Ibid., I.2, p. 88.
18. Ibid., I.3, p. 89.
19. Ibid., 90. See on this topic and its relation to mathematics: Caldecott, *Beauty for Truth's Sake*.
20. Gregory of Nyssa, *Treatise on the Inscriptions*, I.3, pp. 90–91.
21. Ibid., 91.
22. Ibid.
23. For similar reflections, see ibid., 129–30.

Gregory's older brother, Basil, presents similar reflections in the introduction to his homily on Psalm 1. These Cappadocian theologians both focus on cultivation of virtue as the purpose of the Psalms. To them, music exists not for its own sake but serves to support the promotion of virtue. Basil charmingly comments, "The delight of melody He [i.e., the Holy Spirit] mingled with the doctrines so that by the pleasantness and softness of the sound heard we might receive without perceiving it the benefit of the words, just as the wise physicians who, when giving the fastidious rather bitter drugs to drink, frequently smear the cup with honey."[24] For Basil, the Psalms' teaching on virtue is the bitter but beneficial drug while the melody is the honey that makes it palatable. In fact, Basil considers the musical harmony of the Psalms not merely as conducive to ridding oneself of sinful passions, but he also has an eye for the communal benefits of the Psalms. "A psalm," he says, "forms friendships, unites those separated, conciliates those at enmity."[25] The result is that the harmony of the Psalms produces harmony within the congregation: "[P]salmody, bringing about choral singing, a bond, as it were, toward unity, and joining the people into a harmonious union of one choir, produces also the greatest of blessings, charity."[26] The harmony of the choir produces the virtuous harmony of love. The church fathers were not content with the kind of exegesis that is satisfied once it has determined the historical meaning of the text. Instead, they insist that we ask whether one's reading promotes virtue and yields genuine harmony. Interpretation and harmonious character are inseparable.[27]

THE VOICE OF CHRIST

The Psalms are particularly suited for spiritual interpretation because of the multiple ways in which one can discern Christ in them. Michael Fiedrowicz, in his introduction to Augustine's *Expositions of the Psalms*, mentions a five-fold christological interpretation of the Psalms among the Fathers. He explains that the Psalms were interpreted as a word to Christ (*vox ad Christum*); a word about Christ (*vox de Christo*); a word of Christ, spoken by him (*vox Christi*); a word about the Church

24. Basil, of Caesarea, *Exegetic Homilies*, 152.
25. Ibid.
26. Ibid.
27. Fowl, "Virtue," 837. Cf. also Briggs, *The Virtuous Reader*; Treier, *Introducing Theological Interpretation*, 92–96.

(*vox de ecclesia*); and a word of the Church, spoken by the Church (*vox ecclesiae*).²⁸ Of course, only the first three are strictly christological, and I will focus on them. But we should keep in mind that, for Augustine at least, Christ and church should always be viewed together as the "whole Christ" (*totus Christus*). Christ's reprimand of Saul—"Saul, Saul, why do you persecute me?"²⁹ (Acts 9:4)—implied, for Augustine, that Christ identifies with his church.³⁰ The head and the body, the groom and the bride, make up the one total Christ. Jason Byassee, author of a wonderful book on Augustine's interpretation of the Psalms, observes that Augustine's commentary presents "a 'christo-ecclesiological' form of exegesis, premised on the *totus Christus*, the 'whole Christ,' who speaks throughout the Psalter."³¹ So, when the Psalms speak about Christ, the words often need to be applied to those united to him—the church as well as individual believers. Conversely, what the Psalms say about either individual believers or the church often needs to be understood as referring to Christ himself, as well. Thus, Augustine is convinced that proper interpretation of the Psalms takes into account not *just* Christology, but that the Psalms also speak a word about the Church (*vox de ecclesia*) and a word spoken by the Church (*vox ecclesiae*). In what follows, however, I will focus only on the strictly christological interpretation of the Psalms, noting how Augustine's outlook discerns Christ in three ways: the Psalms are words *to* Christ, *about* Christ, and *of* Christ.

Let me first comment on the Psalms as words *to* Christ (*vox ad Christum*). When the Psalms address God, the Fathers have little hesitation in seeing in these words also prayers addressed to Christ. Since Christ is the incarnate Son of God, the Fathers consider it entirely legitimate that Christ is addressed as God in the very words of the Psalms. So when the Psalmist appeals to God for help, forgiveness, and justice, and so on, all of these petitions may be interpreted also as petitions addressed to Christ.³² Thus, the Fathers consciously allow theological convictions to influence their reading of the text.

---

28. Fiedrowicz, "General Introduction," 44–45.

29. Scripture quotations in this article are from the New International Version (NIV).

30. Cf. Matt 25:40; 1 Cor 10:16–17; 1 Cor 12:2; Col 1:24. Cf. Fiedrowicz, "General Introduction," 53–54.

31. Byassee, *Praise Seeking Understanding*, 63.

32. Ibid., 45.

The Psalms also speak *about* Christ (*vox de Christo*). This becomes particularly clear when we look at the Fathers' exegesis of Psalm 1. "Blessed is the man who does not walk in the counsel of the wicked," begins Psalm 1. The immediate question, of course, is: who is "the man" who is the object of the psalmist's speech? Fascinatingly, the very first words of Augustine's commentary on the Psalms are Christ-filled words. "This statement," he says, "should be understood as referring to our Lord Jesus Christ, that is, the Lord-Man."[33] He then continues to speak about Christ's faithfulness in contrast to Adam's lack thereof: "*Blessed is the person who has not gone astray in the council of the ungodly*, as did the earthly man who conspired with his wife, already beguiled by the serpent, to disregard God's commandments."[34] When he then reflects on the man of Psalm 1 as not standing in the way of sinners, Augustine takes this as an opportunity to comment on the incarnation itself: "Christ most certainly came in the way of sinners by being born as sinners are; but he did not stand in it, for worldly allurement did not hold him."[35] Augustine distinguishes here between "coming" and "standing": Christ "came" in the way of sinners since in the incarnation he came in the likeness of sinful flesh, but he did not "stand" in the way of sinners, which is to say he did not become sinful. Without any hesitation, therefore, Augustine begins with a christological reading of the Psalm. The psalmist's voice is here a *vox de Christo*; a voice about Christ.

To be sure, there is no unanimity on this point among patristic interpreters. The great fourth-century defender of orthodox Trinitarian thought, Hilary of Poitiers, explicitly disagreed with this approach that Augustine would later take. "I have discovered," says Hilary, "either from personal conversation or from their letters and writings, that the opinion of many men about this Psalm is, that we ought to understand it to be a description of our Lord Jesus Christ, and that it is His happiness which is extolled in the verses following."[36] We just saw that this is exactly the approach of Augustine, and judging by Hilary's words, this was a common patristic approach. Hilary, however, disagrees, "But this interpretation is wrong both in method and reasoning," he comments, "though doubtless it is inspired by a pious tendency of thought, since the whole of the

---

33. Augustine, "Exposition of Psalm 1," 67.
34. Ibid.
35. Ibid.
36. Hilary, of Poitiers, "Psalm I," 236.

Psalter is to be referred to Him."[37] We must carefully note that Hilary is not objecting to a christological reading. Indeed, he writes, "[T]he whole of the Psalter is to be referred to Him [i.e., Christ]." Hilary nonetheless does not think that the comment, "Blessed is the man," is a reference to Christ, and he gives two basic reasons for this. First, the Son is the one who *gave* the Law, while according to the Psalm, this man's happiness or blessedness depends on his "desire" being in the Law of the Lord. How can one attribute such desire to Christ? Christ's desire, insists Hilary, is not in the Law of the Lord since, as the one who gives it, he is the Law's Lord.[38] Second, the psalmist compares the blessed or happy man to a tree. This presupposes, Hilary explains, that the tree is the greater standard by which the blessed man is measured. How can a tree be happier than the Son of God? How can Christ be happy by becoming like the objects he himself created? The conclusion, insists Hilary, must be that the psalmist is speaking about believers: "[W]e must suppose him, who is here extolled as happy by the Prophet, to be the man who strives to conform himself to that body which the Lord assumed and in which He was born as man. . . ."[39] What we see from this comparison of Hilary and Augustine's readings of Psalm 1 is that the church fathers, while unanimous in reading the Psalms christologically, are not always agreed on the details of *how* to do so.

Athanasius provides us with numerous examples of words *about* Christ (*vox de Christo*) in the Psalter. Thoroughly at home in the Psalms, Athanasius moves back and forth among them with amazing alacrity, and, as he does so, he locates in them many of the particular moments within the economy of the Son's work. Athanasius reads in the Psalms the teaching of the Savior who will come as one who is God (Pss 50:3; 107:20; 118:26–27); the eternal generation of the Son (Pss 45:1; 110:3); the incarnation of God's Son in the flesh (Pss 45:6–7; 87:5); the virgin birth (Ps 45:10–11); the suffering of the Savior (Ps 2:1–2); the death on a Cross (Ps 22:15–18); the representative character of Christ's suffering (Pss 69:4; 72:4, 12; 88:16; 138:8); the ascension into heaven (Pss 24:7; 47:5); the session at God's right hand (Pss 9:7–8; 110:1); the prophecy of Christ's return as Judge (Pss 50:4; 72:1–2; 82:1); and, finally, the calling of

---

37. Ibid.
38. Ibid.
39. Ibid., 237.

the nations (Pss 47:1; 72:9–11).[40] Athanasius regards the *vox de Christo* as nearly omnipresent in the book of Psalms. And while his exegesis tends to be less christological, Basil of Caesarea, too, heaps praise on the Psalms when commenting, "Therein is perfect theology, a prediction of the coming of Christ in the flesh..."[41] The notion that the Psalms present a "word about Christ" receives the unanimous support of the Fathers.

This approach implies great confidence in the inspiration of Scripture. According to the Fathers' interpretation, the Spirit has so shaped the contents of the Old Testament that it already bespeaks New Testament christological realities. This confidence in divine inspiration is what allows the Fathers to read the book of Psalms prophetically. The notion that the Psalter is a book of prophecy is perhaps one of the distinguishing characteristics of pre-modern exegesis. Interpreters like Augustine will often refer to the psalmist as "the prophet." Or, more radically yet, in an unencumbered sort of way, someone like Augustine will simply refer to the Holy Spirit as the speaker of the Psalm.[42] Contemporary sermons and commentaries tend to be much more hesitant in referring to "the prophet" or "the Spirit" as saying something in the text. Such hesitation goes hand in hand with a reluctance to read the Psalms as speaking prophetically about Christ. The modern notion that restricts exegesis to a search for the intent of the human author has a tendency to limit the horizons of interpretation to realities of this world. The almost inevitable result, it seems to me, is that any overarching intentions of the Spirit are excluded from the outset. It is by expanding our attention beyond this-worldly realities and by acknowledging the Spirit's guiding hand in both the authorship and the interpretation of Holy Scripture that we will likely also regain confidence in our discernment of Christ's presence in the Old Testament.

Finally, not only do we have the *vox ad Christum* and the *vox de Christo* in the Psalms, but there is also the *vox Christi*, the voice *of* Christ—Christ himself speaking through the voice of the psalmist. Fiedrowicz makes clear that one of the key elements of patristic exegesis is the attempt to figure out who is speaking in a psalm. Fiedrowicz refers to this as "prosopological exegesis," derived from the Greek word *prosōpon*, meaning "person." Prosopological exegesis, therefore, asks the

---

40. Athanasius, "Letter," nos. 5–8, pp. 103–6. See also no. 26, p. 123.
41. Basil, of Caesarea, *Exegetic Homilies*, 153.
42. Fiedrowicz, "General Introduction," 24.

question: which *person* is speaking in this psalm? Once this has been figured out, much of the rest of the psalm falls into place. We see a striking example of such prosopological exegesis at the very beginning of Hilary's commentary on Psalm 1: "The primary condition of knowledge for reading the Psalms," he starts off, clearly raising a hermeneutical issue right at the outset, "is the ability to see as whose mouthpiece we are to regard the Psalmist as speaking, and who it is that he addresses."[43] With the former of these two issues, the question of whose mouthpiece the psalmist might be, Hilary introduces prosopological interpretation.

We see something similar in Augustine's work. As already mentioned, for Augustine, the doctrine of *totus Christus*—the "whole Christ" as reference to Christ *and* his members—means that Christ can be speaking in these kinds of passages either in his own person (*ex persona sua*) or in our person (*ex persona nostra*).[44] Fiedrowicz puts it this way:

> An important part of Augustine's thought is that the Church was already present in Christ's prayer. His exegesis of the frequently quoted verse of Psalm 21 (21:2[22:1]) shows that for Augustine the cry of Christ on the cross was not only raised "in Adam's name" but had an ecclesial dimension too, in that Christ directed those words to the Father "in the name of his body" equally (*ex persona corporis*). By identifying the Church with even the earthly body of Christ Augustine was able to discover a mysterious involvement of humanity in the event of the cross. We were there (*nos ibi eramus*).[45]

"We were there." This statement shows what is at stake for Augustine—and, really, for the Fathers in general—in prosopological exegesis. By seeing the Psalms as referring to Christ, the church fathers allow God's people to make these Psalms their own, as well.[46] The church is present in the Psalms because Christ himself is present there. Pulling these various strands together, we may say that, for the Fathers, spiritual interpretation is nearly synonymous with christological interpretation.

---

43. Hilary, of Poitiers, "Psalm I," 236.

44. Fiedrowicz, "General Introduction," 52–55.

45. Ibid., 54.

46. Discussing Augustine's exegesis of Ps 100 (101), Louth, "Heart in Pilgrimage," 303, comments: "[I]t is Christ's voice we hear in the psalm, and part of what is meant by understanding the psalm is learning how to join our voice to Christ's; the Christ singing in the psalm is Christ the head of the Church, of which we are the members . . ."

PERSONAL APPROPRIATION

Augustine's *totus Christus* theology makes the Psalms eminently suitable for the life of the church and for individual Christians. Patristic commentators who do not have Augustine's highly developed *totus Christus* theology are, nonetheless, equally convinced that the meaning of the Psalms is intimately connected to the lives of believers. Specifically, I want to point to two elements of this connection. First, I have already mentioned the centrality of the element of virtue for the Fathers when discussing the role of music in connection with the Psalms. But the focus on virtue is not merely a by-product of the Fathers' reflections on aesthetics and harmony; a concern with virtue dominates much of their exegesis. It is central particularly to the Alexandrian tradition (notably Clement and Origen) and to the Cappadocians (Basil the Great, Gregory of Nyssa, and Gregory of Nazianzus), who in this respect follow, at least in part, the first-century Jewish philosopher from Alexandria, Philo. Commenting on the two ways of Psalm 1, Basil explains: "[L]eading us on wisely and skilfully to virtue, David made the departure from evil the beginning of good."[47] Basil's brother, Gregory of Nyssa, places an even greater emphasis on virtue in his *Treatise on the Inscriptions on the Psalms*. He casts the entire book as a treatise on virtue, writing in the preface, "[Y]ou enjoined us to investigate the meaning to be observed in these inscriptions, so that their capacity to lead us to virtue might be obvious to all."[48] Gregory begins the first chapter of Part I with the words, "The goal of the virtuous life is blessedness."[49] He then explains the five books of the Psalms as five stages of ascent in the growth of virtue. In Part II he explains the Septuagint's inscriptions, or headings, above the Psalms, and begins by insisting that these also are meant to lead us on in virtue: "For these too make a significant contribution to us in respect to the way of virtue, as can be learned from the meaning itself of the words which have been inscribed."[50] Gregory is convinced that the Psalms are all about teaching us the virtuous life, and, as a result, the theme of virtue runs throughout his commentary.

---

47. Basil, of Caesarea, *Exegetic Homilies*, 157. See also pp. 160, 161.
48. Gregory, of Nyssa, *Treatise on the Inscriptions*, I.pref.1, p. 83.
49. Ibid., I.1.5, p. 84.
50. Ibid., II.1.1, p. 124.

The emphasis on virtue is not restricted to the Alexandrians and the Cappadocians. It is also present among the Antiochenes. When Theodoret of Cyrus, who likely wrote his *Commentary on the Psalms* between 441 and 448,[51] comments on the word "blessed" in Psalm 1, he explains that this epithet "constitutes the fruit of perfection as far as virtue is concerned. . . . [T]he practice of virtue has as its fruit and goal the beatitude from God."[52] And speaking about the tree growing by the riverbanks, he explains, "You see, champions of virtue reap the fruit of their labors in the future life; but like a kind of foliage they bear sound hope constantly within them . . ."[53]

We may say that the church fathers let their exegesis be guided by the question of how a particular reading advances growth in virtue. Interpretation for them was less a matter of historical investigation than the pursuit of a spiritual purpose. This difference in perspective means an entry into the text rather different from what we are used to. We tend to put historical questions to the text and ask, primarily, what the text *meant*. The Fathers perhaps make us feel uncomfortable by their relative neglect of the historical level of meaning. They are right, however, to search Scripture to see how it can help us rid ourselves of earthly passions and assist our growth in the life of God; in other words, they rightly focus on what the text *means*.

Personal appropriation is not only a matter of growth in virtue, even if that is the overriding and ultimate concern, especially for the Cappadocians. The church fathers are also keenly aware that the book of Psalms reflects a broad range of human emotions, and they believed it quite legitimate to find one's own emotional experiences reflected there. Athanasius's *Letter to Marcellinus* contains a long section in which he reflects on how one can make the Psalms his own. Athanasius praises the Psalter for having "a certain grace of its own."[54] He then comments:

> It contains even the emotions of each soul, and it has the changes and rectifications of these delineated and regulated in itself. Therefore anyone who wishes boundlessly to receive and understand from it, so as to mold himself, it is written there. For in the other books one hears only what one must do and what one

---

51. Hill, "Introduction," 4.
52. Theodoret, of Cyrus, "Commentary on Psalm 1," 47.
53. Ibid., 49. See also p. 50.
54. Athanasius, "Letter," no. 10, p. 107.

> must not do. And one listens to the Prophets so as solely to have knowledge of the coming of the Savior. One turns his attention to the histories, on the basis of which he can know the deeds of the kings and saints. But in the Book of Psalms, the one who hears, in addition to learning these things, also comprehends and is taught in the emotions of the soul. . . .[55]

Athanasius shows himself here as a pastor and physician of the soul who is aware that one cannot read the Psalms without making the various emotions of them one's own. And so he comments that "the one who hears is deeply moved, as though he himself were speaking, and is affected by the words of the songs, as if they were his own songs."[56] Reading the Psalms, for Athanasius, leads to deeper knowledge also of oneself.

Athanasius does not base this emotional appropriation on a *totus Christus* theology. He carefully distinguishes between psalms that prophesy about the Savior, on the one hand, and passages that reflect our own emotions, on the other hand.[57] To be sure, Athanasius then goes on to say that just as the Psalms provide examples that mirror the emotions of our souls, so also Christ provides what Athanasius calls a "type," "image," or "model" for our actions.[58] According to Athanasius, Christ "offered himself as a model for those who wish to know the power of acting. It was indeed for this reason that he made this resound in the Psalms before his sojourn in our midst, so that just as he provided the model of the earthly and heavenly man in his own person, so also from the Psalms he who wants to do so can learn the emotions and dispositions of the souls, finding in them also the therapy and correction suited for each emotion."[59] Christ is the one who stands behind the descriptions of our emotional life in the Psalms; and, what is more, his very life itself offers a description of the life of the soul. Athanasius then goes on to offer page upon page of references to the Psalms connecting them to the various emotional states of the believer. There are psalms for nearly every situation one may encounter and for nearly every emotional expression to which one may wish to give voice.[60] The Psalms, for Athanasius as well

55. Ibid., 108.
56. Athanasius, "Letter," no. 11, p. 109.
57. Ibid., 109–10.
58. Athanasius, "Letter," no. 13, p. 112.
59. Ibid.
60. Athanasius, "Letter," nos. 14–26, pp. 112–23.

as for the other church fathers, offer a glimpse into one's own soul. Thus, the Psalms become a means for healing one's emotional life.

It may be true that in many ways the church fathers inhabited a world quite different from our own. Nonetheless, their exegesis of the Psalms shows an underlying sensibility that we need to retain or, perhaps, retrieve. The underlying sensibility is that the Psalms must be read theologically or spiritually. They are not just human words from the past, whose meaning we can objectively ascertain by painstaking historical research. Instead, in and through the human words of Scripture, the divine author intends to convey eternal, spiritual truth. This interpretive principle—that, in and through the historical or literal meaning of Scripture, God wants to convey spiritual levels of meaning—has several implications. First, we recognize the congruence between the harmonious singing of the Psalms, on the one hand, and the harmony of the cosmos and of the human soul, on the other hand. Singing the Psalms makes us beautiful because it puts us in virtuous harmony with the created order. Second, we recognize Christ at the center of the Psalms. The ultimate reason that we cannot limit our interpretation of the Psalms to their historical meaning is that such exegesis fails to do justice to the newness of what comes in and through the fulfillment of the Psalms in Christ. Finally, union with Christ allows us to appropriate personally the contents of the Psalms and so come to deeper self-knowledge. We ourselves have a place in the Psalms. They speak of us, of our maturation in virtue, and of the wide variety of human emotions. Spiritual or theological exegesis of the Psalms, therefore, yields virtuous harmony, draws us deeper into Christ, and teaches us a deeper knowledge of ourselves.[61]

---

61. I want to thank my colleagues Iain Provan and John Stackhouse for their comments on an earlier draft of this paper.

BIBLIOGRAPHY

Athanasius, Saint. "A Letter of Athanasius, Our Holy Father, Archbishop of Alexandria, to Marcellinus on the Interpretation of the Psalms." In *The Life of Antony and the Letter to Marcellinus*, translated by Robert C. Gregg, 101–30. Classics of Western Spirituality. New York: Paulist, 1980.

Augustine, Saint. "Exposition of Psalm 1." In *Expositions of the Psalms 1–32*, translated and edited Maria Boulding. Works of Saint Augustine: A Translation for the 21st Century 3/15. Hyde Park, NY: New City, 2000.

Basil, of Caesarea, Saint. *Exegetic Homilies*. Translated by Agnes Clare Way. The Fathers of the Church 46. Washington: Catholic University of America Press, 1963.

Billings, J. Todd. *The Word of God for the People of God: An Entryway to the Theological Interpretation of Scripture*. Grand Rapids: Eerdmans, 2010.

Briggs, Richard. *Virtuous Reader: The Old Testament Narrative and Interpretive Virtue*. Studies in Theological Interpretation. Grand Rapids: Baker Academic, 2010.

Byassee, Jason. *Praise Seeking Understanding: Reading the Psalms with Augustine*. Radical Traditions. Grand Rapids: Eerdmans, 2007.

Caldecott, Stratford. *Beauty for Truth's Sake: On the Re-enchantment of Education*. Grand Rapids: Brazos, 2009.

Daley, Brian E. "Is Patristic Exegesis Still Usable? Reflections on Early Christian Interpretation of the Psalms." *Communio* 29 (2002) 185–216.

Fiedrowicz, Michael. "General Introduction." In *Expositions of the Psalms 1–32*, by Saint Augustine, translated and edited by Maria Boulding. The Works of Saint Augustine: A Translation for the 21st Century 3/15. Hyde Park, NY: New City, 2000.

Fowl, Stephen E. "Virtue." In *Dictionary for Theological Interpretation of the Bible*, edited by Kevin J. Vanhoozer et al., 837–39. Grand Rapids: Baker Academic, 2005.

Gregory, of Nyssa, Saint. *Gregory of Nyssa's Treatise on the Inscriptions of the Psalms*. Edited and translated by Ronald E. Heine. Oxford: Clarendon, 1995.

Hilary, of Poitiers, Saint. "Psalm I." In *Homilies on the Psalms*, translated by E. W. Watson et al. Edited by W. Sandy. Nicene and Post-Nicene Fathers II/9. 1899. Reprint, Peabody, MA: Hendrickson, 1994.

Hill, Robert C. "Introduction." In *Commentary on the Psalms*. Vol. 1, *Psalms 1–72*, by Theodoret of Cyrus, translated by Robert C. Hill, 1–38. The Fathers of the Church 101. Washington DC: Catholic University of America Press, 2000.

Louth, Andrew. "'Heart in Pilgrimage': St Augustine as Interpreter of the Psalms." In *Orthodox Readings of Augustine*, edited by George E. Demacopoulos and Aristotle Papanikolaou. Crestwood, NY: St Vladimir's Seminary Press, 2008.

O'Keefe, John J., and R. R. Reno. *Sanctified Vision: An Introduction to Early Christian Interpretation of the Bible*. Baltimore: Johns Hopkins University Press, 2005.

Smith, J. Warren. *Passion and Paradise: Human and Divine Emotion in the Thought of Gregory of Nyssa*. New York: Crossroad, 2004.

Theodoret, of Cyrus. *Commentary on the Psalms*. Vol. 1, *Psalms 1–72*. Translated by Robert C. Hill. The Fathers of the Church 101. Washington, DC: Catholic University of America Press, 2000.

Treier, Daniel J. *Introducing Theological Interpretation of Scripture: Recovering a Christian Practice*. Grand Rapids: Baker Academic, 2008.

5

Social Injustice and the Existence of God

A Commentary on the Old Greek Text of Psalm 57

JANNES SMITH

I OWE PROFESSOR VAN DAM a debt of gratitude for encouraging me to study the Septuagint (LXX) at the University of Toronto. What follows is a verse-by-verse commentary on the LXX text of Psalm 57 (Psalm 58 in Hebrew), comparing the Greek with the Hebrew in an effort to trace how the translator (G) interpreted the parent text.[1] That is to say, the focus is on the meaning of the Greek as originally intended by its translator, not as interpreted later in its reception history. As I have written elsewhere, "The basis for distinguishing the production of a translated document from its reception history is that a translator and a reader of a translation are involved in fundamentally different activities: the former interprets a [Hebrew] source text, and thus the translation stands in a relationship of dependency to its source at its inception, while the latter interprets a [Greek] target text that (s)he has received as a finished product, independent of its source."[2] I have chosen Psalm 57 because it contains four Hebrew words for which Prof. Van Dam contributed lexicographical entries for *New International Dictionary of Old Testament Theology and Exegesis* (*NIDOTTE*). The English translation of each verse is taken from the *New English Translation of the Septuagint* (NETS).[3]

---

1. Unless otherwise specified, verse and chapter references follow the numbering of the Septuagint.

2. Smith, *Translated Hallelujahs*, v.

3. Pietersma and Wright, *A New English Translation of the Septuagint*. A revised edition (2009) is now available, but the text of Ps 57 has remained unchanged.

Since the NETS translators used the *New Revised Standard Version* as their starting point, the NRSV is also supplied to give the reader some impression of the relationship between the Greek and Hebrew texts.

SYNOPSIS

The Psalm asks the sons of men whether they speak righteousness and judge fairly (v. 2). An answer is given to this query, indicating that they have not done so (v. 3). Sinners are described as aliens and liars (v. 4), with wrath like snakes, unable and unwilling to listen (vv. 5–6). However, divine vengeance has left them toothless (v. 7) and sightless under fire from above (v. 9b). Their fate includes disappearance like ebbing water (v. 8a), and removal like melting wax (v. 9a). They will grow weak before God's bow (v. 8b), and when a righteous one will wash his hands in the sinner's blood (v. 11), one may draw the conclusion that God exists (v. 12).

PSALM AS A WHOLE

While the translational character of the Greek Psalm may best be described as isomorphic (morpheme-for-morpheme), a number of small adjustments on the part of the translator have affected the profile of the Psalm. Firstly, his interpretation of *miktam* as *stēlographia* in v. 1 conceives the Psalm as cast in stone. Secondly, whereas the Hebrew Psalm is usually read as addressed to "gods," the Greek, by a different vocalization of the same consonantal text for v. 2, addresses "sons of men." Thirdly, the Hebrew Psalm is often classified as imprecatory, and no doubt the Greek rendition can retain that designation, but G's translation of Hebrew imperatives with Greek indicatives in v. 7 has transformed one imprecation into an affirmation. Fourthly, standard equivalents, which of themselves can hardly be taken to demonstrate interpretive intent, at times have meanings quite at variance with those of their Hebrew counterparts. Finally, departures from isomorphic translation technique are isolated but intriguing.

VERSE 1 [SUPERSCRIPTION]

NRSV: To the leader: Do Not Destroy. Of David. A Miktam.

NETS: Regarding completion. Do Not Destroy. Pertaining to Dauid. For a stele inscription.

Regarding completion

The placement of *lammenatseakh* at the start of a superscription, as well as its association with supervision of temple activities in Ezra and Chronicles,[4] suggests the translation "to the leader" (NIV "for the director of music"). G, however, associated consonantal *lmntskh* with *lanetsakh* "for ever." If *telos* means "end, outcome, completion," and *eis telos* "in the end, in the long run" (LSJ), then one might be led to suppose that *eis to telos* refers to a specified end, but of what is not clear, nor will it have been of concern to the translator. G consistently wrote *eis telos* "completely" for *lntskh* (14x), and *eis to telos* for *lmntskh* (55 times, all in superscriptions). Hence the <*m*> morpheme appears to have triggered the Greek article. One might wonder whether G read *lmntskh* as *lemo-netsakh*. *Lemo*, a fuller form of the inseparable preposition *le*, does not occur in Psalms, so one cannot check how G handled this item elsewhere, unlike *lamo*, which G readily recognized as an alternative for *lahem* "for them." By analogy, *bemo* (11[10]:2) and *kemo* (29[28]:6; 58[57]:5, 8, 9, 10; 61[60]:7, etc.) do occur in the Psalter, and G recognized them as alternatives for *be* and *ke* respectively, but did not mark them as such by articulating the objects of their Greek equivalents. One suspects then that G read *lmntskh* and produced what Flashar called a *Verlegenheitsübersetzung*,[5] writing *telos* for *ntskh*, *eis* for *l*, and *to* to account quantitatively for the <*m*> morpheme. If so, G's equivalent reflects an item-for-item *modus operandi* rather than, for example, an eschatological interpretation of the Psalm.[6]

---

4. For example, see Ezra 3:8–9; 1 Chr 15:21; 23:4; 2 Chr 2:1, 17; 34:12–13.

5. That is, a "translation of embarrassment"; Flashar, "Exegetische Studien," 94: "Wir werden noch öfter der Erscheinung begegnen, dass G da, wo er seine Vorlage nicht verstand oder nicht verstehen wollte, einfach mechanisch Wort für Wort übersetzt und es dem Leser überlässt, einen Sinn aus den Worten heraus zu finden. Eine solche Verlegenheitsübersetzung . . ."

6. *Contra* Rösel, "Die Psalmüberschriften," 138. For a full treatment, see Ausloos, "למנצח in Psalm Headings," 131–9; Pietersma, "Septuagintal Exegesis," 467–71.

Do not destroy

The function of the Hebrew prohibition is difficult to determine. Many translations supply a liturgical direction (NIV "to the tune of"; ESV "according to"; NKJV "set to").[7] Connecting it with 'al tashkhithehu in Isa 65:8 ("As when juice is still found in a cluster of grapes and men say, 'Don't destroy it, there is yet some good in it'" [NIV]), Mowinckel postulated "a well-known ancient ritual to do with the juice of the grape; as this psalm was being recited someone would have been handling the grapes 'which in turn may have been a symbol of the community.'"[8] Intriguing as this suggestion might be, evidence for such a ritual is otherwise lacking. Alternatively, 1 Sam 26:9, 15, might provide a Davidic connection but can hardly be pressed to account for all four superscriptions that contain the prohibition. At any rate, it cannot be demonstrated that G concerned himself with its literary (or liturgical) function, for he simply translated word for word, using a standard equivalent that shares the semantic range of its Hebrew counterpart.[9]

Pertaining to David

NRSV's "Of David" does not specify whether the preposition *le* indicates authorship ("by": e.g., Hab 3:1; Ezek 27:3, 30:3) or topic ("regarding": e.g., MT Jer 23:9; 46:2, 13; 48:1; 49:17, 23, 28). Had G wanted to express the former, he could have written *tou Dauid*, as did Aquila.[10] The genitive also appears in the transmission history of the Greek Psalter, but G consistently used the dative.[11] Given that the dative is his default rendering, its occurrence here need not imply that G had a specific episode from David's life in mind.[12]

---

7. So too, C. Van Dam, שחת, *NIDOTTE* 5:93, where he writes, "It probably signifies the tune (cf. NIV and commentaries)."

8. *HALOT*, sub שחת hif., citing Mowinckel, *Ps. Stud.* 4:46–49.

9. Διαφθείρω appears for 8 of 9 occurrences of the verb שחת, and διαφθορά for 5 of 8 occurrences of the noun שחת in Psalms.

10. Field, *Origenis Hexaplorum*, 184.

11. So A. Pietersma, who argues that the six occurrences of τοῦ Δαυίδ in Rahlfs's *Psalmi cum Odis* are secondary ("David in the Greek Psalms," 213–26; "Exegesis and Liturgy," 103–4).

12. For exegetical links from this Psalm to David's life in rabbinic and patristic literature, see especially Anderson, "King David," 267–80.

For a stele inscription

Like its Hebrew counterpart, *stēlographia* occurs in the LXX only in the titles of six Psalms (15, 55–59). The *Supplement* to LSJ cites what otherwise appears to be the oldest attestation of the word, in a Greek inscription (*I.G.* 9[2].13.4, 14a3) from the first century A.D.[13] One need not conclude, however, that G was the first to use the word, since the noun *stēlographos* "inscriber" is known from an inscription dated to the fourth century B.C. and the verb *stēlographeō* "inscribe" from inscriptions of the third and second centuries B.C., and *stēlographia* is easily formed from these. More difficult to answer is the question why G so interpreted *miktam*, a word whose meaning was already unknown to Aquila and Symmachus and remains obscure to this day. Pietersma has suggested that G's determination to translate a word he did not understand led him to construe *ktm* as *ktb* "write," hence *graphia*, "writing," to which he added *stēlo-* to account quantitatively for the preformative *m*, on the analogy of *eis to telos* for *lmntskh*.[14] That may well be so, but why (at the qualitative level) did he opt for *stēlo-* to fill the slot? One might speculate that G's interpretation of *miktam* was informed by "Do not destroy," which he may have construed as a warning not to corrupt the text, or possibly not to break the stele on which he evidently supposed it was once written, but such speculation, too, leaves questions unanswered.[15]

VERSE 2 [1]

NRSV: Do you indeed decree what is right, you gods? Do you judge people fairly?

NETS: Do you then truly speak righteousness? Do you judge fairly, O sons of men?

---

13. Liddell, *A Greek-English Lexicon*.

14. Pietersma, "A Commentary on Psalm 15," 524–5.

15. The verb is found in a Greek inscription (dated 175–171 BC) with reference to "the 'breaking' of a stone—ἐάν τινα ὑγιῆ λίθον διαφθείρηι κατὰ τὴν ἐργασίαν ὁ τῆς θέσεως ἐργώνης" (Moulton and Milligan, *The Vocabulary of the Greek Testament*, s.v.). It cannot be demonstrated, however, that G intended μὴ διαφθείρῃς to be interpreted in such a manner, since, as noted above, διαφθείρω is his standard equivalent for שחת, nor for that matter can such an interpretation explain the first occurrence of στηλογραφία, in the superscription of Ps 15, which lacks μὴ διαφθείρῃς.

Do you . . . truly?

G frequently handled the *He*-interrogative contextually: where a question expects the answer "No," he wrote *mē*, whether or not the Hebrew had a corresponding negative particle (Pss 29:10; 49:13; 76:8; 77:19, 20; 84:6; 87:11, 12, 13; 93:20).[16] The resulting nuance would have suited the current context rather well: "Surely you do not speak righteousness (do you)?" Instead G opted for *ei*, leading all the daughter versions to translate the first clause as a protasis to the second. Hartley's recent translation of the Greek Psalter has done the same: "If you truly speak righteousness, judge rightly, O you sons of Men."[17] It is not surprising that the Greek text should so be read in its reception history, but it is a mistake to suppose that G would have intended such a reading. Rahlfs supplied a note to clarify, firstly, that *ei* translates not the conditional particle *'im* but the interrogative particle *ha* and, secondly, that *krinete* is not imperative but indicative, since it translates a Hebrew imperfect.[18] A similar instance of *ei* to introduce a direct question is found in 72:11, not for *ha* but for *yesh*: "Is there knowledge in the Most High?" (NETS). It is perhaps an extension of the use of *ei* to introduce indirect questions ("Tell me whether . . . ").[19] *Alēthōs* "truly," like its Hebrew counterpart occurs only here in the Psalter. G's default use of *alētheia* for *'emunah* (21 times out of 22) likely triggered his choice of *alēthōs* for *'umnam*.

then . . . O sons of men

MT's *'elem* is traditionally associated with אלם I "to be dumb" (*HALOT* s.v.; hence Aquila's *alalia*), but how does one speak (*tedhabberun*) mutely? Commentators typically emend to *'elim* "gods," construed as a vocative and referring either to human judges[20] or to heavenly beings re-

---

16. For the use of μή in questions expecting the answer, no, see Smyth, *Greek Grammar*, §2651.

17. Hartley et al., *Psalter according to Seventy*, ad loc.

18. Rahlfs, *Psalmi cum Odis*, ad loc.

19. See Smyth, *Greek Grammar*, §2671. Zerwick, *Biblical Greek*, §401, points to the virtual synonymy of ה and אם in Gen 17:17 (both of which are translated by εἰ) as evidence that the NT use of εἰ to introduce direct questions is "perhaps owing to Hebrew influence."

20. So, e.g., Ridderbos, *Psalmen*, 2:126, citing Exod 21:6, 22:7f, 1 Sam 2:25, Ps 82, and the fact that the king is addressed as "god" in Ps 45:7. For a recent defense, see Day, "Imprecatory Psalms," 169–71.

sponsible for justice on earth.[21] G's choice of *ara* (i.e., inferential ἄρα, not to be confused with interrogative ἆρα) suggests that he read *'ulam* "on the other hand." Both *'ulam* and *ara* are grammatical particles that one would not expect to appear in an opening verse since they presuppose preceding discourse. A consequence of his choice is that it leaves *bene 'adam* "sons of man" as the only candidate for a vocative. The effect is to alter the profile of the Psalm from a complaint against judicial authorities to a litany against humanity.

VERSE 3 [2]

NRSV: No, in your hearts you devise wrongs; your hands deal out violence on earth.

NETS: Indeed, in the heart you devise acts of lawlessness on the earth; injustice your hands braid.

Indeed

In the Hebrew Psalm, *'af* "in fact" marks what follows as the answer to the question of v. 2. *Kai gar* "indeed" translates 8 of 23 occurrences of the particle *'af* and 14 of 35 instances of *gam* "also." Following a suggestion made by his teacher Barthélemy, Venetz has touted the latter equation as evidence for recensional activity analogous to *kaige*, but unconvincingly.[22] *Kai gar* had become a formula well before the LXX was produced.[23]

acts of lawlessness

G's use of *anomia* "lawlessness" to translate not only *'awlah* "wrong, iniquity," but a variety of other words for sinful activity, including *'awen, beliyya'al, zimmah, 'awon, 'athaq, resha',* and *sheqer*, levels the diversity of the Hebrew and more generally reflects the prevalence of *nom-* words, that is, law-related terms, in the Greek Psalter.[24] A number of manu-

---

21. So, e.g., Kraus, *Psalmen*, 1:415; Goldingay, *Psalms*, 2:202–4. For a variation, see Swart and Van Dam, "חמס," *NIDOTTE* 2:179: "the gods of the ANE world (Ps 58:3) act violently against the innocent. . . ."

22. Venetz, *Quinta des Psalteriums*, 80–84; Munnich, "Septante des Psaumes," 77–78; Olofsson, "Kaige Group," 204.

23. Smyth, *Greek Grammar*, §§2813–15, citing Plato, Thucydides, and Xenophon.

24. See especially Olofsson, "Law and Lawbreaking," 291–330; Austermann, *Tora zum Nomos*.

scripts have the singular *anomian*,[25] doubtless a secondary adjustment (since one would not expect a plural abstract "lawlessnesses"): the plural matches the Hebrew and may be read as distributive (so NETS).

injustice your hands braid

MT points the noun *khamas* "violence" as construct and the verb *tefalesun* as second person plural: "you clear a way for the violence of your hands." But G read *khamas* as absolute and construed the verb as third person feminine plural[26] with "your hands" as subject. That G understood the meaning of the Hebrew verb is clear from his choice of *hodopoieō* in 77:20: "He made a path for his wrath." But here, needing an activity of the hands, he opted for *sumplekō* "twist together, braid," which occurs only once in the Psalter (cf. *periplekō* in 49:19 and 118:61). Used in the Pentateuch only for manufacturing the high priestly garments (Exod 28:22; 36:12, 22, 28, 30), its metaphorical sense here and elsewhere in the LXX is also attested in nontranslation Greek literature (LSJ). By construing *yedekhem* "your hands" as subject rather than object, and the verb as third rather than second person plural, G stopped short of producing a Greek idiom for intimacy (*sumplekō tini tas cheiras* "join hands with someone") and instead conceived injustice as a handicraft.

VERSE 4 [3]

NRSV: The wicked go astray from the womb; they err from their birth, speaking lies.

NETS: Sinners were estranged from the womb; they erred from the belly; they spoke lies.

Estranged from the womb

The passive voice may indicate that G read the Niphal (by dittography of preceding *nun*) rather than the Qal of זור.[27] To the Greek reader, the passive verbal phrase *apēllotriōthēsan apo* might suggest (surgical) removal from the womb (if *apo* were construed spatially)[28] or abandonment since

---

25. Rahlfs, *Psalmi cum Odis*, ad loc.

26. That is, by pointing תפלסן with the vowels of the 3rd fem. pl. impf., according to Mozley, *The Psalter of the Church*, 95.

27. So *BHS* ad loc.

28. LSJ *sub* ἀπαλλοτριόω includes the gloss *"remove, in Surgery."*

birth (if *apo* were understood temporally). However, it is unlikely that G intended either interpretation, since the semantic component that *apallotrioō* shares with זור is that of estrangement or alienation, with a nuance of hostility.

they spoke lies

MT has two parallel clauses: "the wicked turn aside from conception" and "those speaking falsehood go astray from birth." Reading *waw* (דברו) in place of *yod* (דברי), G produced a third indicative clause: *elalēsan pseudē* "they spoke lies."²⁹ As Rahlfs notes, *pseudē* "lies" could be accented as the neuter plural form of either the adjective *pseudēs* (ψευδῆ) or the noun *pseudos* (ψεύδη).³⁰

VERSES 5–6 [4–5]

NRSV: They have venom like the venom of a serpent, like the deaf adder that stops its ear, so that it does not hear the voice of charmers or of the cunning enchanter.

NETS: They have wrath in the likeness of the snake, like an adder, deaf and plugging its ears, which will not listen to a voice of enchanters, nor of a charm being administered by a wise man.

wrath in the likeness of the snake

Hebrew *khemah* can mean either "heat" or "poison, venom" of animals or "wrath." In Ps 139:4, G opted for "venom" in the phrase *ios aspidōn* "venom of vipers" (NETS), aided no doubt by the accompanying phrase "under their lips." Here one might have expected him to do the same, but he chose *thumos* "wrath," by no means his default equivalent for *khemah*: *thumos* occurs four times but *orgē* "anger" eight times. Why *thumos*? For one thing, the simile required an item that wicked men have in common with a snake that will not listen: either wrath or venom might apply. For another, G was not the first to make such a choice. A similar passage in Deut 32:33 has *thumos* twice, once for *khemah* "venom" and once for

---

29. *BHS* (ad loc.) proposes to move the *athnach* and to emend Qal participle דברי to Piel perfect דברו to match the syntax of the LXX, but without Hebrew manuscript support.

30. Rahlfs, *Psalmi cum Odis*, ad loc. Both the adjective and the noun occur in Psalms as equivalents for כזב "falsehood, lies."

rosh "poison": "their wine is the wrath of dragons, and the wrath of asps beyond cure" (NETS).

deaf and plugging its ears

In the Hebrew, the wicked are compared to "the deaf adder that stops its ear," to which one might object that it is deaf not by choice but by nature, since the horned viper (to which *pethen* refers) "has no external hearing channel."³¹ Hence (presuming for the moment that his *Vorlage* was consonantally identical to MT), G may have inserted *kai* "and" to clarify that a comparison is being made to a snake that is not only unable (*kōphēs*) but also unwilling (*buousēs ta ōta autēs*) to hear. Certainly v. 6 suggests unwillingness, since G opted for *eisakouō*, which has the nuance of heeding and responding to what is heard.³² However, a simpler alternative is that G was operating from a slightly different Hebrew text, reading *waw* (ואטם) in place of *yod* (יאטם). Thus, construing אטם as a participle functioning as an additional attributive adjective, he wrote *aspidos kōphēs kai buousēs ta ōta autēs* "an adder, deaf and plugging its ears."

a charm being administered by a wise man

G recognized the appositional function of the nominal phrase, casting it in the genitive. However, reading MT's Pual participle ("skilled, expert") as a *min-* prepositional phrase, *mekhakam*, he wrote *para sophou* "by a wise man." Reading *khober* "enchanter" as *kheber* "charm," he opted for *pharmakou*. Then, at pains to preserve the repetition of the Hebrew,³³ and needing a passive verbal form for its agent *para sophou*, he turned *khabarim* into *pharmakeuomenou*.

VERSE 7 [6]

NRSV: O God, break the teeth in their mouths; tear out the fangs of the young lions, O Lord!

---

31. *HALOT* s.v., citing Y. Aharoni, "Animals Mentioned in the Bible," *Osiris* 5 (1938) 475. Of interest is that Prov 23:32 has κεράστης "horned snake" (for צפעני "viper").

32. Louw and Nida, *Greek-English Lexicon*, §24.60. See also Cox, "Εἰσακούω and Ἐπακούω," 251–8.

33. Cf. ἐπαείδων ἐπαοιδήν for חבר חבר in Deut 18:11.

NETS: God crushed their teeth in their mouth; the molars of lions the Lord shattered!

God crushed ... the Lord shattered

In MT, v. 7 begins a modal sequence that extends at least to the end of v. 9 and possibly to the end of the Psalm. The vocatives *'elohim* and *yhwh* are, however, unmarked, and the imperatives are consonantally indistinguishable from perfects. G therefore stayed in the indicative mode, invariably using aorists for what he read as perfects and futures for what he read as imperfects.[34] The effect is to recast the divine response from a plea for action into a reported action. Aquila, however, has the imperative: *ekrizōson, kyrie* "Root out, Lord."[35] G handled הרס "break down, destroy" contextually, using *kathaireō* "take down" in 10:3 and 27:5, but *suntribō* "crush" (more appropriate for removing teeth) here. *Suntribō* is his default equivalent for the verb שבר "break," and translates הרס only here in Psalms, resulting in a Greek allusion to 3:8: *odontas hamartōlōn sunetripsas*, "the teeth of sinners you shattered." *Sunthlaō* "shatter" translates נתץ "tear down, smash" only here in Psalms; G used *kathaireō* in 51:7 and again for its by-form, נתש in 9:7.

their teeth ... the molars of lions

Hebrew *kefir* refers specifically to the young lion able to hunt food for himself and distinguishable by his mane (*HALOT*). In 16:12 (of young lions in hiding) and 103:21 (of dependent young lions), G translated it with *skumnos* "whelp," but here, as in 34:17 and 90:13, he opted for the general label *leōn*. *Malte'oth*, also spelled *metalle'oth*, refers properly to the jawbone,[36] as does *lekhi* in Ps 3:8 (where, however, G misunderstood it and wrote *mataiōs* "in vain"). Here, perhaps guessing its meaning from the parallel noun *odous* "teeth," G chose *mulē* "molars," which shares the first two consonants of its Hebrew counterpart.[37] The semantic distinction between teeth and molars is clear from the (apocryphal) Psalms of

---

34. Similar instances of indicatives where MT has imperatives may be found at 4:2, 7; 29:11; 89:14; 93:1; 141:5.

35. Field, *Origenis Hexaplorum*, 185.

36. So *HALOT* s.v. For a defense of the meaning "fangs," see M. J. Dahood, "Maltā'ôt," 300–303.

37. On the phenomenon of Greek equivalents that sound like their Hebrew counterparts, see Caird, "Homoeophony," 82; also Barr, "Doubts about Homoeophony," 28–35.

Salomon 13:3: "Evil wild animals rushed upon them; with their teeth (*odous*) they tore their flesh, and with their molars (*mulē*) they crushed their bones" (NETS). While breaking their "fangs" (NRSV) would render lions unable to capture their prey, crushing their molars would leave them unable to eat it; either way they would soon perish of starvation.

VERSE 8 [7]

NRSV: Let them vanish like water that runs away; like grass let them be trodden down and wither.

NETS: They shall vanish like water that flows through; he will bend his bow until they become weak.

he will bend his bow

NRSV's "like grass" presupposes the emendation *kemo khatsir badderekh* "like grass on the path,"[38] but G evidently read a text closer, if not identical, to MT. The verb דרך "tread" can mean "to bend the bow by firmly planting the foot in the middle of it" (*HALOT*), but in MT it is the arrows that are trodden rather than the bow. The Hebrew, though difficult, might be translated as follows: "may he keep on aiming his arrows as they wither away." G, for his part, solved the problem by supplying a bow; *toxon* is his standard equivalent for *qesheth* "bow," but here and in 63:3, it translates *khets* "arrow."[39] In both passages, G's choice of *enteinō* "stretch tight" makes clear that he opted for a Greek idiom for bending a bow to shoot.[40]

---

38. See Barthélemy, *Critique textuelle*, 366. He attributes the conjecture to Wellhausen, but prefers MT, calling the use of "arrow" for "bow" an example of catachresis (applying a term to an object that it does not properly denote).

39. Another example of τόξον for חץ occurs in 4 Reigns 13:18, there in the plural. It is of some interest that LSJ's entry includes the meaning "bow and arrows" for the plural τόξα.

40. For ἐντείνω τόξον LSJ cites Aeschylus, *Agamemnon*, 364, and an Aeschylus fragment (*Fragmenta*, 83). For actual shooting, LXX has τοξεύω for ירה "shoot" (2 Reigns 11:20, 24; 4 Reigns 13:17, 19:32; 2 Chr 35:23; Jer 27:14 [MT 50:14]).

until they become weak

Still in interpretive mode, G chose *heōs* "until" for *kemo* "as," as better suited to the imminent demise of the victims of God's bow.[41] *Astheneō* is G's default equivalent for כשל Qal "stumble" (9:4; 26:2; 30:11; 104:37; 106:12; 108:24; cf. *exastheneō* for כשל Hiphil in 63:9). It similarly translates מעד "slip" in 17:37 and 25:1, but more accurately stands for לאה "be weary" in 67:10 and דאב "become faint" in 87:10. Here it stands in for מלל "wither," which occurs twice elsewhere, in 36:2 and 89:6, both times relating to grass, and appropriately translated as *apoxērainō* "dry up" and *sklērunō* "harden" respectively. Here the reference is to humans, so G opted for *astheneō* "become weak, sick," perhaps associating it with the adjective *'umlal* "feeble," which he translated as *asthenēs* in 6:3.[42] The sense of the Greek may be that the sinners grow faint at the sight of God's bow aimed at them.

VERSE 9 [8]

NRSV: Let them be like the snail that dissolves into slime; like the untimely birth that never sees the sun.

NETS: Like wax that melts they will be removed; fire fell, and they did not see the sun.

Like wax

Shabbelul means "snail," which makes its way in *temes* "slime," used adverbially, hence "slimily," that is, with a slimy trail.[43] G, however, read תמס as a Niphal imperfect third feminine singular form of מסס "melt," which he translated with *tēkō* "melt." Thus he guessed the meaning of *shabbelul* from the subject of the other three occurrences of מסס in Psalms, namely *donagh* "wax" = *kēros* (21:15; 67:3; 96:5).

fire fell

The Hebrew next compares the destiny of the wicked to that of *nefel 'esheth* "a woman's stillborn child"; that is, it does not see the sun. But G

---

41. So Mozley, *The Psalter of the Church*, 98, citing Driver: כמו "must . . . have been interpreted from the context as = *until*."

42. Cf. Mozley, *The Psalter of the Church*, 95.

43. GKC, §118q.

read *nefel* as *nafal* "fall" and interpreted *'esheth* as *'esh* "fire," guided perhaps by the melting wax of the first stich. The resulting Greek describes the fate of sinners as death by fire from above.

VERSE 10 [9]

NRSV: Sooner than your pots can feel the heat of thorns, whether green or ablaze, may he sweep them away!

NETS: ^aBefore your thistles take note of the thorn-shrub, as if in anger it will bestorm^b you, as if alive^a.

^aGreek uncertain; ^b*devour* = Rahlfs

your thistles

Siroth can be the plural for either *sir* "cooking pot" or *sirah* "thorn"; NRSV opted for the former and G for the latter. That G knew the meaning of *sir* is clear from 59:10 = 107:10, where he translated it as *lebēs* "cauldron." Here the context gives little direction, unlike in Eccl 7:6: "the crackling of thorns (*sirim*) under the pot (*sir*)" (NIV). The verb *yabhinu* "understand, sense" will not have helped to tip the balance in favor of one or the other, since one would not readily attribute perception to either pots or thorns. The nearby occurrence of *'atad* "bramble," which he glossed as *rhamnos* "thorn-shrub," may well have triggered his choice for a similar plant, *akantha* "thorn," which he otherwise reserved for *qots* "thorn" (31:4 [cf. MT *qayits* "summer"]; 117:12). The Greek term is general (BDAG, MM), but the Hebrew *sirah* refers specifically to the thorny burnet (*Poterium spinosum*).[44]

as if alive . . . as if in anger

The meaning of the Hebrew is obscure, and G makes no effort to enlighten the reader and translates item for item. The preposition *ke* (here *kemo*) is often prefixed to both members of a comparison (as in the English expression "like father, like son"), which here would mean something like "alive and burning alike." Thus NRSV has "whether green or ablaze," referring evidently to the thorns heating the pots. G opted for *hōsei* "as if," which can also be used of comparisons to mean "like, just

---

44. See K. Lawson Younger, *NIDOTTE* 3:246 and the literature cited there.

as" (LSJ) but, unlike the Hebrew preposition, is not repeated. Hence G's isomorphic approach has produced two comparisons. The Greek follows the word order of the Hebrew; *hōsei zōntas* "as if alive" precedes *hōsei en orgō* "as if in anger," but NETS has reversed the order to reflect the fact that *zōntas* is cast as an accusative plural modifying *humas* "you."

it will bestorm you

Rahlfs has *katapietai humas* "he/it will devour you," with no variant in the apparatus.[45] The verb is an odd choice given that it is G's default for בלע "to swallow" and does not overlap with the semantic range of its Hebrew counterpart שׂער (also spelled סער) "to storm." Papyrus Bodmer XXIV (usually cited as 2110) has since provided the variant *kataigieitai* (from *kataigizō* "rush down like a storm" [LSJ]),[46] which is a much better semantic match and also correlates with G's choice of the noun *kataigis* "squall, hurricane" for the same Hebrew root in 49:3, 54:9, 82:16, 106:25, 29, and 148:8, not to mention that *kataigis* appears to have been something of a favorite for G; in the LXX 10 of 29 occurrences are found in Psalms, for a variety of Hebrew nouns. Pietersma has defended its originality and adopted it in NETS.[47] Its subject would appear to be *pyr* "fire" from v. 9 (though one wonders whether G even thought that far), which "storms down" upon the addressees of the Psalm.[48] NETS's barely intelligible translation deliberately reflects the fact that G was more interested in formal correspondence to the Hebrew than coherence in Greek.[49]

VERSES 11–12 [10–11]

NRSV: The righteous will rejoice when they see vengeance done; they will bathe their feet in the blood of the wicked. People will say, "Surely

---

45. Rahlfs, *Psalmi cum Odis*, ad loc.
46. Kasser and Testuz, *Papyrus Bodmer XXIV*, 114, line 22.
47. Pietersma, "Ra 2110 (P. Bodmer XXIV)," 266–67.
48. The sole antecedent for ὑμᾶς "you" in the Greek Psalm is the "sons of men" of v. 2. Since the Hebrew verb has a third-person singular suffix with energic *nun* (ישׂערנו), Mozley calls ὑμᾶς a Greek corruption for ἡμᾶς "us" or αὐτούς "them" (*The Psalter of the Church*, 95), but the former lacks manuscript support and the latter has hexaplaric support, suggesting that it was a secondary correction towards the Hebrew. Hence either the *Vorlage* had a second-person plural suffix, or, if it was the same as MT, G adjusted the pronoun to clarify the antecedent.
49. See Pietersma, "Translating a Translation," 169–82, esp. 174.

there is a reward for the righteous; surely there is a God who judges on earth."

NETS: A righteous one will be glad when he sees vengeance done[c]; he will wash his hands in the blood of the sinner. And a person will say, "If then there is a return for the righteous, then God exists, judging them on the earth."

[c] + *to impious ones* = Rahlfs

when he sees vengeance done

The Greek has a temporal clause referring indefinitely to the future ("whenever that might be"), as it typically does when G understood *ki* to introduce a temporal clause (2:12; 36:24; 48:10, 16, 19; 70:23, 24; 74.3; 101:1; 118:32, 171; 119:7; 126:5). Rahlfs' edition has *ekdikēsin asebōn* "vengeance of (i.e., "for," an objective genitive) impious ones," judging the omission of *asebōn* to be a hexaplaric adjustment towards the Hebrew. But 2110 (not available to Rahlfs), an important witness to the pre-hexaplaric text of the Psalter, also leaves it out, suggesting that its omission in agreement with the Hebrew is not hexaplaric but original.

he will wash his hands

The image of bathing in the blood of the vanquished wicked brings Ahab's prostitutes to mind (1 Kgs 22:38).[50] The Greek has *louō* there but *niptō* here, following normal Greek usage of *louō* for washing the body, *niptō* (earlier *nizō*) for washing hands and feet, and *plynō* for washing clothing (LSJ). G predictably rendered *paʿam* "footstep, instance" with *diabēma* "step" in 16:5, 84:14, 118:133, 139:5, and *pous* "foot" in 56:7, but here (and in 73:3) he opted for *cheir* "hand," producing Greek resembling that of 25:6 and 73:13 (*niptomai en athōois tas cheiras mou* "I wash my hands in innocence"), though there the Hebrew noun is *kaf*, which, unlike *paʿam*, can refer to either the sole or the palm. One wonders then what might have prompted the shift from "feet" to "hands." To associate the shift with G's choice of *enteinō* "stretch" for דרך "tread" (i.e., bending a bow with the hand rather than the foot) in v. 8 is scarcely credible. It is possible that the *Vorlage* had *kappaw* "his hands" as at 25:6 and 73:13 (so BHS), though no Hebrew evidence for such a variant survives. The fact

---

50. See also 1 Kgs 2:5; Ps 67(68):24.

that 73:3 likewise has *cheir* for *pa'am* diminishes the likelihood that the difference is due to the parent text. At 73:3 the choice may be contextual, that is, a more suitable object for the Hebrew imperative *harimah* "lift up." Here context may likewise have played a role; the Hebrew image of wading in the blood of sinners suggests participating in (or at least enjoying) the vengeance carried out on them. G may have written "hands" in order to avoid such a distasteful notion (since vengeance belongs to the Lord). On the basis of a Ugaritic parallel, Dahood translates the Hebrew clause as "wash his hands of blood," but had G so interpreted it, he could have written *apo tōn cheirōn autou nipsetai to haima* "he will wash the blood from his hands."[51] Rather, G may have understood the clause to mean washing one's hands (in the blood of the sinner) for the purpose of making them clean. That is to say, the bloody end of the sinner serves to cleanse the hands of the righteous one, perhaps by impelling him to avoid a similar fate.[52] At any rate, the resulting translation contrasts the hands of the righteous with the hands of sinners in v. 3.

if then . . . then God exists

The repetition of the words *ei* and *ara* from v. 2 creates the illusion that G has produced an *inclusio* not present in the Hebrew psalm. But here the choice of inferential *ara* "then" for emphatic *'ak* "surely" (twice) indicates that *ei* does not introduce a question. In fact, the occurrence of *ei* without formal warrant from the Hebrew suggests an interpretive move on the part of the translator. Perhaps he construed the second inference as deduced from the first ("then . . . so then") and thus cast it as an apodosis to the first ("if . . . then"). Of some interest is the inclusion of the article, making *ho theos* "God" the subject rather than the predicate of *estin*. That is to say, G did not write, "then there is a God" (cf. 13:1: *ouk estin theos* "there is no God"), but "then God exists." The effect of the whole is to make God's existence contingent upon a return for the righteous. G cast the condition as real, in keeping with the gladness of the righteous

---

51. Dahood, *Psalms II*, 63; LSJ *sub* νίζω II. "wash off."

52. Note in that vein the comment of Chrysostom: "For hear the prophet saying, 'The righteous shall rejoice when he sees the vengeance on the ungodly; he shall wash his hands in the blood of the sinner.' Not rejoicing on account of it, God forbid, but fearing that he might suffer the same things, he will render his own life more pure" (*Homilies on Philemon* 3, quoted in Wesselschmidt, *Psalms 51–150*, 36).

one in v. 11: if then there is a return for the righteous [and there is], then God exists.

judging them

MT has a plural participle (*shofetim* "judging") attributed to *'elohim*, an honorific with plural agreement. But G evidently read *shofetam*; that is, singular participle with third-person masculine plural suffix, writing *ho theos estin, krinōn autous* "God exists, judging them." But who is "them"? The omission of *asebōn* "impious ones" (above) leaves the pronoun without an explicit antecedent, and the reader of NETS might be forgiven for thinking that it refers to "the righteous," mistakenly, since the latter is singular. G simply rendered the pronominal suffix with its Greek equivalent, evidently more concerned with formal equivalence than clarity of reference.

BIBLIOGRAPHY

Anderson, G. A. "King David and the Psalms of Imprecation." *Pro Ecclesia* 15 (2006) 267–80.

Ausloos, H. "למנצח in the Psalm Headings and its Equivalent in LXX." In *XII Congress of the International Organization for Septuagint and Cognate Studies: Leiden 2004*, edited by M. K. H. Peters, 131–39. SBLSCS 54. Atlanta: SBL, 2006.

Austermann, F. *Von der Tora zum Nomos: Untersuchungen zur Übersetzungsweise und Interpretation im Septuaginta-Psalter*. MSU 27. Göttingen: Vandenhoeck & Ruprecht, 2003.

Barr, J. "Doubts about Homoeophony in the Septuagint." *Textus* 12 (1985) 1–77.

Barthélemy, D. *Critique textuelle de l'Ancien Testament*. OBO 50/4. Göttingen: Vandenhoeck & Ruprecht, 2005.

Caird, G. B. "Homoeophony in the Septuagint." In *Jews, Greeks and Christians: Religious Cultures in Late Antiquity*, edited by R. Hamerton-Kelly and R. Scroggs, 74–88. SJLA 21. Leiden: Brill, 1976.

Cox, C. "Εἰσακούω and Ἐπακούω in the Greek Psalter." *Bib* 62 (1981) 251–58.

Dahood, M. *Psalms II*. AB 16B. Garden City: Doubleday, 1968.

———. "The Etymology of Malṯā'ôṯ (Ps 58,7)." *CBQ* 17 (1955) 300–303.

Day, J. N. "The Imprecatory Psalms and Christian Ethics." *BSac* 159 (April–June 2002) 166–86.

Field, F. *Origenis Hexaplorum quae supersunt*. CahRB 62. Hildesheim: Olms, 1964.

Flashar, M. "Exegetische Studien zum Septuagintapsalter." *ZAW* 32 (1912) 81–116, 161–89, 241–68.

Goldingay, J. *Psalms*. 3 vols Grand Rapids: Baker Academic, 2007.

Hartley, V. et al., translators. *The Psalter according to the Seventy*. Westport: The WORDSmith, 2001.

Kasser, R., and M. Testuz, editors. *Papyrus Bodmer XXIV*. Cologny-Geneva: Bibliotheca Bodmeriana, 1967.

Kraus, H.-J. *Psalmen*. 2 vols. BKAT. Neukirchener: Neukirchener, 1972.

Liddell, H. G. et al. *A Greek-English Lexicon*. Oxford: Clarendon: 1968.

Louw, J. P., and E. A. Nida, editors. *Greek-English Lexicon of the New Testament Based on Semantic Domains*. 2nd ed. New York: United Bible Societies, 1989.

Moulton, J. H. and G. Milligan. *The Vocabulary of the Greek Testament Illustrated from the Papyri and Other Non-Literary Sources*. Grand Rapids: Eerdmans, 1930.

Mozley, F. *The Psalter of the Church*. Cambridge: Cambridge University Press, 1905.

Munnich, O. "La Septante des Psaumes et le Groupe *Kaige*." *VT* 33 (1983) 75–89.

Olofsson, S. "Law and Lawbreaking in the LXX Psalms: A Case of Theological Exegesis." In *Der Septuaginta-Psalter: Sprachliche und theologische Aspeckte*, edited by E. Zenger, 291–330. Herders Biblische Studien 32. Freiburg: Herder, 2001.

———. "The Kaige Group and the Septuagint Book of Psalms." In *IX Congress of the International Organization for Septuagint and Cognate Studies: Cambridge, 1995*, edited by B. A. Taylor, 189–230. SBLSCS 45. Atlanta: Scholars, 1997.

Pietersma, A. "A Commentary on Psalm 15 in Greek: Text-Production and Text-Reception." In *Die Septuaginta—Texte, Theologien, Einflüsse*, edited by W. Kraus et al., 523–42. WUNT 252. Tübingen: Mohr/Siebeck, 2010.

———. "David in the Greek Psalms." *VT* 30 (1980) 213–26.

———. "Exegesis and Liturgy in the Superscripts of the Greek Psalter." In *X Congress of the International Organization for Septuagint and Cognate Studies: Oslo 1998*, edited by B. A. Taylor, 99–138. Society of Biblical Literature Septuagint and Cognate Studies Series 51. Atlanta: SBL, 2001.

———. "Ra 2110 (P. Bodmer XXIV) and the Text of the Greek Psalter." In *Studien zur Septuaginta Robert Hanhart zu Ehren*, edited by D. Fränkel et al., 262–86. MSU 20. Göttingen: Vandenhoeck & Ruprecht, 1990.

———. "Septuagintal Exegesis and the Superscriptions of the Greek Psalter." In *The Book of Psalms: Composition and Reception*, edited by P. W. Flint and P. D. Miller, 443–75. VTSup 99. Leiden: Brill, 2005.

———. "Translating a Translation, with Examples from the Greek Psalter." In *Translating a Translation: The LXX and Its Modern Translations in the Context of Early Judaism*, edited by H. Ausloos et al., 169–82. BETL 213. Leuven: Peeters, 2008.

Pietersma, A., and B. G. Wright, editors. *A New English Translation of the Septuagint*. New York: Oxford University Press, 2007.

Rahlfs, A., editor. *Psalmi cum Odis*. Septuaginta: Vetus Testamentum Graecum 10. Göttingen: Vandenhoeck & Ruprecht, 1979.

Ridderbos, J. *De Psalmen*. Kampen: Kok, 1958.

Rösel, M. "Die Psalmüberschriften des Septuaginta-Psalters." In *Der Septuaginta-Psalter: Sprachliche und theologische Aspekte*, edited by E. Zenger, 125–48. Herders Biblische Studien 32. Freiburg: Herder, 2001.

Smith, J. *Translated Hallelujahs: A Linguistic and Exegetical Commentary on Select Septuagint Psalms*. Contributions to Biblical Exegesis and Theology 56. Leuven: Peeters, 2011.

Smyth, H. W. *Greek Grammar*. Revised by Gordon M. Messing. Cambridge: Harvard University Press, 1956.

Venetz, H.-J. *Die Quinta des Psalteriums: Ein Beitrag zur Septuaginta- und Hexaplaforschung*. Collection Massorah, Série 1, Études classique et textes 2. Hildesheim: Gerstenberg, 1974.

Wesselschmidt, Q. F., editor. *Psalms 51–150*. Ancient Christian Commentary on the Old Testament 8. Downer's Grove, IL: InterVarsity, 2007.

Zerwick, M. *Biblical Greek Illustrated by Examples*. Rome: Editrice Pontificio Instituto Biblico, 1994.

6

Call Me Father!

The Grief and Desire of a Loving Father

S. Carl Van Dam

WHILE READING MY FATHER's recent book, *The Elder*, I was struck by how powerfully the theme of God's compassion comes through in the book. In thinking about the Lord Jesus as the chief shepherd of his sheep, for instance, we are reminded of how he completely provides for his people and how he actively searches out those who have been scattered or who have wandered astray. As the good shepherd, Jesus Christ even gave his life for the sheep so that they might be able to drink from springs of the living water (Rev 7:17). My father's book also reminds office bearers of, and encourages them with, the truth that the Lord does not leave his under-shepherds to labor on their own. Rather, he sustains them and aids them through the abundant help of his Holy Spirit and his personal revelation in the Word of God.[1]

One of the responsibilities of the elders in Israel was to act as judges in the land and to uphold God's law among the people. It was not simply a matter of maintaining civil justice but of ensuring that the people lived up to the covenant obligations demanded of them by the Author of that covenant. The people of Israel needed to understand that when God's law was transgressed, such transgression was really a matter of rebellion against God himself. As Van Dam reflects, "God was always intimately involved."[2] It is clear from Scripture that the LORD never viewed Israel's

---

1. Van Dam, *The Elder*, 45, 58.
2. Ibid., 77.

sins and transgressions as insignificant but always as something that offended him deeply as a holy, righteous, and good God. Indeed, there are many examples of how seriously the LORD took sin as the just judge of his people. In this article, I would like to briefly explore how Israel's sin affected their LORD, who wanted to have a close relationship with his people, specifically, like the relationship of a father to his children. For this purpose, I will focus on the early chapters of Jeremiah.

FATHER AS FORM OF ADDRESS IN JEREMIAH 2–3

The book of Jeremiah is primarily known as a book of judgment, gloom, and doom for the people of Judah. It is a book that is full of God's words of warning and wrath against his sinful and unfaithful people. The prophet Jeremiah had to bring a message to the people of Judah that they, generally speaking, did not want to hear. They did not want to be confronted with their unfaithfulness, but, instead, they assumed that all would be well since they had the temple of the LORD among them in the city of Jerusalem. They believed the words of the false prophets, that the current peace in Jerusalem would last. After all, they were God's covenant people, were they not? Nothing could go wrong.

However, things had gone horribly wrong. They had completely disregarded the righteous law of the LORD and paid him only minimal lip service, if any at all. They lived a life of idolatry, serving false gods and engaging in immoral and unethical conduct. It was a lawless time in which the poor were oppressed and every man lived for himself and his own benefit.

It is in this kind of environment that the prophet Jeremiah had to proclaim the word of the LORD. What is striking about the early prophecies of Jeremiah is that, although he had to preach words of judgment and wrath, at the same time the love and compassion of the LORD for his people comes through strongly. The LORD is very mindful of his covenant relationship with his people. This is expressed in how he speaks to them and tries to talk some sense into them, as it were. He is not acting as a legalistic judge, who needs to adhere to the letter of the law for the law's sake, but rather he is clearly acting as a father disciplining and punishing his children for their disobedience, or as a husband who is upset at the adulterous conduct of his wife because he loves her and is jealous for her love.

These two metaphors of husband and father are intertwined in the early chapters of Jeremiah. These metaphors, along with various others, are used to heighten the appeal to Judah, that they might realize just how serious their sin against the Lord is. A closer study of the use of the term father will serve to illustrate the depth and character of the profound paternal love that our God has for his covenant children.

The Folly of Sin (Jer 2:27a)

The first reference to "father" is found in Jer 2:27. This verse is part of a longer appeal to Judah, to convince them of the folly of their errant ways. The Lord wonders what fault the people found in him that they did not want to serve him and went to idols instead (Jer 2:5). They have exchanged their glorious God for worthless idols (Jer 2:11). The depth of their folly is compared to preferring a broken cistern over a spring of living water (Jer 2:13). No one in his right mind would act in such a way. Similarly, people who say to wood, "'You are my father' and to stone, 'You gave me birth'"[3] (Jer 2:27) must have lost all sense. Clearly, wood and stone cannot be your father or mother. The basic meaning of this text is clear: rejection of the true God in favor of false gods is foolish. However, there are also a number of interesting features in this text that may not be immediately apparent.

The exact pagan reference that is made here is debated. In the past, some have argued that the wood and stone refer to "local «numina» or gods of tree and stone,"[4] all of which were believed to give life.[5] More recently, though, there seems to be a consensus that the Canaanite fertility cult is meant, usually with Baal as the male god and Asherah as the female goddess.[6] In this fertility cult, normally the male deity would be represented by a stone pillar while the female deity was signified by a wooden pole or tree.[7] In this text, these symbols are reversed, further

---

3. Scripture quotations in this article are from the New International Version (NIV).
4. Olyan, "Cultic Confessions," 255.
5. See, for example, Keil, *Jeremiah 1–29*, 69.
6. E.g., Aalders, *Jeremia*, 1:18; Fretheim, *Jeremiah*, 70; Thompson, *Jeremiah*, 180; Mackay, *Jeremiah*, 161. Lundbom holds that the Canaanite god El, and not Baal, is the "'father' god" (Lundbom, *Jeremiah 1–20*, 285).
7. Zevit, *Religions*, 537.

emphasizing the folly of the people; they do not even know which symbol belongs to which "parent."[8]

Another feature of this description of Israel's foolish disobedience is that God's people are directly attributing to false gods what God had said through Moses about himself earlier in Israel's history.[9] In Deut 32:18, Moses sang, "You deserted the Rock, who fathered you; you forgot the God who gave you birth." These words are spoken in the broader context of Moses describing for the people how the Lord had shown a special love to them, how he had found Jacob in a barren waste, and how he cared for him and guarded him as the apple of his eye (Deut 32:10). The Lord led him to a fruitful land and gave him overflowing abundance. Jacob owed his very existence to the Lord alone. It is the Lord who fathered him and gave him birth, using the metaphors of human birth. Thus, Israel's connection with their God is so vital and so intimate, and yet they simply reject him and desert him in favor of wood and stone. How great is their ungratefulness and folly! How this desertion grieves the Lord who had shown his caring kindness towards them and done everything for them!

Also, take note that the first time that the word father occurs in Jeremiah, it is attributed to a false god made of wood, a mere piece of creation. The Maker of all things, who had revealed himself as a father to his people and had shown to them the love of a father, has been exchanged for a piece of wood. They have attributed to a piece of wood the origin of their life, following the "father" as "procreator" notion of

---

8. Cf. Thompson, *Jeremiah*, 180 and Fretheim, *Jeremiah*, 70. Oosterhoff doubts that satire is meant here and simply holds that the wood and stone are meant to refer to false gods in general (Oosterhoff, *Jeremia 1–10*, 123–4). Yet this view fails to convince, given the clear reversal of the usage of the fertility symbols of wood and stone and the context of showing the foolishness of the people. Mackay agrees that mockery is deliberately meant here with the reversal but says that it is a mockery of the Canaanite religion itself (Mackay, *Jeremiah 1–20*, 161). But the Lord is concerned with his people here and the reversal heightens their folly, however foolish this false religion certainly is.

9. In this calling the wood "father," some have seen a pointed rejection of the adoption of the Davidic king as son by the Lord in Psalm 2:7 (De Jong, *Volken bij Jeremia*, 42 and Van Selms, *Jeremia I*, 56). Oosterhoff questions this link by pointing out that the verb *yld* here refers to a mother bearing a child since the verb should be read according to the kethib (second-person feminine) in line with *'at* and *'eben*, which are both feminine (see Oosterhoff, *Jeremia 1–10*, 123 and Keil, *Jeremiah 1–29*, 69).

the nations around them.[10] Thus, the great folly of the people has been exposed in a very clear and direct way.

Shameless Brazenness (Jer 2:27c; 3:4)

The sinfulness of the people does not remain at the level of folly but is also expressed in shameless brazenness. This aspect comes out in the follow-up to the first usage of father and again in the second usage. After the people are said to address wood as father, thereby showing that they want to serve a false god and turn their backs on the true God, they will nevertheless call upon the LORD when they find themselves in times of trouble. Then they say, "Come and save us!" (Jer 2:27). Israel has the nerve to call upon the LORD after they have rejected him and left him for wood and stone. They think that they can just do what they want and, according to whim and fancy, go from one god to the next and then back to the true God when they need real help. They are forced to recognize the fact that these gods of wood and stone cannot help them in their time of need. They are not able to do anything and cannot even hold themselves in place but need to be nailed down (Jer 10:4). They are completely worthless and useless and, therefore, cannot provide any salvation for the Israelites when they are in trouble.

The second usage of father occurs in Jer 3:4. At the beginning of chapter 3, the LORD uses the metaphor of the unfaithful wife who has left her husband and married another man. The rhetorical question of whether the husband would return to his wife after her unfaithfulness is meant to drive home the seriousness of the situation to the people of Judah. Among men, it is impossible for a man to receive back a divorced wife who has married another man. The relationship between the LORD and his people Judah is now strained to the utmost because of her prostitution with many false gods. Her sister Israel has already received a certificate of divorce and been sent away (Jer 3:8). But the LORD is not yet at that point with Judah, for he is compassionate and desires that Judah would see the error of her ways and still return to him (Jer 3:12).

Therefore, the LORD continues to warn Judah. He tells Judah that the land has been defiled because of her prostitution and wickedness, and, as a consequence of her disobedience, the rains have been withheld from the land; a sign of the covenant curse (Deut 28:22–24) has already

---

10. Cf. Schilder, "Vader," 192, 201–2.

come into effect on the land of Judah. Yet even with such clear warnings from the Lord, Judah "refuses to blush with shame" (Jer 3:3) and even goes so far as to call the Lord "my Father" in v. 4. She uses this intimate name for the Lord as if everything is going well in their relationship. Even though previously Judah had chosen to call wood father, now she uses the correct term for the right God. However, it sounds hollow and fake because her actions do not match her words. She speaks fine words but does all the evil she can (Jer 3:5). As a result, the nice words are a sign of shameless brazenness that is offensive and hurtful to the Lord.

In addition, Judah asks the Lord whether he will always be angry. To her way of thinking, this anger cannot last forever. That she would even ask this question while she does not want to demonstrate any true repentance for her sin shows how little she understands the Lord. By her words, she makes clear that she has not begun to take seriously the holy and righteous demands of the Lord, nor how indebted she is to him because of the love, patience, and faithfulness that he has shown to her over the centuries. She thinks that the Lord will be mollified by a "sweet" request using the right words and the right formula. However, she does not reckon with the fact that the Lord is the true and living God. She has gone after and served false gods who can be swindled and dealt with in a trivial way as they have no real existence anyway. Therefore, she thought that she could get away with the same behavior with the holy and living God. She thought that the Lord would not care what she really thought of him, as shown by her deeds, and that he would be won over by her smooth talk.

Call Me Father! (Jer 3:19)

This third usage of the term father in this early part of Jeremiah is a poignant revelation of the heartfelt compassion of the Lord. He clearly declares to his people how much he wants to show his love to them as his children and how much he wants to hear them respond in love by addressing him as their Father in genuineness of heart, not with the indifference and glibness of one who is unfaithful. The Lord shows that he is disappointed and grieved when his people do not acknowledge him as their gracious Father.[11] The Lord urges this earnest acknowledgement and repentance from the heart upon his people after Judah's shameless

---

11. Schilder, "Vader," 192; Craigie, *Jeremiah 1–25*, 64.

address of God as her Father in Jer 3:6–13. Judah did not learn from the LORD having sent away her sister Israel, and, in the end, Judah's guilt becomes even greater (Jer 3:11).

In the following section (Jer 3:14–18), the LORD clearly reiterates his faithfulness to the covenant that he has established with his people. The LORD declares in Jer 3:14, "I am your husband,"[12] therefore demanding his people return to him. What follows is a series of wonderful promises concerning the return from exile in which the LORD will take the initiative and choose a remnant ("one . . . and two . . ." v. 14) and bring them to Zion. Despite his people's unfaithfulness, the LORD will accomplish his ultimate purpose of renewal and restoration. Israel and Judah will be joined together again, and they will come together in the land that the LORD had given to their "forefathers as an inheritance" (Jer 3:18).

Jeremiah 3:19–20 are forceful and deeply felt words of the LORD to his wayward people. They come somewhat as a surprise right after the wonderful promises that he has just declared in vv. 14–18. Commentators have struggled with how to best understand the connection between these two sections. Verse 19 begins emphatically using the pronoun "I" (*'anoki*) and is connected to v. 18 with the conjunction "and" (*waw*). The LORD has made clear to his people where he intends to go with the chosen remnant, setting before them his promises for the future, but then he moves back to the present[13] and appeals to them by expressing his desire for them. He aims to move his people to love him and treat him as their Father, for he loves them and wants to treat them as sons. He wants to have a vibrant relationship with them as their Father.

The LORD expresses the strong desire[14] that he would have gladly treated his people as sons and given them a desirable land, even the most beautiful[15] inheritance of all the nations. He would have thought it wonderful to give the best of the best to the nation he had set apart. He wanted to treat them as sons,[16] as heirs of the blessings he intended

---

12. Note the play on words here with the use of *ba'al* for husband.

13. Keil, *Jeremiah 1–29*, 97.

14. The verb *'amar* can also be used to denote thinking (said to oneself) and the adverb *'ek* here has an assertive (*HALOT*) or intensive (BDB) force.

15. Literally, "beauty of beauties."

16. The Hebrew text uses the second-person singular for "you" as it refers back to Israel as "woman" in line with much that has preceded. (There is no textual justification for changing the suffix to masculine as some have done.) This use of the feminine has led some commentators go into the matter of daughters acquiring an inheritance in

to give to them. On the basis of Jer 31:9b, where the Lord says, "I am Israel's father, and Ephraim is my firstborn son" (see also Exod 4:22), some commentators conclude that the plural "sons" here includes not only Israel but also the other nations of the world, so that in fact "sons" refers to all men, since the Lord is the Creator of them all.[17] Then Israel is viewed as the most privileged among the sons because Israel receives the most beautiful land. While it is true that Israel is God's special nation that has been set apart,[18] it is doubtful that the use of sons here denotes a plurality of groups of people, since the Lord is addressing Israel alone. This is clear since he uses the feminine singular "you" to refer to his nation.

Van Selms understands Jer 3:19 as the Lord's reflections upon how he could have adopted Israel as his son and heir. It was not sufficient that the Lord declared Israel to be his son by means of a formal statement of adoption. The legal acceptance of this adoption arrangement also needed to be affirmed by the one who was being adopted.[19] This affirmation is referred to in the phrase "call me [the Lord] Father." So, according to Van Selms, the thought in this passage is that the Lord had done his part in adopting Israel, but now he also expects Israel to do her part by responding as an adopted child should—sincerely calling the Lord Father and showing their sincerity by righteous practical living. This calling the Lord Father makes the adoption official and final.

It seems to me that Van Selms' approach misses the mark somewhat. In a very general way, Van Selms is correct that the Lord has done his part but his people have not reciprocated. Yet, these words of the Lord are not, in the first place, about a technical legal arrangement. It is not that the Lord wonders how he could have adopted Israel, but rather the Lord expresses how delighted he is to give his chosen people the best of the best. He wants to show Israel his love and grace but, at the same time, it hurts and grieves him when his people do not respond to his favor with a heartfelt and sincere expression of love in return. There is passion and emotion in these words, which is entirely missed

---

Israel (e.g., Lundbom, *Jeremiah 1–20*, 318; Oosterhoff, *Jeremiah 1–10*, 158), but it seems to me that this issue is not really relevant to the point of this text, which is that God is expressing his love to his nation as a whole, whether to sons or daughters.

17. Keil, *Jeremiah 1–29*, 98; Wambacq, *Jeremias*, 46.
18. See also Mackay, *Jeremiah 1–20*, 196.
19. Van Selms, *Jeremia I*, 80.

in a characterization of these words as a statement about nonreciprocal adoption formulas. In this text, we catch a glimpse of the inner thoughts of the LORD and the depth of his love for his people, as well as of his sorrow at their disobedience.[20] How the LORD would love to have heard his people call him Father! But they were not willing to do this, instead insisting upon going their own way in sinful rebellion.

In the next verse, the LORD switches metaphors by comparing the conduct of his people to a woman who is unfaithful to her husband, the same way that the house of Israel has been unfaithful to the LORD, who had established his covenant with them. The switch in metaphors highlights the emotions that the LORD is feeling due to Israel's sin and unwillingness to return to him in sincere and obedient faith. Concerning Jer 3:19–20, Fretheim writes, "What intimacy God desired in his relationship with the people, and what disappointment is expressed here! While literary purists might deplore the mixing of the parental and marital metaphors here, the effect is almost overwhelming in its pathos. God has been rejected both as parent and as husband! God is like a person who has been rejected not only by his spouse but by his children as well. God suffers the effects of the broken relationship at multiple levels of intimacy."[21] With these words, Fretheim brings out well the reality that God suffers great grief when his children are unfaithful to him. All too often, we fail to have an eye for this divine grief and offense that the LORD takes at our sin. We can think here also of Lord's Day 33 of the Heidelberg Catechism where, as church, we confess that "we have offended God by our sin" and, therefore, in turn, must "grieve with heartfelt sorrow," in addition to also hating sin and fleeing from it.

The rest of Jer 3 shows that there is still hope for the people of Israel. The weeping of contrition and the cry of confession can be heard on the heights (Jer 3:21). The LORD issues the clear and hopeful call to his

---

20. Craigie, Fretheim, and Mackay have seen this aspect of the passage clearly (Craigie, *Jeremiah 1–25*, 64; Fretheim, *Jeremiah*, 85–86; Mackay, *Jeremiah 1–20*, 197).

21. Fretheim, *The Suffering of God*, 116. It should be noted here that modern theology considers that the doctrine of God's impassibility (that God is incapable of suffering) is no longer tenable. It would take us too far afield to go into this debate, but it should be noted that the grief of God as we find it, for example, here and in Eph 4:30, is an example of God accommodating himself to our understanding and should not be taken as a challenge to the doctrine of God's immutability but rather as an expression of God's love in his perfect simplicity (in the sense in which "simple" is used in the Belgic Confession, art. 1).

people to return to him, for he promises to cure them of their backsliding (Jer 3:22). New life with their heavenly Father can only be found through acknowledgement of sin and a genuine change of heart (Jer 3:22–25).

However, this hope will only be truly realized in the distant future. The immediate future for the people of Judah is grim, since there would be no true confession of sin by the people or their leaders. Jerusalem would be destroyed and most of the people taken away to Babylon. Yet even before the exile would take place, the Lord also promises restoration to his people. He speaks of the days when, "I will lead them beside streams of water on a level path where they will not stumble, because I am Israel's father, and Ephraim is my firstborn son" (Jer 31:9). The Lord speaks very directly about the delight that he has in Ephraim his dear son and describes how his heart yearns for him and has great compassion for him (Jer 31:20). The deep love that the Lord has for his people also comes out when he announces, "I will make an everlasting covenant with them: I will never stop doing good to them, and I will inspire them to fear me, so that they will never turn away from me" (Jer 32:40).

CALLING GOD FATHER THROUGH CHRIST

The Lord has truly never stopped doing good to us, and now in the new covenant he has shown us the depth of his love most miraculously and completely in his Son Jesus Christ. While the relationship between God and his people as that of a father with his children was revealed in the old covenant, it was not until the coming of God's eternal Son in the flesh that the identity of believers as sons and daughters of God are more clearly and deeply made known.

It has been debated whether the believers in the old dispensation would have addressed God as Father in their prayers. Van Bruggen, for instance, maintains that texts such as Jer 3:4, 19 point to the fact that the Israelites would have done this.[22] By contrast, Schilder holds the view that there is not a single text in the Old Testament clearly showing that the Israelites would truly call God Father in their prayers.[23] It can be argued that the texts which Van Bruggen brings forward are special

---

22. Van Bruggen, "Abba, Vader!" 32, 34. He also mentions texts such as Ps 89:27 and Isa 64:8 (Van Bruggen, "Abba, Vader!" 30–34).

23. Schilder, "Vader," 203.

instances that do not support being interpreted as indications that addressing God as Father was common in the OT. Certainly, the fact that none of the Psalms, which are the prayers of the Israelites, call upon God as Father in a regular fashion would at least point to addressing God as Father as being unusual, if not nonexistent. It seems difficult to come to a firm and final conclusion, given the nature of the evidence. What is clear is that the intimate covenant bond that the LORD had with his people in the old dispensation has become even closer with the coming of Jesus Christ.

The Apostle John writes in his gospel that those who believe in the Word who became flesh have been given "the right to become children of God" (John 1:12). The eternal Son of God came to this world in order that he might offer himself as the Lamb of God, the atoning sacrifice, which would bring about reconciliation between God and us. It is only through the Son that we may come to know the Father (Luke 10:22). Jesus Christ is the way, the truth, and the life, and no one can come to the Father except through him (John 14:6).

He who enables us to come to God the Father has also taught us to address God as "our Father in heaven" in the prayer that he gave as a model to the disciples (Matt 6:9–13; Luke 11:2–4).[24] Jesus himself also showed the way by addressing God as his Father when he prayed to him.[25] We are privileged to be able to follow his example. He has set us free from sin and has poured out his Spirit upon his church so that we might be enabled to live as God's children. Through the insight given by the Spirit, who proceeds from the Father and the Son, we are equipped to flee from all idolatry and hypocrisy so that we may address God as our Father in all sincerity and humility, not only in words but also in godly conduct. The Spirit, whom Christ has given us, is "the Spirit of sonship and by him we cry 'Abba, Father'" (Rom 8:15). And since we are children, then we are also heirs of the heavenly inheritance that has been prepared for us and which will never spoil or fade but will last forever (Rom 8:17; 1 Pet 1:4). May we always remember and contemplate how

24. For a detailed treatment of the text and place of the Lord's Prayer, see Van Bruggen, "Abba, Vader!" 9–42.

25. The question is sometimes raised whether we can also address God as Son or Spirit. It is possible since the Son and the Spirit are also persons, but the example of Christ is the model that should be generally followed in our own prayers. Moreover, Scripture teaches that both the Son and the Spirit intercede for us before the Father, help us in our prayers, and make our prayers acceptable to him (cf. Rom 8:26–27, 34).

much the Lord loves us and how much we grieve him, yes, also his Spirit (Eph 4:30) when we disobey him. Our heavenly Father desires with all his heart that we should love him above all else, delight in him, and serve him with thanksgiving. When we rejoice in him he will also be filled with joy, taking great delight in us and rejoicing over us with singing (cf. Zeph 3:17).

It is an honor to be able to present these reflections about addressing God as Father on the occasion of my father's retirement as professor of Old Testament. My earthly father has taught me much—from how to walk and swim to how to read Hebrew and study Old Testament theology. However, the most important thing that he taught me was a love for our faithful Lord and Maker. God's mercy and grace have always been central in the life of my father and mother, and they have been a valuable example to me of godly walking and talking. The greatest joy we may share is that we may together call upon the same heavenly Father.

BIBLIOGRAPHY

Aalders, G. Ch. *De profeet Jeremia*. Korte Verklaring der Heilige Schrift. Kampen: Kok, 1923.
Craigie, Peter C. et al. *Jeremiah 1–25*. WBC. Dallas: Word, 1991.
De Jong, C. "De volken bij Jeremia: Hun plaats in zijn prediking en in het boek Jeremia." ThD diss., Kampen, 1978.
Fretheim, Terence E. *Jeremiah*. Smyth & Helwys Bible Commentary 15. Macon, GA: Smith & Helwys, 2002.
———. *The Suffering of God: An Old Testament Perspective*. OBT 14. Philadelphia: Fortress, 1984.
Holladay, William L. *Jeremiah 1*. Hermeneia. Philadelphia: Fortress, 1986.
Keil, C. F., and F. Delitzsch. *The Prophecies of* Jeremiah. Vol. 1, *Jeremiah 1–29*. Translated by David Patrick. Commentary on the Old Testament. Peabody, MA: Hendrikson, 1989.
Lundbom, Jack R. *Jeremiah 1–20: A New Translation with Introduction and Commentary*. AB 21A. New York: Doubleday, 1999.
Mackay, John L. *Jeremiah: An Introduction and Commentary* Vol. 1, *Chapters 1–20*. Fearn, UK: Mentor, 2004.
Olyan, Saul M. "The Cultic Confessions of Jer 2,27a." *ZAW* 99 (1987) 254–59.
Oosterhoff, B. A. *Jeremia*. Commentaar op het Oude Testament. Kampen: Kok, 1990.
Schilder, H. J. "Vader van zijn volk." In *Bezield verband: opstellen aangeboden aan prof. J. Kamphuis bij gelegenheid van zijn vijfentwintig-jarig ambtsjubileum als hoogleraar aan de Theologische Hogeschool van De Gereformeerde Kerken in Nederland te Kampen op 9 april 1984*, 186–205, 425–30. Kampen: Van den Berg, 1984.
Thompson, J. A. *The Book of Jeremiah*. NICOT. Grand Rapids: Eerdmans, 1980.
Van Bruggen, J. "Abba, Vader!" In *De biddende kerk*, edited by C. Trimp, 9–42. Groningen: Vuurbaak, 1979.
Van Dam, Cornelis. *The Elder: Today's Ministry Rooted in All of Scripture*. Phillipsburg, NJ: P&R, 2009.
Van Selms, A. *Jeremia 1–24*. Prediking op het Oude Testament. Nijkerk: Callenbach, 1972.
Wambacq, B. N. *Jeremias Klaagliederen / Baruch Brief van Jeremias*. De Boeken van het Oude Testament uit de grondtekst vertaald en uitgelegd 10. Roermond: Romen, 1957.
Zevit, Ziony. *The Religions of Ancient Israel: A Synthesis of Parallactic Approaches*. London: Continuum, 2001.

7

Wordplay and History in Daniel 5

Al Wolters

I AM DELIGHTED TO be able to contribute to this Festschrift for my good friend and esteemed colleague Cornelis Van Dam, whom I honor as a competent and faithful Old Testament scholar in the same tradition of neo-Calvinist biblical scholarship in which I stand. I owe him a great debt for the welcome which he extended to me when I first came to Hamilton in 1984 as a beginning biblical scholar, and for being a supportive collegial friend ever since. Among other things, he allowed me to audit his course on biblical Aramaic in the winter semester of 1989. It was in that course that I was first introduced to the original text of Daniel 5, one of the few chapters in the Bible that is written in Aramaic. The reflections that follow are a fruit of that initial encounter with the Aramaic text of that chapter.

Before getting into the details of my argument, it will be useful to remind ourselves that the book of Daniel is considered by many scholars (probably the majority today) to be a late composition, written hundreds of years after the events it purports to describe, and containing many historical errors. In the common critical view, the book of Daniel in its present form was compiled by an unknown author around 164 BC, at the height of the religious persecution that the Jews suffered under the Hellenistic king Antiochus IV Epiphanes. It was written to encourage the faithful Jews in their resistance against Antiochus. As encouragement, the author told a fictitious story of some earlier faithful Jews, namely, Daniel and his friends, who had resisted pagan persecution almost four hundred years earlier, at the time of Nebuchadnezzar and Darius the Mede. These faithful Jews had been wonderfully protected and blessed by God. Moreover, Daniel had received prophecies that predicted with remarkable accuracy the historical events leading up to the present persecution under Antiochus; events that were to culminate in the author's own day with the sudden death of Antiochus and the dramatic advent of the kingdom of God. Unfortunately, in telling this story, the author of the book of Daniel made a number of serious historical mistakes, especially in inventing the figure of Darius the Mede who never actually existed as an historical person, and in predicting the coming of the kingdom of God in his own day.

Clearly, this commonly held view of the book of Daniel represents a significant challenge to the traditional Jewish and Christian reading of the book, which accepts the narratives of Daniel and his friends as depictions of actual events that took place in the sixth century BC, and the prophecies received and recorded by Daniel as predictions of later events. From the point of view of such a traditional reading of Daniel, it is significant that the current critical interpretation was first put forward by the third century pagan philosopher and anti-Christian polemicist Porphyry, who proposed it as part of his effort to discredit the Christian Scriptures. Ironically, Porphyry's interpretation of the book began to be accepted by Christian biblical scholars in the nineteenth century, and it is today very widely held in the guild of biblical scholarship, even by conservative scholars who in many other ways defend the essential historicity of the biblical narratives.

It is not part of my present purpose to deal in general with the pros and cons of the critical consensus with respect to the historicity of the book of Daniel. There are others who have done a credible job of defending a sixth-century date for Daniel, although it needs to be acknowledged that, on the traditional reading of the book, there are certain historical problems that still await a satisfactory solution.[1] In my judgment, however, there are even greater problems for the consensus critical reading, not the least of which is the peculiarity that within this view the book of Daniel seems to have been accepted as canonical almost immediately after being regarded as falsified by history. Furthermore, it is significant that a number of the earlier pillars of the critical view, including the supposed nonexistence of Belshazzar, have been shown to be untenable.

1. A good commentary defending an early date of Daniel is Baldwin, *Daniel*.

In any case, I myself find it very difficult to accept that both the historical narratives and the prophetic predictions of this part of the biblical canon should be fundamentally inaccurate and misleading. As a result, I approach the book of Daniel with the assumption that it is historically trustworthy.

With this as background, I turn now to a discussion of what I have called "The Riddle of the Scales in Daniel 5." This is the title of a scholarly article that I published in 1991.[2] In what follows, I will give a popular review of my argument in that essay and then turn to a related topic supporting the historicity of the book of Daniel.

Every reader of the Bible is familiar with the words of the enigmatic handwriting on the wall that appeared at Belshazzar's feast, which Daniel reads as follows: *mene, mene, tekel,* and *parsin* (Dan 5:25-28).[3] The attentive reader, however, will also notice that Daniel's explanation of the handwriting seems to presuppose a somewhat shorter form. He refers to *mene* only once, omits the word "and," and cites *parsin* in the form *peres*, the singular form of *parsin*. There are good grounds for believing that the short form, *mene tekel peres*, is the one actually *written* on the wall, while the long form is the one *read* by Daniel.[4] Therefore, I will proceed on the assumption that the actual writing on the wall gave the short form, not only because of the testimony of the ancient versions, but also because it best elucidates Daniel's explanation, which is a kind of tour de force of riddle interpretation.

However, first I need to explain a few basic facts about the way ancient Aramaic was written. To begin with, words in an Aramaic text were often written in *scriptio continua*, which means that there were no spaces between words. A series of letters could, therefore, be read in more than one way, depending on how the words were divided, just as in English "Godisnowhere" could be read as either "God is now here" or "God is

---

2. Wolters, "The Riddle of the Scales," 155-77.

3. The last part of the inscription is given in some translations as *upharsin*, which is in fact how the Aramaic original reads. However, it needs to be understood that *u* here simply represents the Aramaic word for "and," which also has the effect in this context of changing the first letter of the word *parsin* into *ph*.

4. Apart from the traditional Hebrew text of the Old Testament (the so-called Masoretic Text) there are six independent ancient witnesses to the original text of the handwriting on the wall (the Old Greek, "Theodotion," Josephus, the Vulgate, Jerome in his commentary, and the Peshitta). All but the Peshitta have the short form also in v. 25. For the details, see Wolters, "The Riddle of the Scales," 156.

nowhere." Secondly, it is important to bear in mind that Aramaic, like Hebrew, was written without vowels. That is to say, Aramaic writing consisted exclusively of consonants, and the vowels needed to be supplied by the reader. Just as an English reader can readily interpret the abbreviation "bldg" as "building," so the Aramaic reader could easily read the consonants TQL as *těqēl*, meaning "shekel" (a unit of weight). Of course, the difficulty is that sometimes different words could be read by supplying different vowels. Thus "bldg" in English could be plausibly read as "bulldog" in some contexts; for example, in a list that also included "gryhnd" and "cckr spnl." In cases where there is no context to guide the reader, the consonantal writing of Aramaic words could give rise to significant ambiguity.

If we put the fact that ancient Aramaic writing had no spaces and no vowels together with the evidence that it was the short form of the riddle that was written on the wall, we come to the conclusion that the actual inscription that the Babylonians and Daniel saw on the palace wall was MN'TQLPRS.[5] The reason the Babylonian wise men could not read the inscription was not that they could not recognize the letters but that they did not know how to divide this series of letters into words or know what vowels to supply. Depending on the various possible combinations, these nine letters could be interpreted to represent a number of different Aramaic sentences, including "she has counted the voice of Persia" and "crush whoever has been peeled!"[6] Since none of these made much sense and the Aramaic wise men faced severe reprisals if they got it wrong, they prudently admitted they could not read the inscription.

However, Daniel was enabled by God to read the inscription in a way that immediately persuades all those present. He interprets the nine consonants, MN'TQLPRS, as consisting of three Aramaic words of three letters each, and he then proceeds to interpret each of the three words on three different levels by supplying different vowels at each level. Furthermore, each of these multiple meanings refers to the image of a pair of scales—an image that proves very significant to the date on which Belshazzar's feast took place. In short, Daniel interprets the handwriting as an elaborate wordplay consisting of three sets of double

---

5. The apostrophe represents the Aramaic consonant *aleph*, and Q is the consonant that corresponds to the K of *tekel*.

6. For these and other possibilities, see Wolters, "The Riddle of the Scales," 159–60.

puns, all of which point to a pair of scales.[7] Moreover, he does so on a day when scales had special significance in Babylonian culture.

It would take us too far afield to go into the philological details of my reading of the handwriting on the wall. For present purposes, I will simply lay out my overall conclusions, and refer the interested reader to the argument in my article on the riddle. These conclusions are as follows. For each of the three words that Daniel identifies, he distinguishes three levels of meaning, each following from different vowels that are supplied with the consonants. I will refer to these levels as A, B, and C.

It is the A level that is preserved in the traditional biblical text, the Masoretic Text, which does have a system for indicating vowels. Thus, the A-level interpretation is reflected in the familiar vocalization of our Bible translations: MN' is read as *mene* (more precisely, *měnē'*), TQL as *tekel* (*těqēl*), and PRS as *peres* (*pěrēs*). On this level, it turns out that each of the words refers to a unit of weight. The first refers to the mina (about 500 grams), the second to the shekel (about 8 grams), and the third to the half-mina (about 250 grams).[8] These units should not be regarded as representing coins or symbolizing a succession of kings, but rather as indicating the weight stones used by merchants to weigh out, on a pair of scales, specific amounts of silver in buying and selling merchandise.[9] Many such weight stones have been found in archeological excavations, some of them inscribed with the very words of the riddle: MN', TQL, and PRS. In the context of Daniel 5, these standardized weight stones represent God's standards of justice against which human actions are measured. This first level of meaning is not separately explained by Daniel; it is simply indicated by the traditional vocalization of these words.

The B level of interpretation refers to actions on the part of God. By adding a different set of vowels to the consonants of the three words of the riddle, these words are transformed into Aramaic verbs, with God as the implied subject. For MN', Daniel explains in v. 26 that it means "God has reckoned (or numbered) your kingdom."[10] In this case, the verb translated "has reckoned" is *měnāh*, a variant spelling of the word

---

7. For another clever wordplay in Daniel 5, see Wolters, "Untying the King's Knots," 117–22.

8. It is sometimes argued that *pěrēs* refers to a half-shekel, but this is a mistake. See Wolters, "Metrological PRS-Terms," 239.

9. See Wolters, "The Riddle of the Scales," 161–3.

10. In what follows the translations of Dan 5:26-27 are my own.

for "mina," but now revocalized as *mĕnā'*. In the case of TQL, the B-level meaning is expressed by Daniel's words, "you have been weighed" of v. 27. Here again, a noun designating a weight is transformed into a verb. Underlying this interpretation is the vocalization *tĕqal*, which means "he has weighed," with God as the implied subject and Belshazzar as the implied object. As for PRS, Daniel explains in v. 28 that on this level it means "[your kingdom] has been assessed," assuming the vocalization *pĕras*, "He has assessed." It should be pointed out that this verb does not mean "divide" in Aramaic, as many Bible translations render it, but rather "assess."[11] Daniel thus gives an interpretation that transforms each of the three words of the riddle into verbs describing a divine action of appraisal: he reckoned, he weighed, he assessed. The connection with a pair of scales is made explicit in v. 27: "You have been weighed *on the scales*."

Finally, on the C level, Daniel's interpretation of the riddle again shows that he is revocalizing the three weight names he started out with. In v. 26, he explains the third meaning of MN' as "he paid it out" (not "brought it to an end"), indicating God as the subject and Belshazzar's kingdom as the object. This again presupposes the vocalization *mĕnā'* but it now uses the verb in another of its attested senses.[12] In v. 27, he explains the third meaning of TQL as "you have been found wanting." This presupposes a very ingenious reading in which TQL takes the Aramaic verbal form *tiqqal*, meaning "you are (too) light."[13] To be found too light on the scales is to be found wanting, or not to measure up to God's standards. The third level of meaning for the third word, PRS, is the most dramatic of all. Daniel explains it in v. 28 as follows: "you have been given to the Medes and Persians." He is here alluding to the Aramaic word *pāras*, which means "Persia." This is a direct reference to the critical military situation in which Belshazzar finds himself; namely, that he is under siege by the forces of Persia under Cyrus the Great, which were to enter Babylon that very night and kill him. Daniel mentions both Medes and Persians because these were the two constituent ethnic groups of Cyrus's empire. Thus, each of the C-level meanings refers to the verdict that God pronounces on Belshazzar and his kingdom. The kingdom will

---

11. See Wolters, "Riddle of the Scales," 168–70.

12. Ibid., 171–2.

13. The doubling of the middle consonant would not have been indicated in the consonantal spelling.

be paid out like silver given in payment to Cyrus, Belshazzar himself has been found too light on the scales of God's judgment, and Persia will be the means God uses to carry out his verdict.

We can summarize the foregoing discussion by giving a new and literal translation of the crucial vv. 26–28, indicating in each case the vowels which are explicitly (in the case of level A in the Masoretic Text) or implicitly (in the case of levels B and C) given to the three trilateral roots MN', TQL, and PRS:

26. Mina [*mĕnēʾ*]: God has reckoned [*mĕnāʾ*] your kingdom, and paid it out [*mĕnāʾ*].

27. Shekel [*tĕqēl*]: you have been weighed [*tĕqal*] and found too light [*tiqqal*].

28. Half-mina [*pĕrēs*]: your kingdom has been assessed [*pĕras*] and given to the Medes and Persians [*pāras*].

Thus, we see that each of the three levels of meaning is thematically unified: three weights on level A, three acts of evaluation on level B, and three references to judgment on level C. Furthermore, the central image of God weighing Babylon in the scales of his justice ties the various levels together: level A names the weight stones that symbolize his standards of justice, level B designates the process of weighing that stands for God's acts of judicial appraisal, and level C describes the outcome of that process in the tipping of the scales and the payment of the silver weighed out, representing God's verdict and sentence over Babylon.

It is the central image of the scales that provides us with the connection to the second part of this essay, which has to do with the historicity of the book of Daniel. The connection consists in the remarkable coincidence of the date of Belshazzar's feast and of the annual rising of the constellation Libra (the Scales). This second part could be titled "An Allusion to Libra in Daniel 5," which is the title of another article of mine, published in 1993.[14] If we take seriously the historical reality of the court of Belshazzar on the eve of the Persian conquest as it is depicted in Dan 5, we discover that the reference to a pair of scales takes on unexpected significance in connection with the Babylonian astrology of the time.

That astrology was prominent in Babylonia in Daniel's day does not need to be argued. This is demonstrated clearly by many cuneiform

---

14. See Wolters, "An Allusion to Libra," 291–306.

astrological documents that have been excavated and by the mocking words of Isaiah when he predicted the fall of the neo-Babylonian empire: "Let your astrologers come forward, those stargazers who make predictions month by month, let them save you from what is coming upon you" (Isa 47:13). It is not surprising, therefore, that the book of Daniel pictures the wise men at the courts of both Nebuchadnezzar and Belshazzar as predominately astrologers, especially the group called "the Chaldeans."[15]

A significant feature of Babylonian astrology was the correlation of terrestrial and celestial signs. There is considerable evidence that the Babylonian diviners saw heaven and earth as mirror images of each other, so that an omen on earth had its counterpart in heaven, and vice versa. This belief in a correlation of signs is the basic point of the so-called "Diviner's Manual" published by Oppenheim in 1974.[16] The obvious implication of such a belief for the story of Dan 5 is, therefore, that astrologers at Belshazzar's court would expect there to be a celestial counterpart to the ominous portent that had appeared on the palace wall. Such a counterpart would be particularly apt in the case of a *written* sign, because the astrologers considered the celestial phenomena that they studied to be the *šiṭir šamê*, "the writing of heaven."

It is especially significant, therefore, that the Akkadian name for the constellation Libra is *zibānītu*, meaning "balance" or "scales."[17] In other words, the scales that were so prominent in Daniel's interpretation of the writing on the wall had a counterpart in the scales that belonged to the "writing of heaven," namely the constellation Libra. In fact, our name Libra is simply the Latin equivalent, like its counterparts in Greek, Aramaic, and Hebrew, of the Akkadian *zibānītu*, which had been the standard name of the constellation in Mesopotamia since the second millennium BC.[18] Every astrologer at Belshazzar's court would have known that "the scales," both in Akkadian and Aramaic, was the name of a prominent constellation in the sky.

---

15. See Dan 2:4, 5, 10 and 5:7, 11.

16. Oppenheim, "Babylonian Diviner's Manual," 204, 206–8.

17. See *The Assyrian Dictionary of the Oriental Institute of the University of Chicago*, under *zibānītu*, 2, and W. von Soden, *Akkadisches Handwörterbuch*, under *zibānītu(m)*, B.

18. Wolters, "An Allusion to Libra," 296n24. Even today the constellation is known as "die Waage" in German, "la Balance" in French, and "de Weegschaal" in Dutch.

However, what does this constellation have to do with this story in Daniel? To understand this, we need to take note of two significant dates that have emerged from the cuneiform documents which have come to light over the last century and a half. The first concerns the date of the fall of Babylon. Belshazzar's feast as narrated in Dan 5 takes place on the eve of the fall of Babylon, as the last verse of the chapter clearly states. This was a momentous event in world history, marking the transition from one great empire, the neo-Babylonian, to another, the Persian. We now know from the so-called Nabonidus Chronicle that Babylon fell to the Persians on the sixteenth day of Tashritu of the seventeenth year of Nabonidus, the senior partner with Belshazzar in the "double kingship" of that time.[19] This date works out to October 12, 539 BC in the calendar we use today, and it is quite securely established in the chronology of the ancient Near East.[20] Since Babylonian dates were calculated as beginning with nightfall, not midnight, the sixteenth of Tashritu would have included the evening preceding October 12. Consequently Belshazzar's feast, which took place during the night of October 11–12 according to our calendar, would have taken place, according to the Babylonian calendar, on the sixteenth day of Tashritu, the same day as the fall of Babylon. After all, the whole point of the story is that the execution of God's judgment on Babylon followed immediately after its announcement in the handwriting on the wall. The riddle of the scales therefore appeared on that exact date.

The second date that is relevant for our purposes concerns the annual morning rising of the constellation Libra. In the course of one year, the stars and constellations along the ecliptic ("the path of the moon") become successively visible on the eastern horizon just before sunrise, each appearing, for all practical purposes, on the same date each year. This was the basis of the ancient calendar, in which months and dates were set according to the annual morning rising of the various stars and constellations. These annual morning risings were also significant in Babylonian astrology. According to a widely used Babylonian astrological handbook called MUL.APIN, the annual morning rising of the

---

19. See Nabonidus Chronicle iii 15, in Grayson, *Assyrian and Babylonian Chronicles*, 109. On the "double kingship" see Beaulieu, *The Reign of Nabonidus*, 33–34.

20. See Parker and Dubberstein, *Babylonian Chronology*, 13, 29. Also see such reference works as *Reallexikon der Assyriologie* 1, 383; and Boardman et al., *Persia, Greece, and the Western Mediterranean*, 39, 121, 781.

constellation *zibānītu* (that is, Libra) occurred on the fifteenth day of Tashritu. Modern astronomical calculations show that for the year 539 BC and Babylon's latitude this date was in fact quite accurate.[21]

If we put together these dates, we come to the startling conclusion that the mysterious riddle of Daniel 5, which alludes on three different levels to the image of a pair of scales, appeared *just after* the annual rising of the constellation called "the Scales" (*zibānītu*). In fact, when Daniel says to Belshazzar in v. 27, "You have been weighed *in the scales*," it could also be understood to mean "You have been weighed in *Libra*," the constellation which had just risen in the sky, according to both astrological lore and actual fact, the morning before.

It now becomes clear that Daniel's interpretation of the riddle not only makes fools of the Babylonian wise men in general by deciphering the sophisticated Aramaic wordplay of the enigmatic inscription that had baffled them, but it also turns the tables specifically on the astrologers by interpreting a celestial phenomenon in a thoroughly anti-astrological way. "The Scales" in the sky do not represent mighty gods who determine terrestrial affairs (the Babylonian belief), but they symbolize an instrument in the hand of Daniel's God, "the Lord of Heaven" of v. 22. The message is plain: it is not the stars that determine the fate of nations, but the God of the Jews, whose temple vessels had just been desecrated by Belshazzar in his drunken revelry. The constellation Libra, therefore, becomes a symbol of the sovereign judgment of God, who weighs Belshazzar and his empire in the scales of his justice. With exquisite irony, Daniel simultaneously alludes to another name that the Babylonian astrologers applied to Libra, namely *kikkab kitti u mišāri*, "the star of justice and right," and he turns it against the Babylonian king.[22]

What bearing does the foregoing argument have on the historicity of Daniel? It would be foolish to claim that it proves the factual accuracy of the story told in Dan 5, but it certainly lends unexpected support to such an assumption. It seems a stretch to imagine that the virtual simultaneity of the rising of Libra and the appearance of the riddle of the scales is merely a coincidence, especially since the two phenomena match each other so well.

21. For the technical details, see Wolters, "An Allusion to Libra," 300–302.

22. We find this designation, for example, in the text II R 49, 3, 15f., cited by Jeremias, "Sterne (bei den Babyloniern)," 4:1454.

In any case, the surprising discovery of the relevance of Libra to Daniel 5 is only one of a number of ways in which this chapter seems to be based on historical reality. It is now firmly established that Belshazzar did in fact exist and that he had been entrusted with the kingship by his father Nabonidus.[23] There is no doubt that the prominence of astrologers in the story of Belshazzar's feast reflects the historical reality of the neo-Babylonian court. In fact, Assyriologists have often been impressed by the degree to which Dan 5 is based on historical fact.[24] Similarly, the classic critical commentary on Daniel by Montgomery suggests that the mysterious riddle itself is "based on the correct historical tradition of Cyrus' conquest."[25] Even the enigmatic Darius the Mede has recently been rehabilitated as a historical personage.[26] A good case can also be made for the plausibility of Belshazzar's feast as being part of a Babylonian *akītu* festival on this date.[27] As the German critical scholar Klaus Koch puts it, "Accordingly, the book of Daniel, or at least its older part (the Daniel legends), has command of a relatively good knowledge of Babylonian history in the sixth century."[28]

Although the foregoing essay does not prove the historicity of this part of the Old Testament, I hope that it does show that the belief in such historicity can bear significant fruit for Old Testament scholarship.

---

23. See Dougherty, *Nabonidus and Belshazzar*, and Beaulieu, *The Reign of Nabonidus*, 154–60.

24. For example, Dougherty, *Nabonidus and Belshazzar*, 199–200; Von Soden, "Eine babylonische Volksüberlieferung," 81–89; Shea, "Nabonidus, Belshazzar," 133–49; Wiseman, *Nebuchadrezzar and Babylon*, chap. 3; Millard, "Daniel and Belshazzar," 73–78; Beaulieu, *The Reign of Nabonidus*, 226, 231.

25. Montgomery, *Daniel*, 263.

26. See Koch, "Dareios der Meder," 288–90 and Colless, "Cyrus the Persian," 113–26.

27. See Wolters, "Belshazzar's Feast," 199–206.

28. Koch, "Dareios der Meder," 290 ("Demnach verfügt das Danielbuch oder zumindest dessen älterer Teil, die Daniellegenden, über eine relativ gute Kenntnis der babylonischen Geschichte des 6. Jahrhunderts").

BIBLIOGRAPHY

Baldwin, Joyce G. *Daniel.* TOTC. Downers Grove: InterVarsity, 1978.
Beaulieu, Paul-Alain. *The Reign of Nabonidus, King of Babylon 556–539 B.C.* Yale Near Eastern Researches 10. New Haven: Yale University Press, 1989.
Boardman, John et al., editors. *Persia, Greece, and the Western Mediterranean, c. 525 to 479 B.C.* 2nd ed. Cambridge Ancient History 4. Cambridge: Cambridge University Press, 1988.
Colless, Brian E. "Cyrus the Persian as Darius the Mede in the Book of Daniel." *JSOT* 56 (1992) 113–26.
Dougherty, Raymond Philip. *Nabonidus and Belshazzar. A Study in the Closing Events of the Neo-Babylonian Empire.* 1929. Reprinted, Ancient Near East: Classic Studies. Eugene, OR: Wipf & Stock, 2008.
Grayson, A. K. *Assyrian and Babylonian Chronicles.* TCS 5. Locust Valley, NY: Augustin, 1975.
Jeremias, A. "Sterne (bei den Babyloniern)." In *Ausführliches Lexikon der griechischen und römischen Mythologie*, edited by W. H. Roscher, 4:1454. Leipzig: Teubner, 1909–1915.
Koch, Klaus. "Dareios der Meder." In *The Word of the Lord Shall Go Forth: Essays in Honor of David Noel Freedman*, edited by C. L. Meyers and M. O'Connor, 287–99. Special Volume Series / ASOR 1. Winona Lake, IN: Eisenbrauns, 1983.
Millard, A. R. "Daniel and Belshazzar in History." *BAR* 11 (1985) 73–78.
Montgomery, James A. *A Critical and Exegetical Commentary on the Book of Daniel.* New York: Scribner, 1927.
Oppenheim, A. L. "A Babylonian Diviner's Manual." *JNES* 33 (1974) 197–220.
Parker, Richard A., and Waldo H. Dubberstein. *Babylonian Chronology, 626 B.C.–A.D. 75.* Brown University Studies 19. Providence: Brown University Press, 1956.
Shea, W. H. "Nabonidus, Belshazzar, and the Book of Daniel: An Update." *AUSS* 20 (1982) 133–49.
University of Chicago. The Oriental Institute. *The Assyrian Dictionary of the Oriental Institute of the University of Chicago.* 21 vols. Chicago: The Oriental Institute, 1956–2010.
Von Soden, Wolfram. *Akkadisches Handwörterbuch.* 3 vols. Wiesbaden: Harrassowitz, 1965–1981.
———. "Eine babylonische Volksüberlieferung in den Danielerzählungen." *ZAW* 53 (1935) 81–89.
Wiseman, D. J. *Nebuchadrezzar and Babylon.* The Schweich Lectures 1983. Oxford: Oxford University Press, 1985.
Wolters, Al. "An Allusion to Libra in Daniel 5." In *Die Rolle der Astronomie in den Kulturen Mesopotamiens. Beiträge zum 3. Grazer Morgenländischen Symposion (23.-27. September 1991)*, edited by Hannes D. Galter, 291–306. Grazer Morgenländische Studien 3. Graz: Druck, 1993.
———. "Belshazzar's Feast and the Cult of the Moon God Sîn." *BBR* 5 (1995) 199–206.
———. "Metrological *PRS*-Terms from Ebla to Mishna." In *Eblaitica: Essays on the Ebla Archives and the Eblaite Language*, vol. 4. Edited by Cyrus H. Gordon and Gary A. Rendsburg, 223–41. Publications of the Center for Ebla Research at New York University. Winona Lake, IN: Eisenbrauns, 2002.
———. "The Riddle of the Scales in Daniel 5." *HUCA* 62 (1991) 155–77.
———. "Untying the King's Knots: Physiology and Wordplay in Daniel 5." *JBL* 110 (1991) 117–22.

8

The Epistle of James

Justification or Sanctification?

GERHARD H. VISSCHER

Among all the students and colleagues who have contributed to this volume, there may be some who fit into both categories—as I do. Back in the summer of 1974, I was a young future seminarian in search of some ancient Hebrew, and Cornelis Van Dam had just moved to his second pastoral charge. A couple of times a week throughout that summer I made the trip from Richmond Hill to Brampton to learn that strange, delightful language from our brother. Little did we know that later we would serve side by side for about ten years as Old and New Testament professors.

This article is written out of appreciation for that summer and the many years of collegiality and friendship that followed. At a conference I attended, it was said that the way to honor scholars is not by praise and flattery but by continuing the discussions we have in our labors. "Adulation is for rock stars but patient, searching, truthful dialogue is for those we love." While Cornelis and I have found ourselves in agreement about so very much, this article honors him by continuing the discussion about one of those few areas of disagreement.

As recently as November 2010, when Cornelis and I were traveling to a conference together and riding a train from the airport to our hotel, he suddenly noticed that he was sitting on a bench designated for seniors and the disabled. He promptly stood up, of course considering himself to fit in neither category—until I said, to the delight of those who heard, "Keith, let me tell you something: you are one of those seniors!"

Congratulations, Keith and Joanne, as you enter this new well-deserved period in your lives. May the Lord bless you both.

Now let us turn to this study on the letter of James, which is motivated by a number of factors. First, there is the matter of the classic concerns of Martin Luther with respect to James. Luther once wrote, "Many sweat hard at reconciling James with Paul, but unsuccessfully. 'Faith justifies' [Paul] stands in flat contradiction to 'faith does not justify' [Jas 2:24]. If anyone can harmonize these sayings, I'll put my doctor's cap on him and let him call me a fool."[1] Now I have neither a need for his cap nor a desire to call the doctor a fool, but offering a suggestion as to how to solve the problem is another matter. It is of interest to me, as one who wrote a dissertation on Rom 4,[2] that Luther also posed the question in the light of the relation between James 2 and Romans 4. When he clarifies why he does not consider the book to be the writing of any apostle, Luther cites as his first reason, "Flatly against St. Paul and all the rest of Scripture, it [James] ascribes righteousness to works, and says that Abraham was justified by his works, in that he offered his son Isaac [Jas 2:21], though St. Paul, on the contrary, teaches in Romans 4 [vv. 2–3], that Abraham was justified without works, by faith alone, before he offered his son, and proves it by Moses in Genesis 15 [v. 6]."[3]

Second, there is a position about James that is being defended in our day which suggests that since James is as inspired and infallible as any other NT book, and, since it too speaks about justification, it needs to be reckoned with. In his latest book, Norman Shepherd defends the idea that the best approach is one wherein one examines what James says about justification before even approaching Paul.[4] For a correct biblical view, he suggests, a discussion about justification needs to begin with

---

1. As quoted in Kummel, *The New Testament*, 26.
2. Visscher, *Romans 4*.
3. Kummel, *The New Testament*, 24–25.
4. See Shepherd, *The Way of Righteousness*, 32, where the author summarizes his view by saying, "We can summarize the gospel of James 2:12–26 in four points. First, James 2:24 is talking about justification in the forensic-soteric sense, not in the demonstrative sense. Second, this justification takes place on the Day of Judgment when Christ returns to judge the living and the dead. Third, those who will be justified in that day are those who believe in Jesus Christ as Lord and Savior with a living, active, and obedient faith. Fourth, faith that is not living, active, and obedient is dead faith, and dead faith will not justify and will not save."

James and then move on to a reading of Paul in the light of what James says rather than the other way around, as is the general practice.

In the context of wider scholarship, with these two positions in mind, I would like to suggest that the church's difficulty in understanding James is due to the fact that we have failed to understand that he is speaking more about matters which we today would categorize under "sanctification" than he is about the issue of "justification."[5] To build a case, we need to make a number of excursions.

THE CONTEXT OF THE LETTER OF JAMES

First, we need to consider the most likely context for the Letter of James. During the last two centuries or so, scholars have often departed from what had been largely a consensus view up to that point—namely, that the Letter of James was written by the brother of our Lord Jesus who bore that name. In his commentary, Douglas Moo suggests that there are four main reasons that lead to the thought that the brother of our Lord could not have written this letter.[6] First, if the author was the brother of our Lord, it is thought, he would have mentioned this special relationship he enjoyed. Second, the nature of the letter's Greek and its cultural background lead scholars to doubt that someone in Jerusalem could have written it. Third, the letter's approach to torah seems rather liberal compared to that which James defends in the book of Acts. Fourth, the letter appears to be out of touch with Paul on the topic of justification.

Moo has offered some very good responses to these four points.[7] Concerning the first, there is no reason to believe that James would have thought his familial relationship with the Lord Jesus would have been important for his position in the early church. On the second, while the Greek that James uses may be more polished than what we would expect to see from Koine authors, it is still far from literary Greek. From Martin

---

5. To my knowledge, there is no significant work that has addressed this question. I thank Prof. J. Geertsema, my predecessor at the Canadian Reformed Theological Seminary, for discussions that led to further reflection on this point, and Henry Krabbendam, my predecessor at the Canadian Reformed Church of Ottawa, for his substantial work, *The Epistle of James*. In this work he certainly looks at the question of holiness and James, without making the central point that I am making in this paper.

6. Moo, *James*, 13–20.

7. Ibid.

Hengel's now classic study,[8] we have certainly learned not to force the divide between Palestinian Judaism and Hellenism, but to recognize the significant degree to which Hellenism made its inroads into Palestine. One can think here also of Acts 6; it is surely more than likely that the leader of a church that contained Hebraists as well as Hellenists would have exposure both to Hellenism and to the Greek language.

Regarding the third point, Moo points out that it is hardly accurate to maintain that James was some radical advocate of a Jewish-Christian party. Rather, it is more accurate to say that James "was personally loyal to torah and sought in every way possible to maintain ties between the emerging early Christian movement and the Judaism in which he had been nurtured and in which he ministered."[9] It is hardly difficult to square the Letter of James with such a person, especially when the context of the respective passages is kept in mind. As to the fourth, there are several possible explanations for this most difficult of NT problems. Either James and Paul are each not aware of what the other has written, or one of them is responding to a misunderstood form of the other's theology. More likely yet, the Letter of James is considerably earlier than generally thought and was written before James had any real, direct knowledge of Paul's teaching.

Moo, in fact, suggests that the letter was written in the mid-40s, perhaps just before the Apostolic Council. He posits the view that while James may be reacting to the way in which Paul's preaching has been misunderstood by those who heard him, James himself had not yet engaged in any significant discussion with Paul nor come to realize as yet that Paul's views were behind those he was opposing. Had he known what Paul really preached, as he would have after AD 48, he would have written the letter differently on several points. The other indicator for an early date is the author's lack of any awareness of the conflict over torah, an issue that also arose around AD 47–48. "James's casual references to torah in the letter (1:24–25; 2:8–13) would make more sense if this issue had not yet arisen."[10]

As recently as 2009, Dan McCartney has taken a position very similar to that of Douglas Moo. He also argues that the letter was written by James, the brother of Jesus, before Paul's letters. He suggests that,

8. Hengel, *Judaism and Hellenism*.
9. Moo, *James*, 17.
10. Ibid.

rather than reacting to a form of Paulinism, "similarities may instead be attributed to the fact that both James and Paul operated in a Hellenistic Jewish environment that was experiencing growing pains resulting from an influx of people from a Gentile background. Paul too had problems with Gentile believers who did not always apply their Christian faith to their ethical behavior (see, e.g., 1 Cor. 6)."[11]

McCartney also pays a great deal of attention to similarities between James and other biblical writings. While we cannot recount all his findings here, his conclusion is very relevant to this study. McCartney writes,

> It thus appears that James has features that can be linked to Greco-Roman moral exhortations, and to OT wisdom and poetry, and to OT prophetic material, and to Jewish Second Temple literature, and to certain other NT writings, both Gospels (especially Matthew) and other NT writings (especially 1 Peter). On the other hand, James bears little resemblance to the letters of Paul, beyond what may be expected of their common Christian milieu. Even if the alleged "response" of James to Paul in James 2 is in fact a response to Paul's letters or teaching, it seems to move in a different sphere, deal with different problems, using similar vocabulary differently. All this is best explained if James was written prior to the later heavily Christological development of the church as seen in Paul and 1 Peter, prior to the parting of the ways between Christianity and Judaism, by a person of Palestinian Jewish background who was a disciple of Jesus of Nazareth, but written to a Hellenistic Christian audience, perhaps many of whom were of Gentile origin, but had, by virtue of belief in Jesus as Lord, become reckoned among God's people.[12]

To summarize then, it would appear that the best explanation for the original context of the Letter of James is that it was written

a. from Jerusalem,
b. to Christians dispersed outside of Israel,
c. in the 40s of the first century of the Christian era, and
d. before Paul has written any of his letters.

---

11. McCartney, *James*, 16.
12. McCartney, *James*, 55–56.

It should be noted, by the way, that the view that James wrote prior to Paul is not an obscure position held by only a select few. Several significant scholars, such as Mayor, Zahn, and Schlatter, have held to this position in the past.[13] More recently, it has been defended by Adamson, Johnson, Bauckham, Brosend, and Floor.[14]

IMPLICATIONS

So what happens when we take this position on the Letter of James? In the words of the world's best computer maker, "This changes everything." We need to think especially about the implications this has for the role that James should, or should not, play in the discussions about justification by faith. I would, in fact, argue that James should not play a role in this discussion at all. Here is the argument.

a. Documents prior to Paul do not write as Paul does about justification by faith through grace alone.

There should be no doubt that Christianity has learned much of her present terminology from Paul. While people of Reformed persuasion like to believe that justification by faith through grace alone was a clear doctrine ever since the fall of Adam and Eve, this position is only tenable insofar as we read the Old Testament in the light of Paul's theological constructions. While concepts such as being "righteous" and "holy" are certainly present in the Old Testament and Judaism, it is from Paul that the church has learned and developed such theological constructs as "justification" and "sanctification." Paul is the one who brings together texts from Genesis and Psalms and, more than anyone before him, writes explicitly and consistently about justification by faith through grace alone. One looks in vain to find any kind of Jewish dogmatics for a doctrine of justification by faith. George Foot Moore has chapters on sin and forgiveness, but little on righteousness, and certainly no entry on justification through faith alone.[15] Similarly, the significant text by Ephraim Urbach has nothing on this.[16] Despite their attempts,

---

13. Mayor, *The Epistle of St. James*, cxxi–cliii; Zahn, *Introduction to the New Testament*, 1:91–94; Schlatter, *Der Brief des Jacobus*, 7.

14. Adamson, *James*, 3–52, 195–227; Johnson, *The Letter of James*, 111–21; Bauckham, *James*, 127–31; Brosend, *James and Jude*, 5–6; Floor, *Jacobus*, 14–17.

15. Moore, *Judaism*.

16. Urbach, *The Sages*.

E. P. Sanders and the New Perspective on Paul have not convinced scholarship that a uniform concept of grace was there all along. In fact, the result of all the New Perspective discussion about "works" and "grace" in Judaism is the awareness that, contrary to the claim of Sanders, Second Temple literature in particular is quite content to mix language about grace with language about works. As Stephen Westerholm has suggested, views prevalent in Judaism were after all very similar to the later semi-Pelagian views—which is the very background of the Reformation.[17]

The fact that this thorough analysis of justification by faith through grace, and all the principles of grace, never gets worked out as clearly and as systematically as it does by Paul does not mean that God was not gracious in a previous era, or that the principles of grace were not there throughout redemptive history. We just need to recognize the unique contribution that Paul makes at this point. The Roman context in which Paul needed to defend himself against the charge of promoting evil (Rom 3:8), and the Galatian context in which attempts were made to add circumcision and the like to faith, forced him to think through and write about how justification is through faith alone and how this faith, bringing about union with Christ, will make people fruitful in him. Better yet, God used these contexts to reveal, in greater degree, to Paul and to us the eternal riches of His grace and love in Christ (Eph 3:17–19).

This should not be understood as detracting from the doctrine of the clarity of Scripture. Scripture itself speaks about how previous generations were curious about what would come later in redemptive history (1 Pet 1:10–12). The Lord Jesus reveals the glory, grace, and truth of the Father (John 1:14, 18). God uses men like John and Paul and James to expound it to us in more majestic ways.

b. If James writes before Paul and has formulated such concepts, we should not be surprised that his terms are not equivalent to those of Paul either.

Seen in the context suggested above, we should not be surprised if terms like "justify" and "faith" have a meaning at variance with those of Paul. That appears to be the case, for example, with faith (*pistis*), which does not seem to have a unified meaning in James. In 1:6 and 5:15, James uses

---

17. Westerholm, *Perspectives Old and New on Paul*, 346, 443–44; see also Gathercole, *Where Is Boasting?* 155–56, and Visscher, *Romans 4*, 233–34.

pistis to refer to the prayer of faith as a prayer in which one trusts in God who is the object of such a prayer, but in 2:19 he speaks about demons who believe. In that verse, faith is just an acknowledgement of the existence of God. Paul would hardly call this "faith." However, since James defines faith here in this way, a faith which he himself says is dead (2:17, 26) and useless (2:20), in 2:14–26 he emphasizes the need for works.[18]

c. In fact, the terminology James does use is quite similar to that of the Gospel period, the period in which he writes (according to Moo, McCartney, and others).

There are two interesting volumes written by Alan P. Stanley. The larger volume, originally a PhD dissertation at Dallas Seminary, is called *Did Jesus Teach Salvation by Works?*[19] It should be realized that Stanley argues that "salvation" is a comprehensive term, much more than just a moment of decision and not equivalent to "justification," referring instead to the whole "pilgrimage" of the Christian life.[20] He argues that Jesus clearly does not teach "pre-conversion works" that merit eternal life. It is impossible for anyone, rich or otherwise, to enter the kingdom by works. Only God can string this needle. It is the poor in spirit, sinners, who are granted access. Yet, says Stanley, Jesus certainly did teach "post-conversion works." There are great expectations of those who are clothed with the righteousness of Christ. Almost on every page of the Gospels, in parables and elsewhere, the Lord is speaking about these post-conversion works that are expected of God's people. Stanley writes,

> If by salvation we mean "conversion" and something akin to Paul's justification by faith; and if by works we mean works prior to conversion and thus originating from ourselves then it is clear—Jesus did *not* teach salvation by works. If however we mean final or eschatological salvation and post-conversion works originating from God Himself then, yes, Jesus *did* teach salvation by works—in the same way that James taught *justification by works*. The answer—yes or no—depends on what perspective of salvation we are speaking about. This is exactly the tension we see for example between James 2 and Romans 4.[21]

18. Barth, "Πιστις, εως, η," 3:97.
19. Stanley, *Did Jesus Teach Salvation by Works?* and Stanley, *Salvation Is More Complicated*.
20. Stanley, *Did Jesus Teach Salvation by Works?* 153.
21. Ibid., 333.

And now the point is, when we think about the difference between pre-conversion works and post-conversion works, and put that into Pauline categories, do the words "justification" and "sanctification" not come to mind? Here is Paul's way of saying that there are no pre-conversion works: "For it is by grace you have been saved, through faith—and this not from yourselves, it is the gift of God—not by works, so that no one can boast."[22] And here is Paul's way of speaking about post-conversion works: "For we are God's workmanship, created in Christ Jesus to do good works, which God prepared in advance for us to do" (Eph 2:8–10).

Furthermore, where is it that the words of James find a better temporal context? During or after the writings of Paul? Or during the period of the Gospels? Isn't James just saying, not at all unlike his brother, that post-conversion works are the necessary consequence of faith and conversion? Surely, the best reason that James can write, "a person is justified by what he does and not by faith alone" (2:24), is because he is talking about post-conversion works in a gospel-like fashion. And the best reason that he does not need to qualify his statements vis-à-vis the writings of Paul is because such words have not yet been written.

d. The different ways in which Paul and James use the example of Abraham illustrates the point.

There is a very interesting difference between Paul and James in terms of how they make use of the example of Abraham. Elsewhere, I have illustrated that in the Jewish literature Abraham was seen as a particularly virtuous person. The Hebrew word for "faith" in Gen 15:6 was understood in the sense of "faithful" (Ps 106; Neh 9; Sir 44; *Jub.* 14:4–7; 4Q225; 4QMMT C 25–32; 1 Macc 2:50–53; Philo, *Abr.* 275–276).[23] Abraham was considered faithful to God, in fact, faithful to the Law of Moses even before Moses was born. Today, we would almost speak about the "active obedience of Abraham." In keeping with all that, it should be noted that, prior to Paul, the Jewish literature has quite consistently understood Gen 15:6 in light of Genesis 22. Abraham was seen as righteous because

---

22. All Scripture quotations in this article are taken from the New International Version (NIV).

23. Visscher, *Romans 4*, 161–63. Watson, *Paul and the Hermeneutics of Faith*, 173, points out that even Genesis describes Abram as having "more than enough" works that confirm to the revealed will of God (12:4, 7, 10; 14:14, 20; 17:17, 23; 18:2–3; 20:17; 22:3; 23:19). See also Urbach, *The Sages*, 404–7, 502–3.

of his deeds, the greatest of these being his willingness to sacrifice his son Isaac, the *Aqedah* of Genesis 22.

The noteworthy point here is that it is Paul who first understands Gen 15:6 as a righteousness without works (Rom 4:2), based simply on the act of believing in God, and on his promise (4:13, 14, 16, 20, 21). Says Francis Watson, "Paul sounds a very different note when he insists on taking Gen 15.6 at face value: Abraham's righteousness is constituted merely by his acceptance of God's promise to act on his behalf."[24] However, the even more noteworthy point for our purpose here is that James, in keeping with the literature that exists before Paul, also understands Gen 15:6 in the light of Gen 22.

In that world which was inclined to think of an obedient and righteous Abraham, Paul proclaims the gospel of God's grace most emphatically when he declares Abraham to have been one who was "ungodly, wicked" (*asebēs*, 4:5), who "does not work" but just "trusts God who justifies the wicked" (4:5). James, however, in that earlier context pressed believers to be fruitful in the faith by referring to Abraham, the father of all believers who proved the genuineness of his faith with the reality of his obedient actions. The question I would ask is, do we not usually refer to that as sanctification? Think, for instance, of the Heidelberg Catechism that places this under the section referred to as "Thankfulness" in Lord's Day 32, or of the Belgic Confession that in Article 24 discusses the works which flow out of faith under the heading "Our Sanctification and Good Works."[25]

e. The different ways that Paul and James use the verb "justify" (dikaioō) also illustrates the point.

Several commentators have referred to the fact that James and Paul are using the verb "to justify" (*dikaioō*) in different ways. Thomas R. Schreiner probably says it best when he suggests that Paul uses the word to refer to what Westerholm has called "extraordinary righteousness"—a righteousness that God gives to people who are not righteous of themselves. "Paul shockingly insists that it is the ungodly who are declared to be righteous by virtue of the righteousness of Christ."[26] James, however,

---

24. Watson, *Paul and the Hermeneutics*, 268.
25. See *Book of Praise*, 458.
26. Schreiner, *New Testament Theology*, 601.

uses the verb to refer to "ordinary righteousness"—God then declares him to be right because he does right; he obeys.²⁷

All of this was said some time ago, on pages that many of us have long forgotten about, by Louis Berkhof. Commenting on Jas 2:24, which reads, "You see that a person is justified by what he does and not by faith alone," Berkhof says, "it is quite evident . . . that in this case the writer is not speaking of the justification of the sinner . . . but of a further justification of the believing Abraham . . . The justification of the just by works confirms the justification by faith."²⁸

Again, I would ask whether these words of James do not fit best in a pre-Pauline context. Here are some examples of how the Gospels use the verb *dikaioō* and how the NIV translates these uses. To be sure, there are some that come close to the kind of meaning that Paul gives the verb, though never quite arriving there. Luke 10:29 says of the man to whom Jesus tells the parable of the Good Samaritan, "he wanted to *justify* himself." Luke 16:15 gives us, "You are the ones who justify yourselves in the eyes of men . . ." Luke 18:14 says of the publican in the parable, "this man . . . went home *justified* before God." However, there are other texts that may have more of an affinity with James's intention: Matt 11:19, "wisdom is *proved right* by her actions" (cf. Luke 7:35); Matt 12:37, "For by your words *you will be acquitted*"; Luke 7:29, "All the people, when they heard Jesus's words, *acknowledged that God's way was right*"; so too Jas 2:21, "Was not our ancestor Abraham *considered righteous* . . . ?"; and Jas 2:25, "was not even Rahab the prostitute *considered righteous* for what she did . . . ?" Moreover, there is a very interesting expression in Jas 2:22 about Abraham: "his faith was made complete by what he did (*kai ek tōn ergōn hē pistis eteleiōthē*)." This appears to be the meaning of James, different from Paul's: works justify in the sense that works *complete* faith, *confirm* faith. Moo says something like this when he suggests that one needs to read "James's teaching about 'works' in light of Paul's teaching that Christian works are themselves the product of God's work of grace

---

27. Ibid., argues that it is not quite right to argue that *dikaioō* here means "proved to be righteous" or "shown to be righteous" (as Moo and Davids argue) as the context does not warrant this change in lexical meaning. Schreiner suggests that both James and Paul use the word soteriologically, but Paul thinks of God as declaring those who are unrighteous to be righteous whereas James uses it to emphasize that God declares those who are righteous to be righteous.

28. Berkhof, *Systematic Theology*, 521.

d. James is often perceived as assisting Paul on the doctrine of justification. Might it be more correct to see him filling out Paul's words on sanctification? Rather than placing Jas 2 alongside Rom 4, perhaps it would be more helpful to consider Jas 2 alongside, for example, Rom 6 or Eph 2 or Gal 5:6 ("faith working through love").

e. The Christian church in our day ought to be wary of such language as being justified by a "living, active, and obedient faith," or a "faith that works" and the like. With such qualifiers the danger is very real that one imports something of what we do into God's gracious work and that once again the efforts of human beings are thought to be necessary to supplement the work of Jesus Christ. It is enough to talk simply about a "true faith."

f. In my estimation, the language of a Reformed confession such as the Heidelberg Catechism is much better. Faith is the means, not the basis; we are not acceptable to God because of the worthiness of faith, but only because of the satisfaction, righteousness, and holiness of Christ (Lord's Day 23, a. 61). The origin of all good works is not found in the nature of our faith, but in the fact that by faith believers are grafted into Christ and "it is impossible that those grafted into Christ by true faith should not bring forth fruits of thankfulness" (Lord's Day 24, a. 64). Good works must be there in the lives of the people of God for reasons not inherent in themselves but because Christ renews by his Holy Spirit those whom he has redeemed by his blood (Lord's Day 32). It is not that James ever contradicted that, but he could be misunderstood in that way (e.g., Luther). Similarly, in the gospels, the difference between preconversion works and post-conversion works can sometimes be a subtle one, but it is through the writings of Paul that all of this falls into place.

g. There is no doubt that what James writes is Scripture and, when it is rightly understood in his particular context, it makes a delightful contribution to the significant question of how people who have come to faith can live holy lives and display such holiness before their fellow creatures and the only God.

BIBLIOGRAPHY

Adamson, James B. *James: The Man and His Message*. Grand Rapids: Eerdmans, 1989.
Barth, G. "Πιστις, εως, η." In *Exegetical Dictionary of the New Testament*, edited by Horst Balz and Gerhard Schneider, 3:91–97. 3 vols. Grand Rapids: Eerdmans, 1993.
Bauckham, Richard A. *James: Wisdom of James, Disciple of Jesus the Sage*. New Testament Readings. London: Routledge, 1999.
Berkhof, Louis. *Systematic Theology*. 4th rev. ed. Grand Rapids: Eerdmans, 1974.
Book of Praise: Anglo-Genevan Psalter. Winnipeg: Premier Printing, 1995.
Brosend, William F., II. *James and Jude*. New Cambridge Bible Commentary. Cambridge: Cambridge University Press, 2004.
Floor, L. *Jacobus, Brief van een broeder*. Kampen: Kok, 1992.
Gathercole, Simon J. *Where Is Boasting? Early Jewish Soteriology and Paul's Response in Romans 1–5*. Grand Rapids: Eerdmans, 2002.
Hengel, Martin. *Judaism and Hellenism: Studies in Their Encounter in Palestine during the Early Hellenistic Period*. Translated by John Bowden. 1974. Reprint, Eugene, OR: Wipf & Stock, 2003.
Johnson, Luke Timothy. *The Letter of James*. AB 37A. New York: Doubleday, 1995.
Krabbendam, Henry. *The Epistle of James: Tender Love in Tough Pursuit of Total Holiness*. 2 vols. Theologisches Lehr- und Studienmaterial 9. Bonn: Verlag für Kultur und Wissenschaft, 2006.
Kummel, Werner Georg. *The New Testament: The History of the Investigation of Its Problems*. Nashville: Abingdon, 1972.
Mayor, J. B. *The Epistle of St. James: The Greek Text with Introduction, Notes and Comments*. New York: Macmillan, 1897.
McCartney, Dan. *James*. Baker Exegetical Commentary on the New Testament. Grand Rapids: Baker Academic, 2009.
Moo, Douglas J. *The Letter of James*. The Pillar New Testament Commentary. Grand Rapids: Eerdmans, 2000.
Moore, George Foot. *Judaism*. 2 vols. 1927. Reprint, Peabody: Hendrickson, 1960.
Schlatter, A. *Der Brief des Jacobus*. Stuttgart: Calwer, 1932.
Schreiner, Thomas R. *New Testament Theology: Magnifying God in Christ*. Grand Rapids: Baker Academic, 2008.
Shepherd, Norman. *The Way of Righteousness: Justification Beginning with James*. LaGrange, CA: Kerygma, 2009.
Stanley, Alan P. *Did Jesus Teach Salvation by Works? The Role of Works in Salvation in the Synoptic Gospels*. The Evangelical Theological Society Monograph Series 4. Eugene, OR: Pickwick Publications, 2006.
———. *Salvation Is More Complicated Than You Think: A Study on the Teachings of Jesus*. Colorado Springs: Authentic, 2007.
Thielman, Frank. *Theology of the New Testament: A Canonical and Synthetic Approach*. Grand Rapids: Zondervan, 2005.
Urbach, Ephraim E. *The Sages: Their Concepts and Beliefs*. Cambridge: Harvard University Press, 1979.
Visscher, Gerhard H. *Romans 4 and the New Perspective on Paul: Faith Embraces the Promise*. Studies in Biblical Literature 122. New York: Lang, 2009.
Watson, Francis. *Paul and the Hermeneutics of Faith*. London: T. & T. Clark, 2004.
Westerholm, Stephen. *Perspectives Old and New on Paul: The "Lutheran" Paul and His Critics*. Grand Rapids: Eerdmans, 1988.
Zahn, T. et al. *Introduction to the New Testament*. Translated by J. M. Trout et al. 3 vols. Edinburgh: T. & T. Clark, 1909.

9

The Lamb's Scroll of Life in Revelation 5

Jakob Geertsema

In Revelation 5 we learn about the scroll that the Lamb took and opened. There are two main interpretations of this scroll. The more common interpretation reasons that the scroll contains the events of God's reign through Christ Jesus, from his ascension to his return. I call this the *events view*. The other explanation, mostly rejected or ignored, takes the scroll to be the Book of Life with the names of those purchased for God with the blood of Christ. This view will be called the *life view*. This study gives much attention to the description of Christ Jesus as "the Lamb who was slaughtered." This is the exegetical key for a correct understanding of Rev 5:1–10 and supports the argument for a distinction between the scroll and the seals, whereby each have their own distinctive content.

I am thankful for this opportunity to honor our Old Testament colleague, Dr. C. Van Dam. I present my arguments with the aim to abide by what we both learned, and tried to practice and teach, at the Canadian Reformed Theological Seminary for a number of years; namely, the need to explain a passage of God's Word carefully and precisely, in its closer and increasingly wider biblical contexts, in a Christ-centered manner, and possibly also in the light of the historical situation—all for the benefit of God's covenant people.

THE COMMON VIEW: THE SCROLL CONTAINS ESCHATOLOGICAL HISTORY

A Brief Description

In Greek, the word rendered in Rev 5:1 as "scroll" is *biblion*—that is, "book." In the apostolic era, books generally were in the form of a number of papyrus sheets attached together and rolled up around a stick, called a scroll.[1] In Rev 5, the scroll in God's right hand is at the center of the events and, indeed, it plays an important role throughout Revelation. Therefore, a good understanding of its content is needed. Before the time of the Reformation, the content was often seen as being the Old and New Testaments. Interestingly, the seven seals were taken as the cover, or veil, preventing people from understanding the Scriptures correctly, since they can only be understood when revealed by Christ Jesus. From the time of the Reformation until the present, the content of the scroll was often seen as the entire book of Revelation itself, or at least as a part of it.[2]

Scholars such as D. E. Aune and G. K. Beale place themselves in this latter category. Aune writes at the end of his explanation of Rev 5, "The scroll and its contents therefore include the entire eschatological scenario extending from 6:1 through 22:9."[3] Similarly, Beale writes that the scroll "concerns a predestined plan that is eschatological in nature, since its contents are revealed in Rev 6–22 and are summarized in 4:1 as 'what must take place after these things....'"[4] Aune also mentions the difference of opinion among interpreters regarding which part(s) of Revelation appear on the scroll.[5] Is it Rev 6–22? Is it the part that begins after all seven seals have been opened, namely, Rev 8 and following? Or does it begin with the opening of the first seal in Rev 6:1? And where does it end? Whatever differences of opinion there may be on the starting and ending points, these scholars agree that the content of the scroll refers to events.

---

1. Pictures of sealed scrolls are shown in Finegan, *Light from the Ancient Past*, 2:410–11.

2. Aune, *Revelation*, 344. More detailed is Stefanovic, *Sealed Book*, see esp. his summary on 112–17.

3. Aune, *Revelation*, 374.

4. Beale, *Revelation*, 341–42.

5. Aune, *Revelation*, 344.

Mention should also be made of G. B. Caird. He rejects the view that the scroll contains a smaller or larger part of Revelation, but favors the "theory" that the scroll contains "God's redemptive plan, foreshadowed in the Old Testament, by which he means to assert his sovereignty over a sinful world and so to achieve the purpose of creation."[6] At the same time, he asserts that the opening of the seals implies the opening of the scroll, the content of which is events.[7]

When we compare this view of Caird and others like him[8] with that of Aune and Beale, we can conclude that while these views may differ in form, in fact what Caird describes as the content of the scroll is *materially* the same as what we read in Rev 6–22. It is important to realize that this material agreement is based on their shared assumption that the opening of the seals implies, and is essentially identical with, the opening of the scroll.[9]

Some Weak Points

The first weak point is the obvious lack of unity among events-view proponents regarding the exact extent of the content of the scroll. Is it all or only a part of Revelation? Does it start with 6:1 or 8:1? And how far does it go? In addition, if the content begins with the opening of the first seal or after all seven seals are opened, does this mean that chapters 4 and 5 are not included? That would be awkward as chapters 4 and 5 form a unity with what follows, at least with 6:1—8:1. Moreover, it would also be awkward to take chapters 4 and 5 with 1–3. Someone may argue that we should not demand such exactness from the apostle; however, that argument becomes weak when there is an alternate explanation in the life view that does not have these difficulties.

Aune himself mentions another problem. Dealing with the scroll's content, he writes, "the text of 5:1—8:1 . . . contains no *explicit* indication of the contents of the scroll."[10] In other words, the idea that the

---

6. Caird, *Revelation of St. John*, 71–72.

7. Ibid., 71.

8. Farmer, *Revelation*, 62, writes that "most commentators are in general agreement with G. B. Caird."

9. Aune, *Revelation*, 345; Beale, *Revelation*, 339; Caird, *Revelation of St. John*, 70–71.

10. Aune, *Revelation*, 343; emphasis added. After expressing doubt regarding the identity of the scroll of Rev 5 and the one of Rev 10, he adds, "An important clue for the contents of the scroll is Ezek 2:9–10, the model for this passage, in which the contents of

scroll's contents are made known through the "opening" (breaking) of the seals is an implicit assumption rather than an explicit assertion. Linked with this is the further supposition that when the seals are broken the scroll is also thereby opened and its contents disclosed. This is also an assumption without any "explicit indication."[11] This supposition may appear to be quite logical, but that does not alter the fact that it is still an assumption.

A final weak point of the events view is that there is no explicit mention in Revelation of the opening of the scroll as an opening of a "book of events." This is strange in light of the scroll's great importance. By contrast, the life view does not have this problem, since Rev 20:12, 15 specifically mention the opening of the Book of Life.

THE ALTERNATE VIEW: THE SCROLL IS THE BOOK OF LIFE

The manner in which Rev 5:1–12 speaks about the book, or scroll, and its seals needs careful attention. It is freely translated below;[12] some phrases are italicized for the sake of emphasis.

> 5:1 John saw, upon the right hand of God, seated on his heavenly throne, *a book* written on the inside and on the back, *thoroughly sealed with seven seals*.
>
> 5:2 And he saw a strong angel proclaiming with a loud voice, "*Who is worthy to open the book and break its seals?*"
>
> 5:3 And no one in heaven or on earth or under the earth was able *to open the book or to see it* [= its contents].
>
> 5:4 So he wept intensely because no one was found worthy *to open the book or to see it* [= its contents].

---

the scroll shown to Ezekiel are described as 'words of mourning, lamentation, and woe,' i.e., the message of divine judgment that the prophet will announce." It is true that there is a formal similarity between the scrolls in Ezek 2 and Rev 10: both are open scrolls that the prophets, Ezekiel and John, have to eat. However, the problem with making Ezek 2 the basis for the events view is that it fails to account for the difference between the *closed* scroll of Rev 5, which is taken by the ascended Lamb, and the *open* scroll of Rev 10, which is eaten by the prophet.

11. Aune, *Revelation*, 343.

12. Throughout this article I provide my own translation of Scripture passages, although I did also consult the NIV to see how that translation worded particular verses.

5:5   And one of the elders said to me, "Stop weeping. Look, *the lion of the tribe of Judah, the root of David*, has won the victory *to open the book and its seven seals.*

5:6   John saw, in the midst of the throne, *a lamb* standing as *having been slaughtered.*

5:7   And he came and *took* [the scroll] from the right hand of the one seated on the throne.

5:8   And when *he had taken the book*, the four living beings and the twenty-four elders worshipped the Lamb, each with a harp and a bowl full of incenses, which are the saints' prayers.

5:9   And they sang a new song: "*Worthy are you to take the book and open its seals*, because you were slaughtered, and you purchased us for God with your blood, from every tribe and language and people and

5:10 nation; and you made them a kingdom and priests for our God; and they will reign on the earth.

5:11 [A multitude of angels sings . . .]

5:12 "Worthy is the Lamb who was slaughtered to receive power and wealth and wisdom and strength and honor and glory and praise."

The Seals: Connected to, but Distinct from, the Scroll

In the above passage, the verb *to open* is key with respect to both the scroll itself and the seals. In v. 2 it says, "open the book and break the seals." By mentioning the scroll first, the expected order is reversed. Normally, one would first break the seals in order to open a book. The order in v. 2 thus demonstrates the greater importance of the scroll.[13] Verses 3 and 4 confirm this since both read "open the scroll and look (into) it," without mentioning the seals. Finally v. 5 offers the same counterintuitive order: "to open the scroll and its seven seals."[14]

---

13. Mounce, *Revelation*, 143.

14. This is the reading of the great majority of the manuscripts; only a few read "open the scroll and break its seals." See Comfort, *New Testament Text and Translation*, 824, who, unsure himself, says that the textual critics favor the shorter reading. Indeed, based on the great majority of both manuscripts and textual critics, the shorter reading seems to be the better choice.

Furthermore, there are two striking changes both in and after v. 5. The first is that here the apostle no longer speaks of *breaking* the seals, but he applies the verb *to open* to both the scroll and the seals. This gives the impression that both are significant. Both need to be opened, and thus each seems to have its own specific content and revelatory function. As we will shortly see in more detail, the scroll, as Book of Life, is opened in 20:12, but the seals are opened as described in 6:1, 3, 5, 7, 9, 12, and 8:1.

Interestingly, in antiquity, personal seals made of stone or other hard material were engraved with names or pictures of gods, animals, or other objects, which carried certain meanings. Seals like this were still used in the apostolic age. For instance, Emperor Augustus used a variety of seals over time, each with its own unique engraving and presenting its own message.[15] In a similar way, the first seal in Rev 6 might show a rider with a bow while the second portrayed a rider with a sword, and so on. This example from antiquity supports the idea that the seals have their own content and message, distinct from those of the scroll itself.[16]

However, there is another striking change at v. 5 that supports the idea of a distinction between the contents of the seals and the scroll. After Rev 5:5, the apostle John does not speak anymore of *opening* the scroll. In the vv. 7, 8, 9, 12, the text reports that the Lamb came and *took* the scroll. Moreover, this taking, not opening, of the scroll by the Lamb is obviously the climax of this chapter. Verse 8 records the excited, joyful reaction of the elders and living creatures as they worship the Lamb who

---

15. "The principal device on ancient seals was usually pictorial—a favorite deity, a mythical hero, animals, and later, portraits. The seal devices of several prominent men of Roman times are known; Augustus first used a sphinx and later a portrait of Alexander the Great." Hornblower and Spawforth, *Oxford Classical Dictionary*, 1376.

16. Examples are the two stones of the high priest's ephod, each with six names of Israel's tribes, "for a memorial" (Exod 28:9–14); and his breastplate with twelve stones, each with one name, "for making decisions" (Exod 28:15–21). It is also noteworthy that Aune, *Revelation*, 322, quotes a study by T. Birt, stating that "the term *anoixai* [to open] is a technical term for breaking the seal . . ." so that the two formulations, *breaking a seal* and *opening a scroll*, "are virtually synonymous. . . ." However, the expression *opening a seal* does not occur anywhere else in the NT and is not found in the Septuagint. Moreover, when consulting the *Thesaurus linguae graecae* (*TLG*), with only one exception, I did not find this formulation anywhere else except in places where Rev 5 and 6 are discussed. The conclusion can be that the expression *anoigein sfragida*, "opening a seal" occurs sporadically in Greek literature, but that this does not prove to be the case in Rev 5 and 6. It is noteworthy that Birt remarks in the above mentioned note that in Rev 5:2 *et passim* the scroll's opening as unfolding its contents is not in view at all.

has taken the scroll. Accordingly, in v. 9 they sing, "You are worthy 1) to *take* the scroll and 2) to *open* the seals." The climactic action of *taking* the scroll indicates that it is the most important *event* in Rev 4–5, which is foundational for the rest of Revelation.

To read Rev 5:1–10 in this way might seem improbable in the context of the common events view, but it fits well in the life-view context. Not only does it do justice to the change of verb, from breaking to opening seals, but it also reckons with the scroll's opening at the final judgment. The taking of the scroll in Rev 5, combined with the fact that it is not opened until 20:12, indicates that the Lamb's *possession* of the scroll is sufficient for the time being. This central position of the Lamb in Rev 5 is stressed as well by the fact that in v. 12 the angels are said to glorify the Lamb, while in v. 13 the entire cosmos directs its doxology "to him who is seated on the throne *and to the Lamb.*"

At the same time, the events of God's rule through Christ, including his judgments, do not disappear. They do not issue forth from the scroll *per se*, but rather from the opening of the seals, the blowing of the trumpets, and the outpouring of the bowls. Yet predominant in all of this is the Lamb who was slaughtered for, and takes care of, his own. It is to him that our attention must now turn more closely.

The Scroll Is the Lamb's Book of Life

The three descriptions of Christ Jesus in vv. 5–6 each have their own distinct features. In these verses, one of the elders tells John not to weep, since "the Lion of Judah's tribe" who is "the Root of David" has overcome. He won the victory to open both "the scroll and the seals." The first title for Christ is taken from Gen 49:9, from the context of father Jacob's blessing for his son, Judah. The second comes from Isa 11:1, 10, from the context of a prophecy about the coming Davidic Messiah, anointed with the Spirit of God to bring about a kingdom of justice for the needy, as well as peace for creation. Both have a *royal* messianic character. An important feature of the Lion of Judah's tribe is waging God's war and defeating his enemies: ". . . your hand will be on the neck of your enemies" (Gen 49:8, cf. Rev 5:5). With less emphasis, this aspect is also present in the description of Christ as the Root of David. In Isa 11:4b it says, "He will strike the earth with the rod of his mouth; with the breath of his lips he will slay the wicked." However, the main feature of this description is that he, anointed with the Spirit of the Lord, will bring about the realm of peace in God's earthly creation. These two titles point out that the Messiah will win God's battle against the enemies and bring about the kingdom of God on a renewed earth. These two features take effect both in the judgments that bring punishment and in the realization of God's glorious kingdom.

However, the third description as "the Lamb who was slaughtered" is the central and most significant one. It is specifically this *priestly* feature of offering himself as a sin-offering to God that prompted the animated reaction of the elders and the living creatures. It is noteworthy that this priestly work, along with its effect of purchasing God's people for God, is the main content of the song of praise. "You are worthy to take the scroll and open its seals; for you were slaughtered, and *purchased* [us][17] for God with your blood out of every tribe and language and people and nation . . ." Therefore, although no names are explicitly mentioned, indeed, the bearers of those names are certainly referred to here. Those whom the Lamb purchased are those whose names are written in God's Book of Life, which now becomes the Lamb's Book of Life. This emphasis on the Lamb in Rev 5 runs throughout Rev 6–22,[18] occurring some twenty-six times in Revelation. At the same time, the risen and ascended Lamb is not without power; John saw him with seven horns on his head. Moreover, it is this Lamb who opens the seals, bringing judgment upon the world.

In a special way, chapters 7 and 14 reinforce this central position of the Lamb with his saints. First, concerning Rev 7, the 144,000 of Israel are sealed with "the seal of the living God" (v. 2), indicating God's ownership and protection. Then 7:9–17 speaks about an uncountable multitude from every nation, tribe, people, and language. The 144,000 sealed of God's Israel are, most likely, the same as the multitude praising God and the Lamb.[19] Furthermore, the terms nation, tribe, people, and

17. One, most likely two, of the oldest manuscripts, as well as the group of Coptic manuscripts, miss the object; all other manuscripts read "us" as the object. Cf. Comfort, *New Testament Text and Translation,* 825, and Beale, *Revelation,* 360. Even if this object is not original, from early times the absolute majority has understood that "us" was the correct object. We follow this majority. See also the "us" in 1:5.

18. The Lamb theme is also central in Hebrews. See Heb 2:10–13, 14–18; 5:7–9; 7; 9:11–14, 23–28; 10:5–14; 12:22–24.

19. Swete, *Apocalypse,* 99–100; Beale, *Revelation,* 424–28; Greijdanus, *Openbaring,* 170. It should be noted that Greijdanus speaks of the 144,000 as being part of the innumerable assembly mentioned in Rev 7:9. Thus, he makes a strong connection, but not a complete identification, between the two groups.

language are also used in 5:9 for those purchased by the Lamb, and in 7:9 these saints are said to "stand before the throne and *before the Lamb* clothed in white robes." Moreover, the robes they wear are made white in the blood of the Lamb (7:14), the very same blood used to purchase them in 5:9. All these connecting points serve to confirm the identity of the sealed servants of God in 7:1–17 and the purchased saints in 5:1–12, both of whom belong to the Lamb.

Second, in chapter 14, John sees "the *Lamb* standing on Mount Zion, along with 144,000 with his name and his Father's name on their foreheads." These saints are identical to those sealed with God's seal in 7:3. After all, seals and names are closely related to each other.[20] There is also an identity marker between these saints of 14:1–5 and those of 5:1–12; the expression "the ones purchased," which is used in 14:3 and in 14:4, first occurred in 5:9. These very similar formulations indicate that the 144,000 of the Lamb marked with the seal of the living God are identical with the purchased ones of 5:9 for whom the Lamb was slaughtered.[21]

Chapter 14 presents a few additional descriptions of these purchased saints. They "did not defile themselves with women, for they kept themselves pure [lit. virgins]" and "no lie was found in their mouths; they are blameless" (vv. 4–5). The purity and integrity of these saints resounds in 21:27 where it says, "Nothing impure will ever enter it [New Jerusalem], nor will anyone who does what is shameful or deceitful."[22] Then, significantly, it is added, "but only those whose names are written in the *Lamb's book of life*." Again, based on this connection between Rev 14 and 21 as well as the previous connection between Rev 14 and 5, we can conclude that those purchased by the Lamb with his blood for God are precisely the same as those whose names are written in the Lamb's Book of Life.[23] Considering this, we can agree with W. Sattler, who writes that it "will not be too bold [to conclude] that the scroll with the seven seals contains the names of these servants of God, and that, in other

---

20. Cf. 3:12 where Christ promises to write on every one who overcomes "the name of my God and . . . my new name."

21. Beale, *Revelation*, 412–13, 744.

22. The words "lie" in 14:5 and "deceitful" in 21:27 are different renderings of the same Greek word *pseudos*.

23. Although John's Gospel does not mention the Book of Life in connection with the Lamb, all that this combination of the Lamb and "Book of Life" means in Revelation is present in this Gospel, too; see 1:29, 36; 6:39; 10:11, 15, 28–30; 13:1; 17:1, 2, 6, 9, 24.

words, it is the heavenly register of those sealed with the seal of God, and thus the book of life."[24]

The Lamb's Book of Life in Revelation 13

Revelation 13:7 depicts a sharp contrast between the anti-Christian beast, a servant of the dragon, and the saints against whom the beast makes war. The beast conquers the saints, but, remarkably, he did not gain authority over them so that they would worship him. The beast does gain such authority "over all the inhabitants of the earth," but these inhabitants are further defined as "everyone whose name has not been written from the foundation of the world in *the book of life of the Lamb who was slaughtered*."[25] God's wrath and the wrath of the Lamb were on all those whose names are not in the Book, but those recorded in the Book remain faithful to the Lamb. Thus, it is clear that the saints who did not come under the beast's authority and who did not worship him are the purchased and protected ones who went through the great tribulation, as described in Rev 7.

It is noteworthy that here the Book of Life is identified as the possession of "the Lamb who was slaughtered." Automatically this descriptor, "*the Lamb who was slaughtered*," reminds us of the place where it first occurred, namely, in 5:6, 9, 12. Significantly, 13:8 is the only other place where we find this expression, and it is found in combination with a book or scroll. When a specific expression is used in two separate places, it is safe to conclude that the same matter is dealt with in both places. Surprisingly, this logical conclusion is not made in commentaries, most likely due to the fact that commentators generally view the scroll in Rev 5 as containing events, thus not connecting it to the Book of Life. However, as we have seen, the events view is not based on explicit fact but on implicit assumption. Therefore, we can justly conclude that

---

24. Sattler, "Das Buch," 43–53. In particular, on page 47 he writes, "Die Folgerung wird nicht zu kuehn sein, dasz das Buch mit sieben Siegeln ... die Namen dieser Gottesknechte enthaelt, dasz es, mit andern Worten, das himmlische Verzeichnis der mit dem Siegel Gottes Versiegelten (7:3), also das Buch des Lebens ist."

25. The NIV's rendering of v. 8 is, "All inhabitants of the earth will worship the beast—all whose names have not been written in the book of life belonging to the Lamb that was slain from the creation of the world." The NIV renders the English in the same order as in the Greek text. However, it is better to take the phrase "from the creation of the world" with "written" rather than with "slain." Not only does "names written before the foundation of the world" make more sense, but it is found in 17:8 too.

in 13:8 it is explicitly stated that the book of the Lamb who was slaughtered *is* the Book of Life. A parallel text in 17:8 confirms this, although the formulation there is shorter. In sum, the Lamb and the Book of Life belong together.

The Lamb's Book of Life in Revelation 20 and 21

In the context of the final judgment, and in contrast to the books of the deeds, "also another book was opened, that of life" (v. 12). As people are judged, their deeds are taken into account (v. 13), but in the end it is the Book of Life that is decisive. This is made clear in v. 15, which says, "if one is not found written in the Book of Life, he is thrown into the lake of fire." Thus, similar to 13:8 and 17:8, these verses show that ultimately it is not the deeds of man that determine their salvation, since all have sinned and fall short of the glory of God.[26] Rather, it depends on God's electing good pleasure in Christ Jesus. The phrase "in Christ" refers not only to his person but also to his work, particularly his self-sacrifice as an act of total obedience in suffering death as the payment price for sin. Thus, also these verses concerning the judgment in Rev 20 demonstrate an undeniably strong link with Rev 5:6–12. The Lamb only takes God's Book of Life based on the fact that he has been slaughtered and so paid the purchase price for God's people. The names of these purchased ones are written in God's Book, and the final judgment is precisely the right and necessary moment for the Lamb's Book of Life to be opened.

What is said in Rev 20:12 and 15, including the preceding words about the Lamb and his Book of Life, finds its final climactic fulfilment in 21:27, in the context of God's new earth: nothing unclean and no one wicked will be there, but only that which is clean and those who are holy to the glory and praise of God and of the Lamb.

GOD'S BOOK OF LIFE IN THE REST OF SCRIPTURE

The Book of Life is also mentioned in Exod 32:32, Ps 69:28, Dan 12:1, Phil 4:3, and it is alluded to in Luke 10:21 and Heb 12:23. A brief look at these other occurrences of the Book of Life in Scripture will underline our discoveries thus far.

To begin with, Exod 32:32 describes the intercession of Moses for Israel after their sin with the golden calf. Moses begged for the Lord's

---

26. Rom 3:23.

forgiveness and added, "... if not, then blot me out of *your* book that *you* have written."²⁷ The "your" and "you" stress that this is God's special book, listing those who belong to him as his precious possession, not only in this life but also after it.²⁸

Next, Ps 69 is clearly messianic. It is quoted seventeen times in the New Testament, mostly with respect to Christ. Faced with hostile enemies who seek to kill him, David implores God, "Let them not share in your salvation" (v. 27). Then he adds, "May they be blotted out of the book of life, and not be listed with the righteous" (v. 28).²⁹ They are wicked enemies of God, and of his anointed servant, and they cannot have their names in God's Book. For God's Book of Life contains only the names of those who are holy and faithful servants of God and his Messiah. Here there is a connection with Christ's warning and promise in the letter to Sardis. First he says, "I have not found your deeds complete in the sight of my God" (3:2), but then he continues, "He who overcomes will . . . be dressed in white. I will never blot out his name from the book of life, but will acknowledge his name before my Father and his angels" (3:5). Furthermore, the idea of Ps 69:28 also occurs in Rev 21:27 where we read, "Nothing impure will ever enter it, nor will anyone who does what is shameful or deceitful,³⁰ but only those whose names have been written in the book of life of the Lamb."

Turning to the book of Daniel, we read in Dan 12, "At that time Michael, the great prince who protects your people, will arise. There will be a time of distress such as has not happened from the beginning of nations until then. But at that time, your people—everyone whose name is found written in the book—will be delivered." This book of names in Daniel is clearly connected with Rev 13:8; 17:8; 21:27, and so, indirectly, with the scroll in 5:6–9.

Then, in Phil 4:3 the Apostle Paul says that the names of his fellow workers and his own are in the Book of Life. This is his conclusion based on their sincere dedication to the Lord and his church, which is the re-

---

27. Although the NIV omits it, I add the original emphatic "your" of both the Masoretic and Greek Texts.

28. See Deut 14:1–2, which implies that God's children remain his precious possession after this life.

29. In the Hebrew OT it is Ps 69:29 and in the LXX Ps 68:29.

30. See also Rev 21:8, the royal messianic Ps 101, and Ps 104:35a.

sult and proof of God's gracious work in them (cf. 2:13). In other words, they show the marks of those written in the Book of Life.

There are also two occasions in Scripture where the Book of Life is not explicitly mentioned but clearly implied. The first one is Luke 10:20 where the Lord addresses his enthusiastic apostles as they return from their mission during which even demons submitted to them in Christ's name. Christ's response is both realistic and encouraging: "Do not rejoice that the [evil] spirits submit to you; but rejoice that your names are written in heaven." In other words, their certainty is not to be in their own accomplishments, since Christ Jesus worked through them. Having their names written in heaven, that is, in the Book of Life, is a matter of God's undeserved, electing good pleasure in Christ. In the following verses this is clearly expressed: "Full of joy through the Holy Spirit, Christ said, 'I praise you, Father, Lord of heaven and earth, for you have hidden these things from the wise and learned, and have revealed them to little children. Yes, Father, for this was your *good pleasure*. All things have been committed to me by my Father; and no one knows who the Son is, except the Father; and no one knows who the Father is, except the Son and those to whom the Son chooses to reveal him'" (vv. 21–22). These words of Christ provide a significant and rich description of what the Book of Life means.

The second allusion is found in Heb 12:24, which speaks about the New Testament covenant people who "have come to Mount Zion, the city of the living God, . . . and to the church of the firstborn, whose names are written in heaven. . . ." This is the same comforting, strengthening, and exhorting message as that which is found in Rev 7, among other places.

THREE ADDITIONAL OBSERVATIONS

In the first place, since the Book of Life became the book of the slaughtered Lamb, there is also a fitting explanation for the fact that the scroll in 5:1–10 was *sealed*. It could not be taken and opened before the vicarious sacrifice for sin was brought to God to satisfy his justice. However, having been slaughtered, the Lamb was worthy and had the covenantal right to take and open the Book of Life. In connection with this, it is interesting that Oecumenius, the sixth-century bishop of Tricca, once said, "So the fact that the scroll was closed and sealed indicates . . . the lack of a free approach [to God] by those whose names were written in the scroll."[31] By contrast, with the events view it is much more difficult to account for the sealing of the scroll. The events view understands the contents of the scroll to refer, in large measure at least, to the judgments that are described with the opening of the seals, the blowing of the trumpets, and the outpouring of the bowls. However, the judgments associated with the first four seals are often mentioned in the Prophets;[32] those associated with the trumpets have similarities with the plagues in Egypt,[33] as do the outpouring of the bowls.[34] In other words, the judgments described in Revelation are not special plagues that need to be hidden.[35] They were already prophesied and foreshadowed in the Old Testament. Moreover, in the Gospels we read that Christ Jesus himself prophesied that such judgments would come before his parousia.[36] So, if they were already foretold, at least in part, what was the reason for keeping them sealed away with seven seals? Obviously, the life view is not burdened by these complications.

Second, scholars have noted that the scroll with the seven seals has formal similarities with the final testaments, or wills, of the ancient world.[37] This comparison has validity, also according to W. Sattler.[38] He remarks that Revelation's author wants us to know that the Book of Life, which is identical to the scroll with seven seals, has to be taken as God's testament. The inheritance promised in the testament is both the New Jerusalem and eternal life with God and Christ on the new earth, while the heirs are those whose names are written in the Book of Life as the testament of God.

---

31. Oecumenius, *Commentary on the Apocalypse*, 60–62.

32. Ezek 5:17 and 14:10, 21, mention sword, famine, wild beasts, and plague, though not in the same order; and three of the four judgments: Ezek 6:11, 12; 7:15; Jer 14:12; 21:7, 9; 24:10; 27:8.

33. Beale, *Revelation*, 465.

34. Mounce, *Revelation*, 291; Beale, *Revelation*, 809–10.

35. They cannot be seen as the sealing, or shutting up, of the seven thunders of Rev 10:4 or with Dan 12:4, 9.

36. Matt 24:6–8; Mark 13:7–8; Luke 21:10–11.

37. The idea of a doubly written contract, rather than a testament (Beale, *Revelation*, 344–6) is correctly rejected by Van de Kamp, *Openbaring*, 178, since it takes away the idea of securing, which is present in the seven seals. As Mounce, *Revelation*, 142, writes, "sealed with seven seals [is] to insure the secrecy of its decrees."

38. Sattler, "Das Buch," 51–52. See also Keener, *The IVP Bible Background*, 778.

Third, the life view also makes more sense in connection with John's intense weeping, as described in Rev 5:4. If, according to the events view, the scroll remained sealed and the judgments of God's plan would not unfold, that certainly would be a bad thing, worthy of grief and tears. However, if, according to the life view, God's Book of Life could not be opened, then no one would be eternally saved. And *that* would give more than ample reason for *much* lamenting!

CONCLUSIONS

Summary

Revelation 5 confronts us with the following question: what is the content of the scroll? The common view identifies this content with the book of Revelation in its entirety, or at least a significant section of it. This view is based on the hypothesis that with the opening, or breaking, of the seals, the scroll is also simultaneously opened and its content revealed. This interpretation, however, is based not on explicit information in the text but rather on assumptions. In fact, after v. 5, the text no longer speaks about *opening* the scroll, but about *taking* it (vv. 7, 8, 9, and 12). Moreover, it is specifically "the Lamb who was slaughtered and purchased [us] with his blood for God" who is worthy to take the scroll. His slaughter points to his vicarious self-sacrifice for sin. Thus, it is the Lamb, along with his purchased sheep, who is central not only in Rev 5 but also in the Rev 7 and 14:1–5. Besides, Rev 13:8 speaks of "the book of life of the Lamb who was slaughtered," thereby identifying the scroll of Rev 5 as God's Book of Life that the Lamb took, so that it became the Lamb's Book of Life. The scroll as the Lamb's Book of Life returns in 20:12, 15, in the context of the final judgment, and in 21:27, in the context of the New Jerusalem.

When the scroll of Rev 5 is understood as the Lamb's Book of Life, then there is also a good explanation for the fact that the scroll was sealed with seven seals. Its content must be kept secret until the final day when the dead are raised and everyone will be judged (Rev 20:11–15). At the same time, the seven seals also point to a sealed testament, namely, God's testament describing the inheritance for, as well as the names of, all his heirs.

The Events Book Remains

Accepting the interpretation of the scroll as the Book of Life does not entail a wholesale rejection of some kind of events book. The *scroll* is not the book of events, but the book of Revelation itself remains fully what it was and is, namely, the events book that describes the outworking of God's plan in the history of heaven and earth from Christ's ascension to his return as the Judge of heaven and earth. By the same token, once we view the Lamb and his Book of Life as a central theme in the book of Revelation, we need not view Rev 7 and 14 as interludes. In fact, they are high points on the main thematic line that is being developed from Rev 4–22. The Lamb and his purchased ones form the main line from Rev 4–5 through to Rev 21–22. We also conclude that reading the book of Revelation with the Lamb's Book of Life as a focal point brings out the majestic glory of God the Father on the throne in heaven and of his Son, our Saviour, the Lamb.

An Application

Taking the Lamb's Book of Life as a focal point also provides a strong message of comfort for the Lord's people. The prophecy of Revelation describes three series of judgments: the seven seals, the seven trumpets, and the seven bowls full of God's wrath. But each time, before the judgments are executed, those whom the Lamb had purchased with his death are strengthened. Before the seals are opened (Rev 6), the Lamb reveals to his people (Rev 5) that he has received, from the Father, God's Book of Life with their names and that he holds it—or, perhaps better, holds *them*—in his caring hands. They are well kept by him who first bought them. Before the trumpets are sounded (Rev 8–9), the Lamb shows those believing in him that they are sealed with the seal of the living God (Rev 7), and that they belong to the great multitude who stand before the heavenly throne, in white robes, victorious, with palm branches in their hands. Before the bowls of God's wrath are poured out and the terrifying dragon and his beasts attack (Rev 16), the Lamb gives another comforting picture (Rev 14) in which God's people may look ahead and see themselves standing with the Lamb on Mount Zion, with their Lord's name and the name of his Father on their forehead. Thus, each time again, before another cycle of judgment commences, the Lamb-Shepherd first strengthens his feeble sheep, saying, as it were,

"Do not give up the battle. Do not be overwhelmed by the judgments. Look at me. I will bring you there. I have your names in my book!"

Deep gratitude is due to God for having given us this book of Revelation from Christ Jesus, his Son, the Lamb who has been slaughtered, and who on that basis assures us as his church that he was worthy to take, and will execute, the Book of Life as the guarantee of our salvation to the everlasting glory of our triune God.

BIBLIOGRAPHY

Aune, David E. *Revelation 1–5*. WBC 52A. Waco: Word, 1997.
Beale, G. K. *The Book of Revelation: A Commentary on the Greek Text*. NIGTC. Grand Rapids: Eerdmans, 1999.
Berkowitz, L., and K. A. Squitier. *Thesaurus linguae graecae: Canon of Greek Authors and Works*. 3rd ed. New York: Oxford University Press, 1990.
Caird, George B. *A Commentary on the Revelation of St. John the Divine*. London: Black, 1966.
Comfort, Philip. *New Testament Text and Translation Commentary*. Carol Stream, IL: Tyndale House, 2008.
Farmer, Roland L. *Revelation*. Chalice Commentaries for Today. St. Louis: Chalice, 2005.
Finegan, Jack. *Light from the Ancient Past: The Archeological Background of Judaism and Christianity*. 2nd ed. Princeton: Princeton University Press, 1959.
Greijdanus, S. *De openbaring des Heeren aan Johannes*. Korte Verklaring. Kampen: Kok, 1938.
Hornblower, Simon, and Antony Spawforth. *The Oxford Classical Dictionary*. 3rd ed. Oxford: Oxford University Press, 1996.
Keener, Craig S. *The IVP Bible Background Commentary: New Testament*. Downers Grove, IL: InterVarsity, 1993.
Mounce, Robert H. *The Book of Revelation*. Grand Rapids: Eerdmans, 1977.
Sattler, W. "Das Buch mit sieben Siegeln: Die Bücher der Werke und das Buch des Lebens." ZNW 21 (1922) 43–53.
Stefanovic, Ranko. *The Background and Meaning of the Sealed Book of Revelation 5*. Andrews University Seminary Dissertation Series 22. Berrien Springs, MI: Andrews University Press, 1996.
Suggit, John N., translator. *Oecumenius: Commentary on the Apocalypse*. The Fathers of the Church 122. Washington, DC: Catholic University of America Press, 2006.
Swete, H. B. *The Apocalypse of St. John*. Grand Rapids: Eerdmans, 1968.
Van de Kamp, H. R. *Openbaring: Profetie vanaf Patmos*. Kampen: Kok, 2000.

10

Bavinck on Creation

JAMES VISSCHER

IT IS AN HONOR to be asked to participate in this collection of essays dedicated to Cornelis Van Dam. Our friendship goes back almost fifty years. During that time we have studied together, worked together on various committees and magazines, and even traveled together to far-off places. I was also privileged to be a member of General Synod Smithville 1980 that appointed him as Professor of Old Testament at the Theological College of the Canadian Reformed Churches in Hamilton, Ontario.

This appointment has been richly blessed by the Lord. Dr. Van Dam has proven himself a most able teacher. He is widely known for his deep knowledge of his field of study; his clear, comprehensive, and exacting teaching style; his lucid writings; and his deep love of the churches that entrusted him with this important task. Moreover, Dr. Van Dam also has a childlike awe and respect for the Word of God. For him, to be able to pass along the riches of the Old Testament Scriptures to generations of future ministers represents both a great honor and a weighty responsibility. He has done his utmost to impress upon his students that the Old Testament is not just ancient literature. It is part of the written, inspired, and infallible Word of God. Students need to embrace its contents in faith. They need to know it intimately, preach and teach it faithfully, and defend it robustly.

Dr. Van Dam has himself promoted the reliability of the Word of God in general, and the Old Testament in particular, against all who seek to undermine or deny its teachings. That applies also to the area of origins, creation, and evolution. On numerous occasions, he has defended the biblical account of creation as representing an historic and reliable account. Indeed, it can be said that the early chapters of Genesis, including both the creation and flood accounts, have always been of great interest to him.[1]

It is with that in mind that I deemed it fitting to direct my attention to one of the great theologians in the Dutch Reformed tradition, Herman Bavinck, highlighting what he has written on the same subject. To that end, it is necessary to read and survey what he has penned, especially in the second volume of his *Reformed Dogmatics*,[2] but also in his one volume systematic theology called *Our Reasonable Faith* and in a number of his monographs.[3]

BASIC THOUGHTS

Bavinck gave the subtitle "God and Creation" to the second volume of his *Dogmatics*. He did so because while the first part of it discusses God in relation to his incomprehensibility, knowledge, names, attributes (both incommunicable and communicable), and the Holy Trinity, in the second part he writes about God in relation to earth and heaven. Concentrating on that second part, we turn first to chapter 8, entitled "Creation." One can say that this chapter is both introductory and preliminary as in its opening paragraphs Bavinck sets out a number of basic thoughts. The first is that "the creation proceeds from the Father through the Son and in the Spirit so that, in the Spirit and through the Son it may return to the Father." The second is that "the purpose and goal of creation is to be found solely in God's will and glory." The third is that "a doctrine of creation is one of the foundational building blocks of a biblical and Christian worldview."[4] Throughout chapter 8, Bavinck comes back to these three basic thoughts.

---

1. See *Clarion* 37 (November 25, 1988) and 38 (March 31, 1989).
2. Bavinck, *Reformed Dogmatics*.
3. Bavinck, *Our Reasonable Faith*. The original Dutch title for this work is *Magnalia Dei*. It is unfortunate that the publisher did not insist on that title or some equivalent translation into English. Additional material written by Bavinck and translated into English on this subject can be found in Bavinck, *Essays on Religion*.
4. Bavinck, *Reformed Dogmatics*, 2:426.

THE TRIUNE GOD

Bavinck is insistent on the fact that the Triune God is "the author of creation."[5] He traces the development of this teaching back to Athanasius and the three Cappadocians, along with Augustine. Together, these men make a "sharp distinction between the Creator and the creature and avoid all Gnostic mingling."[6] He states,

> All things originate simultaneously from the Father through the Son in the Spirit. The Father is the first cause; the initiative for creation proceeds from him. Accordingly, in an administrative sense, creation is specifically attributed to him. The Son is not an instrument but the personal wisdom, the Logos, by whom everything is created; everything rests and coheres in him (Col. 1:17) and is created for him (Col 1:16), not as its final goal but as the head and master of all creatures (Eph 1:10). And the Holy Spirit is the personal immanent cause by which all things live and move and have their being, receive their own form and configuration, and are led to their destination, in God.[7]

While thus stressing that creation is a work of the Triune God, Bavinck also recognizes that this work stands in a special or peculiar relationship to the Son. He pays special attention to "Word" and "Wisdom" as OT references to the Son, and shows how the NT elaborates on the Son's preeminent role, citing biblical expressions from such passages as John 1:3; Col 1:15–17; and Rev 1:17; 21:6; 22:6. Bavinck sums up this section by stating, "thus the world finds its idea, its principle (*arche*), and its final goal (*telos*) in the triune being of God."[8]

THE PURPOSE OF CREATION

Along with declaring creation a work of the Triune God, Bavinck is insistent that creation has a purpose and goal, namely, the will and glory of God. Of course, in some ways this is reminiscent of his overall approach, and, like John Calvin, he never tires of this central theme: "The world is the product of his will (Ps 33:6; Rev 4:11); it is the revelation of his perfections (Prov 8:22–23; Job 28:23–24; Ps 104:1; 136:5–6; Jer 10:12) and

---

5. Bavinck, *Reformed Dogmatics*, 2:420.
6. Ibid., 2:422.
7. Ibid., 2:423.
8. Ibid., 2:425.

finds its goal in his glory (Isa 43:16ff.; Prov 16:4; Rom 11:36; 1 Cor 8:6)."[9] It is also through this teaching of creation that faith is strengthened, trust in God is confirmed, consolation is received, praise and thanksgiving is inspired, and humility and meekness are stimulated.

Bavinck comes back to creation and the glory of God later on in chapter 8 when he elaborates on the matter of "creation out of nothing." He admits that this phrase, or the Latin expression *creatio ex nihilo*, cannot be found in the Scriptures, but affirms that Scripture clearly teaches this matter.[10] For in it God is clearly presented as the one who "merely by speaking, by uttering a word of power, calls all things into being."[11] The visible world rests in God, and he is the one who brings everything into existence. He does so solely by his word. Needless to say, all of this advances his glory. That the glory of God is also the intention of creation is borne out in chapter 8 where Bavinck, returning to the subject of creation's end or purpose, asks, "What goal did he [God] have in mind for creation?"[12] Various answers have been given to this question. Some say that the world is an expression of God's love and goodness, while others say that he made it for man. Scripture, however, says that God made it for his own praise and glory. Thus, Bavinck adds, "The Reformed tradition made the honor of God the fundamental principle of all doctrine and conduct, of dogmatics and morality, of the family, society, and the state, of science and art. Nowhere was this principle of the glory of God more universally applied than among the confessors of the Reformed religion."[13]

WORLDVIEW

After dealing with the authorship and goal of creation, Bavinck introduces us to the matter of a right doctrine of creation as the basic building block for a true biblical worldview. He shows that neither pantheism nor materialism is adequate to this task.

Pantheism, at least the ancient Greek version, seeks the origin of all things in either some sort of eternal, immutable being, or in some kind

---

9. Ibid., 2:407.
10. Ibid., 2:416.
11. Ibid., 2:417.
12. Ibid., 2:431.
13. Ibid., 2:434.

of an eternal becoming.[14] Later pantheists, such as Schelling, taught an absolute identity between God and world. Hegel went in the same direction and said that one could see the appearance of the absolute in the finite and accidental. Schleiermacher rejected the distinction between creation and God or creation and providence; whether the world was eternal or temporal made no difference to him, provided everything depended on God.[15] Bavinck describes materialism as seeking "the final elements of all being in eternal (without beginning) and indestructible material atoms, and attempts to explain all phenomena of the entire universe in light of atomic processes of mechanical and chemical separation and union in accordance with fixed laws."[16] In the end, Bavinck deems both pantheism and materialism to be lacking any semblance of exact science and having more in common with philosophy or systems of belief. Rather than being opposites, they are two sides of the same coin,[17] yet neither presents a solution when it comes to origins. Pantheism cannot explain how matter came from mind. Neither can materialism "explain how purely material, and therefore unconscious, inanimate, unfree, aimless atoms could produce that spiritual world of life, consciousness, purpose, religion, morality, and so on, which surely thrusts itself upon our inner consciousness with no less force than the physical world upon our senses."[18] At the end of the chapter, Bavinck argues that only a creation-based worldview has any warrant or validity. He states that "pantheism attempts to explain the world dynamically; materialism attempts to do so mechanically. However, both strive to see the whole as governed by a single principle. In pantheism the world may be a living organism (*zōon*), of which God is the soul; in materialism it is a mechanism that is brought about by the union and separation of atoms. But in both systems an unconscious blind fate is elevated to the throne of the universe."[19]

Scripture, however, presents a radically different worldview. In it, heaven and earth remain distinct. All things have their own nature and task, and they rest on divinely established ordinances. There is, thanks

14. Ibid., 2:408.
15. Ibid., 2:411.
16. Ibid., 2:412.
17. Ibid.
18. Ibid., 2:415.
19. Ibid., 2:435.

to God, both great diversity and profound unity. Bavinck cites Augustine with approval, for Augustine insisted that while the world is a unity, it is not a uniformity. In it there is "an infinitely varied diversity," all because God is "supremely true, supremely good, and supremely beautiful."[20] He also quotes Calvin, "There is no spot in the universe wherein you cannot discern at least some sparks of his glory," as well as Zanchius, who saw the world as a "splendidly clear mirror of his divine glory."[21] This kind of a worldview, says Bavinck, has "overcome both the contempt of nature and its deification."[22] He adds,

> But the Christian looks upward and confesses God as the Creator of heaven and earth. In nature and history he observes the unfathomability of the ways of God and the unsearchability of his judgments, but he does not despair, for all things are subject to the government of an omnipotent God and a gracious Father, and they will therefore work together for good to those who love God. Here, accordingly, there is room for love and admiration of nature, but all deification is excluded. Here a human being is placed in the right relationship to the world because he has been put in the right relation to God.[23]

THE MATERIAL WORLD

Bavinck gives to chapter 10 the title "Earth: The Material World." Here again, with some introductory remarks he sets the stage for what he discusses in detail throughout the chapter. His opening includes the following segments: "all religions have creation stories; all scientific systems are rooted in religious beliefs . . . The creation narrative in Genesis is utterly unique . . . The interpretation of Genesis 1–2 has a rich and diverse history . . . The six-day period is best divided into three parts: creation, separation, adornment . . . The Bible does not provide us with a scientific cosmology—using the language of ordinary experience—but spiritually and ethically, the earth (with humanity) is the center of the universe." Bavinck continues, "The data of natural science must be taken seriously by Christians as general revelation, but only special, biblical revelation can describe the true state of the world . . . It is important,

20. Ibid., 2:437.
21. Ibid., 2:438.
22. Ibid.
23. Ibid.

however, to insist on the historical rather than merely mythical or visionary character of the creation story in Genesis. The science of geology is still young ... The reality of a cataclysmic flood ... complicates matters considerably. Theology should neither fear the sure results of science nor, in immoderate anxiety, make premature concessions to the opinions of the day."[24] In these remarks, one can already ascertain some of the main elements of Bavinck's thought on the earth and its beginning, including that creation stories are common, science is not neutral, the biblical account is unique and historical, science must be respected, and only Scripture can explain the world.

CREATION STORIES

Launching into the actual contents of chapter 10, we find that Bavinck first examines the biblical and Babylonian creation stories. He is quick to deny that the creation account as given in Genesis originated in Babylon and thus "bears a mythological character."[25] Indeed, he points out that there are numerous points of difference between these two accounts. When Genesis opens, God exists, whereas in the Babylonian story the gods come out of, and are a result of, the chaos. In Genesis it is the divine Word that creates, whereas creation emerges out of the chaos in Babylonian mythology. In the Genesis account, the ordering of the earth is completed in six days, while the Babylonian myth includes no ordering over a specific time span. In the end, the only resemblance that Bavinck can find between Genesis and the Babylonian account is "that in both stories a chaos precedes the formation of heaven and earth."[26] For the rest, he is quick to deny any sort of common identity or origin and insists that "the creation narrative in Genesis is utterly unique."[27]

In what way is it unique? Bavinck responds by saying that from the very beginning it was "created by God as earth."[28] The earth is not just matter or primeval matter or chaos: "The state of the earth in Genesis 1:2 is not that of positive destruction but of not-yet-having-been shaped. There is no light, no life, no organic creature, no form and configuration

24. Ibid., 2:473.
25. Ibid., 2:476.
26. Ibid., 2:477.
27. Ibid.
28. Ibid., 2:478.

in things."²⁹ These things only happen when God begins his work on the first day.

In this connection, Bavinck also distinguishes between a first creation, or "what God did 'in the beginning' (Gen 1:1; cf. John 1:1)," and a second creation, or what God "did 'by the words of his mouth' in six days (Gen 1:3ff)."³⁰ He states, "the first creation (*creatio prima*) is immediate, an act of bringing forth heaven and earth out of nothing. It absolutely does not presuppose the existence of available matter but occurred 'with time' (*cum tempore*). But the second creation, which starts with verse 3, is not direct and immediate; it presupposes the material created in verse 1 and links up with it. It occurs specifically 'in time' (*in tempore*), and that in six days. Hence, this second creation already anticipates the works of preservation and government."³¹

THE DAYS OF CREATION

From creation stories, Bavinck proceeds to deal with the six days of creation. First, he defends the old pattern of this creation work whereby it is divided into three parts: *creation* (Gen 1:1–2); *separation*, or what happens on the first three days between light and darkness, heaven and earth, land and sea; and *adornment*, or what happens on the days four, five, and six.³² Thereafter, he dwells for a moment on aspects related to each of these three parts.

From commenting on the biblical account itself, he next moves on to theology and remarks that "Christian theology has always treated this six-day period with special fondness."³³ He then cites the names of numerous theologians in the early church, as well as from the Reformation and post-Reformation periods, who have all written on this subject. He admits, however, that they did so from an Aristotelian-Ptolemaic worldview, which is to say, from the perspective that the earth is at the center of the universe and the stars all rotate around it. Bavinck highlights the fact that the Ptolemaic worldview had a bearing on how one explained the six-day period. On this subject, there were two schools of thought. The

---

29. Ibid.
30. Ibid., 2:479.
31. Ibid.
32. Ibid., 2:480.
33. Ibid., 2:482.

one—promoted by such notables as Philo, Clement, Origen, Athanasius, Augustine, and others—rejected the temporal character of the six days and regarded it as visionary. They defended the view that the entire world was created by a single stroke of God's power. The other school—which included Tertullian, Basil, Gregory of Nyssa, John of Damascus, as well as later Roman Catholic and Protestant theologians among its members—held to the literal view of the creation narrative. Concerning these two schools, Bavinck notes that, "the alternative exegesis of Augustine was consistently discussed with respect and never branded heretical."[34] In spite of the differences, Bavinck concludes, "there was perfect agreement in the matter of worldview."[35] Members of both schools of thought spoke geocentrically because Scripture speaks geocentrically, using the language of ordinary daily experience. While in an astronomic sense, the earth may no longer be at the center of the universe, in a religious and ethical sense, it remains central.[36]

Then, however, came the Copernican worldview, and Bavinck is bold enough to state that "Christian theology, then, has no objections to the Copernican worldview."[37] Yet he is quick to add, "The situation is very different, however, with the hypotheses assumed nowadays by science with respect to the genesis of our solar system and the earth."[38] He cites and interacts with the views of Kant and Laplace who posited that the universe in the beginning was one large blob of gaseous chaos and parts of it broke away due to temperature and rotation and took on a spherical shape. He opines that "this hypothesis is insufficient to explain the origin of the universe, of motion, and of organic beings."[39] This is a critical comment that Bavinck makes not just with respect to the views of Kant and Laplace, but also when it comes to the views of others. He cites the case of George Howard Darwin, a son of Charles Darwin, who tries to explain the origin of the solar system as being related to meteoric activity but in the end "says nothing about the origination of the sun and the first planet."[40] Hypotheses may have their uses but they fail to explain

34. Ibid., 2:483.
35. Ibid.
36. Ibid., 2:484.
37. Ibid., 2:485.
38. Ibid.
39. Ibid., 2:486.
40. Ibid., 2:488.

existing matter. Indeed, what natural science cannot teach us is given us by revelation: "The truth is rather that Scripture tells us the story of an actual state, while natural science is offering us assumptions that are not scientifically tenable."[41]

GEOLOGY

It needs to be highlighted that in this last statement Bavinck begins to move into the area of science and even expresses a negative judgment on it. In other words, he moves beyond the realm of theology, drifting into the realm of science and from there into the science of geology in particular. In chapter 10, he makes a number of comments on "the formation of the earth," and he notes that geology has formed a hypothesis about different periods of earth's development, starting with the Azoic period, followed by the Paleozoic, the Mesozoic, the Tertiary or Cenozoic, and the Quaternary eras. Bavinck comments that this theory about geological periods is grounded both in the Kantian hypothesis and in the study of the strata of the earth's crust.[42]

Yet, at the same time, he acknowledges that the stage is now set for a serious conflict between revelation and science. In particular, he refers to two points of conflict: the one having to do with *time* and the other with *order*. With respect to the former, he refers to the church fathers who said that the time between creation and the fall of Rome amounted to 5,611 years, and to scholars after the Reformation who were of the opinion that the creation of the world took place somewhere between 3950 and 4004 BC. He mentions that there has also been serious controversy between theologians, both ancient and more modern, about whether creation took place in the spring or in the fall. Finally, he

41. Ibid., 2:487. Here Bavinck appears to overstate his case. It is one thing to assert that Scripture says something. It is another thing to label something in natural science as "not scientifically tenable." Such a negative judgment requires more knowledge of, and interaction with, the findings of natural science.

42 Ibid., 2:489. Davis A. Young, while acknowledging that Bavinck had much appreciation for geology, critiques him on several points. He claims that Bavinck used out-of-date information and was not knowledgeable when it came to fundamental geological principles. In part, this is said to be due to the fact that he relied too much on German writers whose understanding of geology could be called into question. There is also the fact that the Free University, where Bavinck taught in his later years, did not even have a geology program. Young favors the approach of British and American Presbyterians who were more receptive to the findings of geology as a whole and to an old-Earth view in particular. See Young, "The Reception of Geology."

gives a few examples of men who even defended the date of creation as being either March 25 or October 26. After surveying these advocates of a relatively young creation, Bavinck turns to the time frame suggested by geology. He writes that "the figures assumed to the age of the earth are fabulous—as among some pagan people."[43] Thereafter, he mentions men whose time projections go from 20 million years to 560 million years to 2,000 million years to an unlimited number. Obviously, the time frames coming from theologians and geologists differ greatly. Not only that, but there is little doubt that Bavinck sides with the theologians and supports an early or young-earth view.[44] In an article in the *Methodist Review*, he goes on record as saying, "To reckon with millions of years, in the past or in the present, is child's play and unworthy of mature minds, and is at best of no greater value than the gigantic numbers of Indian mythology."[45] When considering the order of created things, Bavinck again sides with the theologians and states that Scripture moves forward from light and darkness, to waters above and below, to dry land and sea, to vegetation. By contrast, geology reverses this order.

RECONCILING SCIENCE AND SCRIPTURE

Can science and Scripture be reconciled? Bavinck describes the various attempts to do so: the ideal theory, which sees Gen 1 as poetry and not history; the visionary theory, which approaches Gen 1 as a visionary presentation; the restitution theory, which separates Gen 1:2 and 1:3, inserting geological eras into the period before v. 2; concordism, which considers the days of creation to be periods of long duration; and the antigeological approach, which tries to fit the geological periods into the six creation days, the period between Adam and Noah, and during the flood.

After describing, interacting with, and in some cases critiquing these theories, Bavinck does not consider that they are totally opposed to one another but that there may be elements of truth in them. Still, he

---

43. Bavinck, *Reformed Dogmatics*, 2:490.

44. He considered the figures coming from geologists to be far-fetched. He had little use for Darwin's "incalculable number of years." He stated, "as a matter of fact, there are other reasons as well why the human race cannot have existed many thousands of years before Christ." These "other reasons" have to do with population projections, lack of archaeological support, and the absence of human evidence. Ibid., 2:520–23.

45. See Bavinck, "Creation or Development," 869.

does feel compelled once again to stress that "Scripture does not speak the language of science but that of daily experience; that also in telling the story of creation it assumes a geocentric or anthropocentric viewpoint."[46] Furthermore, he adds, "when Scripture, from its own perspective precisely as the book of religion, comes in contact with other sciences and also sheds light on them, it does not all at once cease to be the Word of God but remains that Word . . . And for that reason Christian theology, with only a few exceptions, continued to hold onto the literal historical view of the creation story."[47] Yet, notwithstanding the historical character of the creation story, Bavinck notes that "not a single confession made a fixed pronouncement about the six-day continuum, and that in theology as well a variety of interpretations were allowed to exist side by side."[48] He then quotes Augustine with approval when he urges believers not to be too quick to declaring a theory to be in conflict with Scripture.

At the same time, he acknowledges that geology "may render excellent service to us in the interpretation of the creation story."[49] He even adds that "Scripture and theology have nothing to fear from the facts brought to light by geology and paleontology."[50] But then he adds, "for the time being it would seem advisable for geology—which is a relatively

---

46. Bavinck, *Reformed Dogmatics*, 2:495.

47. Ibid.

48. Bavinck, *Reformed Dogmatics*, 2:496. As we shall soon see, Bavinck did not believe that the six days of creation were necessarily twenty-four hour days; nevertheless, he was convinced that his views were within the parameters of the confession. In taking this approach he is not alone. Abraham Kuyper was of the opinion that the first three days were far from ordinary and that only with the fourth day did they become "ordinary." Anton Honig, Bavinck's successor in Kampen, believed that the first three days were "creation days" and were longer than our days. Gerhard C. Aalders, who taught OT at the Free University of Amsterdam from 1920 to 1950, also said that the first three days were extraordinary and called them "God's days." Klaas Schilder, successor to Honig, refused to take a position on this matter and called it "an incidental question." Elsewhere he appears to side with Aalders and his view that they were not "ordinary 24-hour days." For more details on the view of these theologians, see Rogland, "Ad Litteram," who concludes his article by stating, "Accordingly, even proponents of twenty-four hour creation days treat the question primarily as an exegetical one, rather than as a test of orthodoxy or confessional fidelity. Hence the charges of 'doctrinal drift,' 'perverting and twisting the Scriptures,' or even 'heresy' which one encounters in some American Presbyterian circles appear to be largely (if not entirely) absent from discussion of the issue in the Dutch Reformed tradition" (233).

49. Bavinck, *Reformed Dogmatics*, 2:496.

50. Ibid.

young science and, though it has already accomplished a lot, has still a vast amount of work to do—to restrict itself to the gathering of material and to abstain from forming conclusions and framing hypotheses."[51] After these remarks, which he considers provisional, Bavinck proceeds to voice his opinion that probably "the creation of the heaven and earth in Genesis 1 preceded the work of the six days in verses 3ff. by a shorter or longer period,"[52] and that "the first chapter of Genesis, however, hardly contains any ground for the opinion that we are dealing here with a vision or myth. It clearly bears a historical character."[53]

THE CHARACTER OF THE CREATION DAYS

While Gen 1 is historical, Bavinck is also of the opinion that the days of Gen 1 have "an extraordinary character." In the case of the first three days, he says, "however much they may resemble our days, [they] also differ significantly from them and hence were extraordinary cosmic days."[54] With regard to the sixth day, he remarks that "it is very difficult for us to find room on the sixth day for everything Genesis 1–2 has occur in it if that day was in all respects like our days. For occurring on that day are the creation of the animals (Gen 1:24–25), the formation of Adam (Gen 1:26; 2:7), the planting of the garden (Gen 2:8–14), the announcement of the probationary command (Gen 2:16–17), the conducting of the animals to, and their naming by Adam (Gen 2:18–20),

---

51. Ibid.
52. Ibid.
53. Ibid., 2:499.

54. Ibid. Bavinck concedes that "Scripture speaks very definitely of days which are reckoned by the measurement of night and morning and which lie at the basis of the distribution of the days of the week in Israel and its festive calendar." But then he continues, "Nevertheless Scripture itself contains data which oblige us to think of these days of Genesis as different from our ordinary units as determined by the revolutions of the earth." He supports this view by saying, "In the first place we cannot be sure whether what is told us in Genesis 1:1–2 precedes the first day or is included within that day.... In the second place, the first three days (Gen 1:3–13) must have been unlike ours.... the Book of Genesis itself tells us that sun and moon and stars were not formed until the fourth day.... In the third place, it is certainly possible that the second series of three days were constituted in the usual way. But if we take into account... then it seems not unlikely that the second series of three days also differed from our days in many respects.... Finally, it deserves consideration that everything which according to Genesis 1 and 2 took place on the sixth day can hardly be crowded into the pale of such a day as we know the lengths of days to be." See Bavinck, *Our Reasonable Faith*, 172–73.

Adam's deep sleep and the creation of Eve (Gen 2:21–23)."[55] He says later that "the creation days are the workdays of God."[56]

At this point, however, one senses that a certain tension creeps into Bavinck's position. Elsewhere he insists, as we have seen, that the creation account has to be regarded as "historical" and that "the literal historical view of the creation story" needs to be embraced, but when it now comes to the ordinary understanding of the word "day," he is prepared to stretch its meaning. Yet doing that raises the question as to whether or not one can still claim to be "historical" when one reinterprets the word "day" and regards it as undefined or as an extended period of time.[57]

After speaking about creation days, Bavinck begins to wind down his discussion. He revisits geology and dwells on the matter of earth layers. He also brings in the flood as having brought great changes to the earth. In summary, he says that "from the moment of creation in Genesis 1:1 to the flood, Scripture offers a time span that can readily accommodate all the facts and phenomena that geology and paleontology have brought to light in this century."[58] In the final analysis, he insists that "theology has nothing to fear from thorough, multifaceted research."[59]

EVOLUTION

Still, Bavinck is not finished, for in his next chapter, called "Human Origins," he covers some of the same ground again, but he also deals directly with the matter of creation and evolution, as well as with Darwinism. As such, he notes that evolution is not a new teaching, going back as it does to the Greeks. Yet in the eighteenth century it was refashioned to include the theory of the descent of humanity from animal ancestry. Among the names that Bavinck lists as evolutionists are Lamarck, Spenser, Huxley, and, especially, Charles Darwin.

After he summarizes some of the main elements of Darwinism, Bavinck launches into a critique of it. It includes the following four

---

55. Bavinck, *Reformed Dogmatics*, 2:500.

56. Ibid.

57. C. Van Dam himself has also written on this subject. He insists "there is nothing in Scripture to suggest that these days were anything other than days as we reckon days, days that include daytime and nighttime." See Van Dam, "Days of the Creation Week," 94.

58. Bavinck, *Reformed Dogmatics*, 2:506.

59. Ibid., 2:507.

points: "the theory of descent has proved completely unable to make the origin of life somewhat understandable"[60]; "Darwinism has also proved incapable of explaining the further development of organic entities"[61]; "in Darwinism the origin of humanity is an insoluble problem"[62]; and "Darwinism above all fails to provide an explanation of humanness in terms of psychic dimension."[63] In one of his final salvos, Bavinck remarks, "the theory of the animal ancestry of humans violates the image of God in man and degrades the human into an image of the orangutan and chimpanzee. From the standpoint of evolution humanity as the image of God cannot be maintained."[64]

---

60. Ibid., 2:516. Elsewhere Bavinck states that "Accordingly, experience, empirical investigation, can tell us nothing about the origin of things . . . the theory of evolution, consequently, lacks the potential of explaining the origin of things. It tacitly proceeds from the idea that those things in their undeveloped state eternally existed. The theory of evolution begins with an assumption which is quite undemonstrable and, accordingly, also takes its position on faith." See Bavinck, *Our Reasonable Faith*, 164–65.

61. Ibid., 2:517. On the matter of development, it should be noted that Bavinck says that "creation and development do not therefore exclude each other. Creation, rather, is the starting point of all development. Because God has created a world inexhaustible in its rich differentiation and variety, in which the various kinds of creatures have their own natures, and in that nature each has received its own thought and property and law, therefore and only therefore evolution is possible. All such evolution takes its point of departure, and at the same time its direction and its purpose, from this creation." See Bavinck, *Reasonable Faith*, 174. Elsewhere he writes that "Christianity did not replace or dispute this idea of development but took it over and enriched it." See Bavinck, *Essays on Religion*, 106. Bavinck also wrote, "the descendance theory of Darwin may be an indispensable link in the doctrine of development; it finds no support in facts. Man always has and still does form a distinct species in the world of creatures." See Bavinck, "Creation or Development," 859.

62. Bavinck, *Reformed Dogmatics*, 2:519.

63. Ibid.

64. Ibid., 2:520. With regard to humanity, Bavinck writes that "the conformity between these and similar phenomena is so strong and surprising that, with the abandonment of faith in creation and the neglect of other data, the thought could easily arise that man gradually evolved from an animal. Nevertheless, this hypothesis must be strictly distinguished from the facts on which it rests. In the theory of man's animal descent, we are not dealing with an observable and well-established fact but with an argument built on the facts mentioned above; in other words, a hypothesis. . . . If man's animal descent were a fact, it would be accepted in spite of all this. But such is definitely not the case. There are no direct proofs. No one has ever observed them . . . As far as we can determine, human beings have always been human and animals always animals. One cannot speak of a slow, gradual transition. Thus far the 'missing link' has not been found." See Bavinck, *Essays on Religion*, 114–15.

CONCLUSIONS

After this lengthy survey, what have we learned? A number of things come to mind:

1. Bavinck's stress on creation being a work of the Triune God represents a serious attempt to do justice to the person and work of the Father, the Son, and the Holy Spirit.

2. Bavinck's desire to see the glory of God as creation's goal lends weight to the importance of the created realm.

3. Bavinck's attempt to fashion a sound theology of creation advances the cause of Christian worldview studies.

4. Bavinck's repeated defense of the biblical account of creation rests on the premise that it is historical.

5. Bavinck's view that the creation days are extraordinary days is not an isolated one, and while reflecting a line of interpretation that has long been present and even respected in the Christian church, it raises questions about just how far one can go in reinterpreting the meaning of the word "day" in Genesis and still be considered "historical."

6. Bavinck's interaction with geology, while laudable, raises questions about how far a theologian should wander from his chosen field of study.[65]

7. Bavinck's critique of Darwinism still has much to commend it, especially when it comes to the crucial matter of the origin of life.[66]

---

65. Cornelius Van Til went on record as saying that "it was especially in the locus de creation that Bavinck 'weakened his own position.' He did this by trying to absorb the results of science too uncritically into his own thought." See Van Til, "Bavinck the Theologian," 51. Brian Mattson, in his review of Van Til's review, believes that Van Til may have overstated his case. See Mattson, "Van Til on Bavinck," 111–27.

66. After his death, a controversy erupted as to whether or not Bavinck changed his mind on the historicity of the creation account as found in Gen 1–3. Some quoted him as saying towards the end of his life that "the creation story, as announced in the Scripture, is difficult to accept as such." Dr. H. W. van der Vaart Smit, one of his students and friends, goes to great lengths to deny that such a change ever took place. See van der Vaart Smit, *Bavinck's Schriftbeschouwing*, 1. In light of the fact that during the 1930s there was a great deal of controversy about the opening chapters of Genesis in the Reformed Churches of the Netherlands, it is not surprising that attempts were made by men on both sides of the issue to claim that Bavinck, as the preeminent Dutch theologian, was on their side.

BIBLIOGRAPHY

Bavinck, Herman. "Creation or Development." *Methodist Review* 83 (1901) 849–74.
———. *Essays on Religion, Science, and Society.* Grand Rapids: Baker Academic, 2008.
———. *Our Reasonable Faith.* Grand Rapids: Eerdmans, 1956.
———. *Reformed Dogmatics.* 4 vols. Grand Rapids: Baker Academic, 2004.
Mattson, Brian G. "Van Til on Bavinck: An Assessment." *WTJ* 70 (2008) 111–27.
Rogland, Max. "*Ad Litteram*: Some Dutch Reformed Theologians on the Creation Days." *WTJ* 63 (2001) 211–33.
Vaart Smit, H. W. van der. *Bavinck's Schriftbeschouwing in Verband met de Eerste Hoofstukken van Genesis.* Wageningen: Veenman, 1933.
Van Dam, Cornelis. "What Did the Days of the 'Creation Week' Consist Of?" *Clarion* 38:5 (March 3, 1989) 94–95.
Van Til, Cornelius. "Bavinck the Theologian: A Review Article." *WTJ* 24 (1961) 48–64.
Young, Davis A. "The Reception of Geology in the Dutch Reformed Tradition: The Case of Herman Bavinck (1854–1921)." In *Geology and Religion: A History of Harmony and Hostility*, edited by Martina Kölbl-Ebert, 289–300. Geological Society Special Publication 310. London: The Geological Society, 2009.

11

Specious Pacification and Pleasant Consensus
Calvin's Ecumenical Efforts in 1549

JASON VAN VLIET

WHEN I FIRST ENTERED seminary in the autumn of 1992, Dr. Cornelis Van Dam was serving as Principal and as Professor of Old Testament. In both capacities, he cultivated our hearts and minds, preparing us to be preachers of God's Word and pastors in Christ's church. Over time, my wife and I have come to know him even better. He solemnized our marriage, and later he also provided much appreciated guidance during my further studies. During all the years of our acquaintance, it has been evident to me, and I am certain to many others, that Cornelis Van Dam had a heart of service not only for the federation of churches he served, the Canadian Reformed Churches, but indeed for Christ's catholic church throughout the world. For him, ecumenical effort is not only a duty, but also a delight. With this in mind, I dedicate this essay to him.

In the first half of 1549, John Calvin dealt with three separations that strained his emotions, at times, to the breaking point. He grieved the first separation more deeply than words can express. The second was a clear confirmation of a longstanding severance, but it was painful nonetheless. The third rift was, thankfully, overcome; however, the path toward this unity was an arduous journey.

What were these three separations? The first occurred on 29 March 1549. On that dark day, Calvin's beloved wife, Idelette, succumbed to her long-lasting illness and passed on into everlasting blessedness. Her Jean, though, was left behind. To his close friend, Pierre Viret, he wrote that her death was "exceedingly painful"[1] to him, adding despondently, "truly mine is no common source of grief."[2] To his older confidant, Gillaume Farel, he confided the true depths of his despair when he sighed, "I do what I can to keep myself from being overwhelmed with grief."[3]

The second severance was between those adhering to Rome and those advocating the Reformation. To be sure, that separation was more than three decades old by that time. However, it became all the more entrenched when, in the same spring as Idelette's death, Calvin published his response to Emperor Charles V's *Augsburg Interim*. His treatise was entitled *The Adultero-German Interim* to which he appended *The True Method of Christian Pacification and Reforming the Church*.[4] As the titles indicate, Calvin offers neither commendation nor cooperation for Charles V's attempt to restore some semblance of religious unity in his empire. He swiftly dismisses it as a "specious pacification" that will only lead people away from the true Author of peace, Jesus Christ.[5]

Yet even as Calvin was busy refuting this imperial effort toward religious unity, he was redoubling his own efforts to cultivate consensus among Reformers on that most divisive issue of the sixteenth century, namely, the Lord's Supper. With the Swiss in general, and Bullinger in particular, Geneva's Reformer saw the potential for concurrence. Therefore, on 20 May 1549 he traveled to Zürich. Shortly thereafter the *Consensus Tigurinus* was adopted. What few had thought possible, Bullinger and Calvin produced. In fact, two weeks before this *Consensus* was reached, Calvin was already rejoicing in anticipation. On 7 May 1549, after receiving a draft document on the Supper from Bullinger, he dashed off a note to him exclaiming, "I have scarcely ever received anything more pleasant from you"![6]

Thus, the question arises, was Calvin consistent in his ecumenical endeavors in 1549? Why was he so patient and persistent with the Zürich

---

1. Calvin to Viret, 7 April 1549, *CO* 13:230; Calvin, *Letters*, 2:216. The common abbreviations for the collected works of Calvin are used in this essay: *CO* and *OS*.

2. Calvin to Viret, 7 April 1549, *CO* 13:230; Calvin, *Letters*, 2:216.

3. Calvin to Farel, 11 April 1549, *CO* 13:228; Calvin, *Letters*, 2:217. A helpful description of Idelette and her loyalty to Calvin can be found in van den Berg, *Friends of Calvin*, 123–33.

4. *CO* 7:545–674; English translation in Calvin, *Tracts*, 3:189–358.

5. *CO* 7:591; Calvin, *Tracts*, 3:241.

6. Calvin to Bullinger, 7 May 1549, *CO* 13:226; Calvin, *Letters*, 2:225.

theologians, while at the same time so direct and dismissive with the *Augsburg Interim*? Was Calvin's ecumenical enthusiasm reserved only for those with whom he felt personally comfortable? Did the Reformer of Geneva not desire concord for all of Christendom? Furthermore, and from a different angle, did Idelette's death have any impact on Calvin's ecumenical outlook, either for good or ill? These are the questions we will pursue below.

AN APPARENT, BUT UNSATISFACTORY, ANSWER

However, from the outset, it may seem futile to place Calvin's response to the *Augsburg Interim* side by side with his work toward the *Consensus Tigurinus*. Are we really comparing apples with apples? Three considerations initially suggest that the comparison is not valid. First, the *Interim* advocated a nearly wholesale return to the teachings, sacraments, and ceremonies of Rome. Only two key concessions were made to the Reformers: for the time being, clergymen who had married could remain in their matrimonial state, and those congregations celebrating the Eucharist by giving both bread and cup to their members could continue with that practice.[7] By contrast, the *Consensus* sought to iron out some of the finer points of Reformed sacramentology, such as whether the Lord's Supper was an instrument of, or a testimony to, God's grace.[8] Second, earlier in the 1540s, Calvin had already exerted earnest effort in building bridges with papal theologians. The colloquies in Haguenau, Worms, and Regensburg testify to that. However, those colloquies did not bring the two sides any closer together.[9] Therefore, theoretically, by 1549 Calvin could excuse himself from expending any more energy on seeking common ground with papal theologians. Using admittedly anachronistic terminology, Geneva's Reformer might have said, "Been there, done that." Third, the *Interim* clearly arose within a political context. Emperor Charles V made no bones about the fact that he sought ecclesiastical concord because, to his way of thinking, "discord, rancour, wars, difficulties, and grievances of the States"[10] had all proceeded from

---

7. *CO* 7:588; Calvin, *Tracts*, 3:238–39. These two exceptions were also highlighted by Charles V in his preface, see *CO* 7:551; Calvin, *Tracts*, 3:192.

8. Rorem, "Did Calvin Compromise?" 87–90.

9. For a thorough treatment of Calvin's role in these colloquies see Stolk, *Johannes Calvijn en de godsdienstgesprekken*.

10. *CO* 7:549; Calvin, *Tracts*, 3:190.

religious dissension. By contrast, the *Consensus* seems to be motivated by ecclesiastical and ecumenical, not political, concerns. Considering these three factors, it might seem wiser to avoid all comparison between *The True Method* and the *Consensus Tigurinus*. The two documents appear to arise out of circumstances that are too dissimilar.

However, a closer look indicates that such avoidance is unnecessary, as three more considerations come to the fore. First, both the *Interim* and Calvin's response in *The True Method* speak about the sacraments just as extensively as the *Consensus* deals with the same topic. Of the twenty-six chapters in the *Interim*, no less than thirteen of them deal with the sacraments. Second, although modern minds may think that the *Consensus* dealt with sacramental minutiae, the hearts of the sixteenth century felt differently. At one point, the rift between Geneva and Zürich concerning the Lord's Supper seemed so deep that Calvin felt he was being accused of departing "from the pure and simple doctrine of the Gospel."[11] In fact, in 1548 the rift between Bullinger and Calvin grew into gorge. Calvin insisted that the sacraments were instruments of grace, while Bullinger fervently refused to embrace any kind of instrumentalism. In the words of Paul Rorem, this mutual intransigence resulted in nothing less than "an impasse."[12] By the same token, "impasse" is also a good way to sum up Calvin's feelings about the Colloquy of Regensburg 1541.[13] Third, concerning both the *Interim* and the *Consensus*, it appears that political considerations played a major role. As mentioned above, Charles V had a politically vested interest in the success of the *Interim* and he was not shy to express it.[14] However, it is also fair to say that political and military concerns were a major factor in motivating Bullinger and Calvin to seek—yet again—some kind of common ground on the sacraments. With the crushing defeat of the Schmalkaldic League at Mühlberg, the Protestant forces were down in numbers and back on the defensive. Consequently, in the summer of 1548, Calvin wrote to Bullinger, "May the very fewness of our numbers incite us to alliance!"[15] Thus, both in content and in context, Calvin's *True Method of Christian Pacification*

---

11. Calvin to Bullinger, 26 June 1548, *CO* 12:728–29; Calvin, *Letters*, 2:170.
12. Rorem, "Did Calvin Compromise?" 80.
13. Calvin to Viret, 3 August 1541, *CO* 11:261–63; Calvin, *Letters*, 1:279.
14. *CO* 7:549; Calvin, *Tracts*, 3:190.
15. Calvin to Bullinger, 26 June 1548, *CO* 12:730; Calvin, *Letters*, 2:172.

and the *Consensus Tigurinus* overlap sufficiently to justify a more detailed comparison between the two.

THE TRUE METHOD OF CHRISTIAN PACIFICATION AND REFORMING THE CHURCH

What follows is a highly selective summary of some key points brought forward in *The True Method*. Our lens of scrutiny will only focus on one question: why does Calvin refuse, in no uncertain terms, to make any concessions along the lines of what the emperor and his theologians had proposed in the *Augsburg Interim*? Early on in his treatise, Geneva's Reformer clarifies that it is not because he has run out of patience with the slow pace of moral reform within the ranks of the priests and monks. And if the issue is simply renewal of piety, then Calvin is willing to be temporarily satisfied with initial reform, so long as further reform would be pursued in the future.[16] Neither is it a matter of disputing over mere words or doctrinal trivia. As Calvin says, "we dispute not about words"; in fact, he adds, "I would easily give up all contest about the word."[17] Rather, there is something much more fundamental at stake here.

The remarkable thing about the opening sentences of *The True Method* is how much they concentrate on Jesus Christ. Calvin begins: "'Specious indeed is the name of peace,' says Hilary, 'and fair the idea of unity; but who doubts that the only peace of the church is that which is of *Christ*?'—truly an admirable sentiment which ought to arise in our mind whenever we treat of establishing peace and concord among Christians, and especially when the object sought is consent in doctrine."[18]

From what follows in succeeding paragraphs, it is clear that the emphasis in this quotation must fall firmly on the word "Christ." Division in the church is nothing less than a "foul and dreadful rending of the body of Christ."[19] However, if a certain proposal to mend what is rent is not properly composed, then, in spite of all its appeal, the "specious pacification" will leave the church with "a half Christ."[20] And the final

---

16. *CO* 7:593; Calvin, *Tracts*, 3:242; see also *CO* 7:552; Calvin, *Tracts*, 3:193. There, Charles V acknowledges that the Roman Catholic Church needed to focus on renewal of piety.

17. *CO* 7:598; Calvin, *Tracts*, 3:249; *CO* 7:597; Calvin, *Tracts*, 3:247.

18. *CO* 7:591; Calvin, *Tracts*, 3:240; emphasis mine.

19. *CO* 7:591; Calvin, *Tracts*, 3:240.

20. *CO* 7:591–92; Calvin, *Tracts*, 3:241.

condition will be worse than the first. Indeed, there are those who, out of ecumenical zeal, announce that "provided what is fundamental remains safe, the loss of other things is tolerable."[21] For his part, Calvin does not endorse such an approach to church unity. He writes, "They speak thus just as if Christ had given himself up to be divided at their pleasure,"[22] and that only compounds the calamity, as it is not only the body of Christ, the church, that is rent, but proponents of specious pacification also threaten to subdivide the head of the church, Christ himself! To be sure, every urgent summons for pacification among Christians has a certain appealing ring to it. However, for Calvin, all ecumenical endeavors must promote, protect, and praise the entire undivided Christ. If not, the proposed pacification may be appealing, but it is equally misleading. In a word, it is *specious*.

Referring more specifically to the *Augsburg Interim*, there are two main areas in which the speciousness of the imperial ecumenism becomes apparent: the doctrine of justification and the manner of worship. Concerning the first, the *Interim* contains a surprisingly Protestant-sounding affirmation of justification by faith when it asserts in the sixth chapter, "With such faith toward God, whosoever leans on the divine mercy and merit of Christ, and commits himself to the same, receives the promise of the Spirit, and is so justified by faith in God, according to the Scripture, that not only is sin forgiven him, but he is also sanctified and renewed by the Holy Spirit."[23]

However, rather than quickly chiming in with his assent, Calvin first cautiously ascertains how his opponents speak about the nature of human beings after the fall. So long as they "leave man freedom of the will" to either embrace or eschew God's grace, "they transfer to man that which belongs to the grace of God."[24] Furthermore, this type of synergistic concurrence between the efforts of the human will and the expression of divine grace can only result in one thing—a conscience that loses tranquility and languishes in uncertainty.[25] As serious as it may be, this lack of assurance is not the worst consequence. Those who promote salvation by synergism "assail the glory of Christ, which he has

---

21. *CO* 7:593; Calvin, *Tracts*, 3:242.
22. *CO* 7:593; Calvin, *Tracts*, 3:242.
23. *CO* 7:558; Calvin, *Tracts*, 3:199.
24. *CO* 7:594; Calvin, *Tracts*, 3:243.
25. *CO* 7:595–8; Calvin, *Tracts*, 3:245–48.

been pleased so to connect with our salvation, that he who detracts from the one violates both."[26] Indeed, they are again guilty of subdividing; this time subdividing salvation between God and human beings, rather than expecting "the whole entire from Christ."[27]

Concerning worship, we might expect that Calvin would demonstrate greater flexibility on this issue. After all, different groups of Christians worship in slightly different ways, often due to historical, cultural, and traditional factors. Yet so long as they are all worshipping the same Christ, should there not be room for a unity that embraces liturgical diversity? Moreover, did not Calvin himself argue that there should be some breathing room for "freedom of conscience"[28] in matters pertaining to worship? To be sure, he did, but that does not mean, in turn, that all worship becomes *adiaphora*. Far from it. There may be those who think that the manner of worship is "frivolous" when compared to weightier matters such as the doctrine of salvation. According to Calvin, such persons have misplaced priorities, as he affirms when he writes, "I say that it [the worship of God] is to be preferred to the safety of men and angels!"[29]

There are two essential characteristics of true worship. First, it must be spiritual, rather than merely ceremonial, and, second, it must be performed in accord with the will of him who is being worshipped, not the wills of those who are worshipping.[30] This second item, the problem of self-willed worship,[31] (*ethelothrēskia*), is vividly expounded as Calvin turns to the topic of the Lord's Supper. The Church of Rome contended that the sacrament involved a transformation of the bread and wine into the body and blood of Christ. The Reformers maintained that the bread remained bread, and the wine remained wine. However, would it not be possible for both views to coexist within the walls of the church? Clearly, Calvin's answer is "No!" Why? Again, the answer concentrates on Christ: "Christ orders us to take and eat bread,"[32] and as the Reformer makes clear, that also means that we do not physically eat the body of Christ, but just as the Lord himself said, we eat *bread*.

26. *CO* 7:607; Calvin, *Tracts*, 3:260.
27. *CO* 7:595; Calvin, *Tracts*, 3:245.
28. *CO* 2:889–90; Calvin, *Institutes*, 4.10.31.
29. *CO* 7:607; Calvin, *Tracts*, 3:260.
30. *CO* 7:607; Calvin, *Tracts*, 3:260.
31. *CO* 7:609–10; Calvin, *Tracts*, 3:263. Here Calvin is alluding to Col 2:23.
32. *CO* 7:621; Calvin, *Tracts*, 3:278.

For Calvin, compromising with transubstantiation would involve departing from the words of Christ and thereby diminishing the reverence that ought to be paid to him.[33]

Much the same applies to the question of whether to celebrate the sacrament in one kind, that is, bread only, or two kinds, that is, bread and wine. Whether out of charity or expediency, the fact remains that the Emperor Charles was willing to compromise on this issue. The Reformer Calvin was not. In fact, partaking of both bread and wine was sufficiently significant that he was willing to shed his own blood over the matter, and he encouraged others to do likewise![34] What could possibly make Calvin so adamant about such a seemingly external matter? The answer, once again, focuses directly on Christ. To begin with, it was Christ who commanded both "Take and eat," as well as, "Drink from it all of you." Therefore, "though a thousand dangers impended, I maintain that it would not be lawful to make any change in the perpetual and inviolable edict of Christ."[35] What is more, whoever restricts people to half the sacrament, "derogates as much from Christ," and by "lacerating the ordinance," Christ himself is also divided and that can never be.[36] Thus, just as with the doctrine of justification, Calvin refuses to compromise on the matter of celebrating with both bread and wine, not because he himself is rigidly stubborn, but because he is eager to avoid anything which would subdivide Christ or present a half Christ to his congregation.

In sum, then, this is why he calls the *Augsburg Interim* a specious pacification. At first sight, any plan to unite Christians is an appealing prospect. Yet, upon further inspection, if that plan involves dividing Christ according to the desires of sinful human beings, then indeed the plan is not only specious, it is spurious.

CONSENSUS TIGURINUS

In 1541, Calvin published a *Short Treatise on the Lord's Supper*.[37] Over the course of fifty-two carefully organized paragraphs, he outlines the doctrine of the sacrament. Beginning with the fifty-third paragraph, though,

---

33. *CO* 7:622; Calvin, *Tracts*, 3:278–79.
34. *CO* 7:626; Calvin, *Tracts*, 3:284.
35. *CO* 7:626; Calvin, *Tracts*, 3:283.
36. *CO* 7:626; Calvin, *Tracts*, 3:284.
37. *CO* 5:433–60; English translation in Calvin, *Tracts*, 2:163–98.

he unveils his purpose in writing this treatise. There have been debates about the Lord's Supper, yes, even "alienation"[38] over the Eucharist among Reformers such as Luther, Zwingli, and Oecolampadius. "Hyperbolical forms of speech"[39] and a failure in "having the patience to listen to each other"[40] have led to separations over the Supper that should, in Calvin's opinion, be overcome. In 1544–1545, there was another heated exchange between Luther and the Zürich theologians when the former published his *Kurzes Bekenntnis vom heiligen Sakrament* and the latter responded with their *Wahrhaftes Bekenntnis der Diener der Kirche zu Zürich*. At the same time, there was a more positive development when Bullinger also wrote *De Sacramentis* (1545). That document, being more pedagogical and less polemical, caught Calvin's eye. Two years later, on 25 Feb 1547, Calvin sent a letter to Bullinger that contained an extensive commentary on *De Sacramentis*. Eventually, Bullinger responded,[41] but at the beginning of 1548 the prospects for consensus were "bleak," as Paul Rorem puts it.[42]

However, the advent of the *Augsburg Interim*, first privately circulated and then publicly promulgated in June 1548, spurred the two theologians back into ecumenical action. Letters were exchanged and pamphlets were printed, namely, Bullinger's *Annotations*, Calvin's *Response*, and finally Bullinger's *Notes*.[43] Much progress was made, but one sizeable obstruction blocked the path leading toward agreement. The obstacle was whether the Supper was an instrument of God's grace (Calvin's position) or a testimony to God's grace (Bullinger's position).[44] At the beginning of 1549, there was no obvious way to remove this im-

38. *CO* 5:459; Calvin, *Tracts*, 2:196.

39. *CO* 5:459; Calvin, *Tracts*, 2:196.

40. *CO* 5:460; Calvin, *Tracts*, 2:197.

41. There is some uncertainty surrounding this letter from Bullinger. Calvin refers to it in his reply to Bullinger (Calvin to Bullinger, 1 March 1548, *CO* 12:666; Calvin, *Letters*, 2:160). However, there is no extant copy of Bullinger's letter. For more details see Rorem, "Did Calvin Compromise?" 79–80.

42. Rorem, "Did Calvin Compromise?" 80. For further details concerning the history leading up to the *Consensus Tigurinus*, consult this article. The author provides an excellent overview of the events.

43. *Ioannis Calvini Propositiones de Sacramentis. Annotationes breves adscripsit Henricus Bullingerus, CO* 7:693–700; *Calvini Responsio ad Annotationes Bullingeri. Scripta Mense Ianuario 1549, CO* 7:701–8; *Henrici Bullingeri Annotata ad Calvini Animadversiones, CO* 7:709–16.

44. Rorem, "Did Calvin Compromise?" 83–4.

pediment as each man held firmly to his conviction. Nevertheless, somehow by end of May, the deed was done and the *Consensus Tigurinus* paved the way for a more harmonious cooperation between Geneva and Zürich. How did they do it? Once more, what follows is a highly selective summary of some key points of the *Consensus*, as well as of the correspondence between Bullinger and Calvin in the months leading up to the *Consensus*. Our focus will be on this question: what convinced Calvin that he could make concessions[45] on certain matters, such as instrumentality, without compromising the fundamental truths of the Supper?

Interestingly enough, the *Consensus* starts with the same emphasis as the *True Reform*, concentrating on Christ. The first article commences with this assertion, "Seeing that Christ is the end of the law, and the knowledge of him comprehends in itself the whole sum of the gospel, there is no doubt that the object of the whole spiritual government of the church is to lead us to Christ."[46] This focus on Christ is sustained throughout the next four articles, as the list of their titles below illustrates:[47]

- Art. 1 – The Whole Spiritual Government of the Church Leads Us to Christ
- Art. 2 – A True Knowledge of the Sacraments from the Knowledge of Christ
- Art. 3 – Nature of the Knowledge of Christ
- Art. 4 – Christ, A Priest and King
- Art. 5 – How Christ Communicates Himself to Us

---

45. Scholars have debated whether the *Consensus* represents a victory for Calvin, a compromise on his part, or simply an indication of the firmness, as well as the flexibility, of his ecumenical approach. A nice summary of the debate, including references to those involved, can be found in Davis, *Clearest Promises of God*, 31–41. The debate continues, but one thing ought to be clear by now: the *Consensus* is not purely and entirely the sacramental view of Calvin. Indeed, Calvin himself acknowledged this when he later wrote the following words to Bucer: "You wish piously and wisely, to explain more clearly and fully the effect of the Sacrament, and what the Lord bestows through it. Nor indeed was it owing to me that they were not fuller on some points. Let us bear therefore with a sign what we cannot correct" (Calvin to Bucer, June 1549, *CO* 13:439; Calvin, *Letters*, 2:235).

46. *OS* 2:247; Calvin, *Tracts*, 2:212.

47. *OS* 2:247–48; Calvin, *Tracts*, 2:212–13. In the Latin original the title of the fourth article is even more emphatically Christocentric: *Christus sacerdos. Christus rex.*

This Christocentric start is by no means accidental. Already back in March 1548 and again on the eve of the *Consensus* in May 1549, Calvin writes to Bullinger saying that "we all unanimously profess the same Christ," and therefore it is incumbent upon them to keep striving for unity "in a solid peace."[48]

Added to that, in the second article of the *Consensus*, self-willed worship (*ethelothrēskia*) is excluded from the start. The agreement states that "he only can discourse aptly and usefully of their nature, virtue, office, and benefit, who begins with Christ."[49] The implication is that—since the Lord's Supper is indeed the *Lord's* Supper, that is, proceeding from Christ as well as pointing to him—the only true knowledge concerning this sacrament is knowledge gained by listening to Christ and carefully following his instructions. Moreover, it was precisely a problem on this point that Calvin identified with the *Augsburg Interim*. Whether it was the matter of transubstantiation or celebrating in one kind, the heart of the issue was not only the sacramental practice as such, but more so the self-willed approach to worship that had led to these practices.

Therefore, already in the first two articles of the *Consensus*, two key principles are laid in place. Both sides agree that they will proceed, focusing intensely on the fullness of Christ while, at the same time, shunning all inclination toward self-willed worship. These are the fundamentals that give both Calvin and Bullinger the confidence to build a consensus concerning the Lord's Supper. Of course, there is still the obstacle mentioned above, that is, the question of whether the sacrament is an instrument or a testimony. Already in 1548, Calvin felt that this difference came down to the fact that he held to "a greater communication of Christ in the Sacraments than you [Bullinger] express in words."[50] Yet, when he phrases it in that way, it raises a pertinent question: did Bullinger actually hold to a greater communication of Christ, that is to say, a more instrumental view of the sacrament than he chose, or dared, to express in words? In other words, did Calvin and Bullinger agree, for the most part, about instrumentality, even though they differed concerning terminology? On two later occasions, Calvin suggests that this may be the case. Just before his trip to Zürich in 1549, Calvin expresses his

---

48. Calvin to Bullinger, 1 March 1548, *CO* 12:666; Calvin, *Letters*, 2:160. Calvin to Bullinger, 7 May 1549, *CO* 13:266; Calvin, *Letters*, 2:225.

49. *OS* 2:247; Calvin, *Tracts*, 2:212.

50. Calvin to Bullinger, 1 March 1548, *CO* 12:666; Calvin, *Letters*, 2:160.

joy to Bullinger that "hardly anything—or at least very little—hinders us from agreeing *now even in words*."[51] This implies that in the past they had basically agreed in their views, but they did not fully realize it because the harmony of their convictions was obscured by the disparity of their expressions. Similarly, after the *Consensus* was put in place, and as Calvin was assuring Bucer that he has not abandoned the truth concerning the Supper, Geneva's Reformer admits that he had "framed the words differently," but his colleague in Strasbourg should not think that the truth confessed therein had been altered.[52] Sometimes in life, preferred terminology can be sacrificed for the sake of true pacification. As both Paul Rorem and Thomas Davis have demonstrated, Calvin's willingness to forego terms such as *instrumentum* and *per* and to embrace alternate vocabulary such as *organum* provided a pathway along which the work towards consensus could proceed.

Yet it was not merely the omission of certain words that had to be dealt with. There was also the not inconsiderable aspect of suspicion. It is remarkable how often Calvin mentions this, in one way or the other, in his letters to Bullinger during the latter half of the 1540s. The following phrases can be found sprinkled throughout their correspondence: lying "under suspicion . . . without any ground for it,"[53] "baseless suspicions,"[54] "preconceived opinion,"[55] "unprofitable distrust,"[56] and "over-scrupulousness."[57] Doubtless, the charge of baseless suspicion could be leveled in both directions. For example, Calvin was rather uncharitable himself when he implied that Bullinger's silence on the matter of the Lord's Supper was tantamount to presenting his throat to be cut by the imperial sword.[58] Undoubtedly, Calvin's relish for rhetoric not only had the power to persuade, but it also had the potential to alienate. Moreover, so long as Bullinger and Calvin went back and forth in correspondence, they could not seem to clear that last hurdle, namely,

---

51. Calvin to Bullinger, 7 May 1549, *CO* 13:266; Calvin, *Letters*, 2:225; emphasis mine.

52. Calvin to Bucer, June 1549, *CO* 13:439; Calvin, *Letters*, 2:235.

53. Calvin to Bullinger, 26 June 1548, *CO* 12:729; Calvin, *Letters*, 2:171.

54. Calvin to Bullinger, 21 January 1549, *CO* 13:165; Calvin, *Letters*, 2:210.

55. Calvin to Bullinger, 21 January 1549, *CO* 13:165; Calvin, *Letters*, 2:210–11.

56. Calvin to Bullinger, 21 January 1549, *CO* 13:165; Calvin, *Letters*, 2:211.

57. Calvin to Viret, 20 July 1549, *CO* 13:334; Calvin, *Letters*, 2:240.

58. Calvin to Bullinger, 19 September 1547, *CO* 12:590–91; Calvin, *Letters*, 2:144.

the instrumentality of the Supper. By all accounts, in the end, it was not so much the difference of opinion or the disparity in terminology that stood in the way, but it was that "unprofitable distrust."[59] When, toward the end of May 1549, Calvin finally donned his cloak and traveled to Zürich, this last obstacle was removed. Just as it is in the twenty-first century, so it was in the sixteenth century, when it comes to building trust, nothing can replace a face-to-face meeting. As Calvin said to Bucer later on, "suddenly the light broke out" and, according to another letter sent to Myconius, the *Consensus Tigurinus* was a done deal in less than two hours.[60]

Given the decades of debate and the profusion of paper devoted to this one topic, the Lord's Supper, the speed at which the *Consensus Tigurinus* was finalized seems almost too good to be true. However, perhaps it should not be so surprising. After all, in the end, it appears that Bullinger and Calvin "merely" had to discover and articulate the unity that already existed between them. They did not have to create a consensus *ex nihilo*.

THE TRUE REFORM AND THE *CONSENSUS TIGURINUS* COMPARED

We have reached the point where it is helpful to take stock of and sum up our discoveries. Briefly put, the central issue is this: in 1549, Calvin had no patience for the emperor's attempt to reunite the portion of Christendom under his jurisdiction, but, at the very same time, he appeared to bend over backwards in order to attain harmony between the theologians of Zürich and Geneva. Why? Simplistically, one might answer that obviously the papal theologians were Calvin's foes and the Zürich theologians were his friends. It is only natural to seek concord with friends before searching for common ground with foes. Granted, but there is more. Prior to 1549, Calvin had worked hard to build bridges with both papal theologians (e.g., the Colloquies of Haguenau, Worms, and Regensburg) and Reformed colleagues (e.g., *The Short Treatise on the Lord's Supper*). *Both* efforts resulted in an impasse. Still, Calvin resolutely pressed on with Zürich, just as surely as he decisively shut the door

---

59. Calvin to Bullinger, 21 January 1549, *CO* 13:165; Calvin, *Letters*, 2:211.

60. Further details concerning these letters can be found in Rorem, "Did Calvin Compromise?" 84. Calvin to Bucer, June 1549, *CO* 3:440; Calvin, *Letters*, 2:235–36. Calvin to Oswald Myconius, 6 Dec 1549, *CO* 3:456–57.

in the emperor's face. Again, why? Based on the above analysis, there are three primary reasons:

1. In the struggle toward the *Consensus Tigurinus*, Calvin was always confident that the Zürich theologians and he embraced the same Christ and the whole Christ. By contrast, as Calvin saw things, agreeing with the *Augsburg Interim* would entail subdividing Christ and proclaiming a "half Christ"[61] from the pulpit. It was bad enough that the body of Christ, the church, was divided. Geneva's reformer was not about to start severing the head of the church, the Christ, as well.

2. Like the other Reformers, Calvin was an adamant proponent of worshipping according to God's will. The *Interim* advocated self-willed worship, even if it did not use that term. Therefore, *de facto*, Calvin would not entertain the thought of conceding ground on any liturgical proposal contained therein. Quite the opposite was true with the Zürich theologians. Like him, they, too, held that Savior-willed worship was a *sine qua non*.

3. The differences between Calvin and Bullinger concerning the Lord's Supper turned out to be more a matter of perspective than principle. Baseless suspicions and dissimilar dialects in theological terminology had been obscuring the fact that these two Reformers already agreed on the principal points of sacramentology. It would have been a shame if distrust and diction had been permitted to prolong division within the church. Thankfully, the Tigurinian *tête-à-tête* in the spring of 1549 prevented that from happening.

IDELETTE'S DEATH

We began by identifying three separations that Calvin had to deal with in 1549. Thus far, we have only analyzed two of them: the rift with Rome and the fissure with Zürich. Yet there was also that tragic, and humanly speaking premature, separation that Jean experienced when his beloved Idelette was taken out of this life and out of his arms. Chronologically, all three events converge rather closely. However, our attention will rest on the interaction between just two of them. On 29 March 1549, Calvin

---

61. *CO* 7:591–2; Calvin, *Tracts*, 3:241.

sat anxiously by his wife's deathbed in Geneva. A mere eight weeks later, he walked apprehensively into a room in Zürich to greet Bullinger and his colleagues. Is there a plausible connection between these two events? Indeed, there is.

On 7 May 1549, while still in deep grief over Idelette's death, Calvin received a letter from Bullinger outlining, yet again, his views on the Lord's Supper. By that point, Bullinger and Calvin had been going back and forth on this topic for months, yes, even years. So, how did Calvin respond to yet one more missive on the Lord's Supper? Did he roughly shove it to the side so that he could concentrate on his personal grief instead? Did the whole debate seem tedious and tangential to him now that Idelette was no longer with him? After all, what's more important—the finer points of sacramentology or your own beloved spouse? Remarkably, Calvin reads Bullinger's letter . . . with interest. In fact, no sooner does he finish reading it than he grabs his quill to scribble a few words to Bullinger: "As time does not permit me to reply to your letter now, I am merely desirous of telling you that I have scarcely ever received anything more pleasant from you, as it served to alleviate a very trying domestic grief, which, occasioned by the death of my wife a little before, was causing me very much sorrow. For I am very glad that hardly anything—or at least very little—hinders us from agreeing now even in words."[62]

The exuberance in Calvin's expression is almost tangible. Why does he respond with such enthusiasm to *this* particular letter from Bullinger? Was this letter so radically different from all the other letters and pamphlets on the Lord's Supper that he had received from Zürich's Antistes? To be sure, Bullinger, like Calvin, was constantly trying to refine the rough edges of his position and remove any misunderstandings. However, as Calvin seems to indicate himself, this breakthrough has more to do with the "very trying domestic grief" on his side than it has to do with any radical doctrinal change coming from Bullinger's side. As often happens, the death of a loved one puts things into perspective. Mortality has a dramatic and decisive way of demarcating the difference between essential and nonessential. Yes, Bullinger's letter alleviated Calvin's grief, but it works the other way as well. Idelette's death sufficiently altered Calvin's outlook on life that he could see his way clear to compromise on a word such as *instrumentum* and still maintain the

---

62. Calvin to Bullinger, 7 May 1549, *CO* 13:266; Calvin, *Letters*, 2:225.

truth of the *sacramentum* itself. Thus, providentially, as death snatched Idelette from Jean's loving arms, the path was already being prepared for a most pleasant consensus. Evidently, sometimes absence can make the heart grow fonder, also in ecumenical efforts.

BIBLIOGRAPHY

Berg, Machiel A. van den. *Friends of Calvin*. Translated by Reinder Bruinsma. Grand Rapids: Eerdmans, 2009.

Calvin, John. *Corpus Reformatorum. Ioannis Calvini Opera Quae Supersunt Omnia*. 59 vols. edited by G. Baum, et al. Brunsvigae: Schwetschke, 1863–1900.

———. *Institutes of the Christian Religion*, edited by John T. McNeill. Translated by Ford Lewis Battles. 2 vols. Philadelphia: Westminster, 1960.

———. *Joannis Calvini Opera Selecta*. Edited by P. Barth and G. Niesel. 5 vols. Monachii: Kaiser, 1952–1967.

———. *Letters of John Calvin*. Edited by Jules Bonnet. 1858. Reprint. Eugene, OR: Wipf & Stock, 2007.

———. *Tracts and Treatises of John Calvin*. 3 vols. Translated by Henry Beveridge. Eugene, OR: Wipf & Stock, 2002.

Davis, Thomas J. *The Clearest Promises of God: The Development of Calvin's Eucharistic Teaching*. AMS Studies in Religious Tradition 1. New York: AMS, 1995.

Rorem, Paul E. "The *Consensus Tigurinus* (1549): Did Calvin Compromise?" In *Calvinus Sacrae Scripturae Professor: Calvin As Confessor of Holy Scripture*, ed. Wilhem H. Neuser, 72–90. Grand Rapids: William B. Eerdmans, 1994.

Stolk, J. M. *Johannes Calvijn en de godsdienstgesprekken tussen rooms-katholieken en protestanten in Hagenau, Worms en Regensburg (1540-1541)*. Kampen: Kok, 2004.

12

Wellsprings of the Offices

Roelf C. Janssen

Cornelis Van Dam's *The Elder: Today's Ministry Rooted in All of Scripture*[1] is a well structured, clearly written, and thorough exposition on the office of elder, its scriptural underpinnings, and the implications of these roots for the practice of the office today. It is certainly a book that should be in every Reformed pastor's library.

In this book Van Dam argues that there is a link between today's elder, both ruling and teaching, and the elder of the old covenant. He also argues in favor of a direct link between today's teaching elders, or pastors, and the Aaronic priests of the old covenant. These are very appealing conclusions. However, it is worth noting that this particular paradigm for connecting today's offices to Scripture is not typically found in the branch of the Calvinist tradition in which Van Dam is active. Furthermore, this paradigm has implications for the exercise of the offices today that are at odds with the practices of some Reformed churches in the Netherlands. This is worthy of further investigation.

As this article will indicate, in Van Dam's study, two branches of the Calvinist tradition meet: the Scottish and American Presbyterian and the Dutch Reformed. In what follows, I will refer to the former as the Westminster tradition and the latter as the Dort tradition. Both traditions trace themselves to John Calvin, but the polities of these traditions are distinct, perhaps even so distinct as to be irreconcilable.[2] In *The*

---

1. Van Dam, *The Elder*.
2. For more on this, see Janssen, *By This Our Subscription*, 298–99, esp. n. 725.

Elder, Van Dam describes what is traditionally the exegetical approach of the Westminster tradition, but he does so within the context of the Dort tradition. This raises the following question: will this exegetical foundation fit well underneath the Dort building?

This essay begins with an overview of the positions held in the Dort tradition, especially during the twentieth century in the Netherlands and in North America.[3] This overview will demonstrate that the paradigm flowing from Van Dam's exegesis is not found in the Dort tradition. Next, we will review Van Dam's *The Elder*, and reflect on the question of whether the paradigm it presents and its implications will dovetail with the Dort tradition of church polity. Finally, some comments will be made on the effect that exegesis has had, and can have, on church polity.

THE ROMAN CATHOLIC STREAM

The Dort tradition traces itself back to positions held by the sixteenth-century Reformers, especially John Calvin. However, the views of these Reformers were developed within the context of the Roman Catholic tradition. For many centuries, the practice of the offices flowed from the spring of Scripture through the stream of the Roman Catholic Church. Therefore, in the first place, it is proper to take note of the Roman Catholic teaching about the offices.

As Te Velde explains, the Roman Catholic tradition confronted the Reformers with three distinct offices: bishop, priest, and deacon. It also promoted hierarchy within the offices and a sharp distinction between clergy and laity. The *Catechism of the Catholic Church* contains authoritative statements about the offices. The bishop is said to be the direct representative of Christ as teacher, shepherd, and priest. The Catholic priests are described as the New Testament equivalent of the Old Testament priests. The deacons are understood to be servants of, and assistants to, the bishops and priests.[4]

---

3. In providing this overview of the Dort tradition, grateful use has been made of research done by Mees te Velde, professor of church polity at the Theological University of the Reformed Churches in the Netherlands (liberated). The results of his research have been published in a series of articles for a popular audience, but not (yet) in an academic publication. See Te Velde, "De afbakening."

4. Te Velde, "Afbakening," 140–1. *Catechism of the Catholic Church*, arts. 1558, 1564, and 1570.

THE REFORMED STREAM

The Reformers rejected as unscriptural both the idea of hierarchy among the offices, as well as the distinction between clergy and laity. They also balked at the Roman Catholic understanding of the individual offices. Te Velde has pointed out that originally the only office was that of the minister, although in Lutheran circles civil authorities also held a position. However, already in 1538, the Reformed Church in Strasbourg had three offices: preachers, elders, and deacons. The idea of three offices became the basic pattern for the churches of the Calvinist Reformation. As Calvin tried to systematize the data of Scripture, he found it to be a difficult task. Much of what Calvin has written on the offices is prefaced with comments such as "in my opinion" and "possibly." This may well suggest that a neat and tidy scheme cannot be deduced from Scripture.

In addition, Te Velde explains that the Reformers worked primarily with the Scriptural data found in Eph 4:11, Rom 12:6–8, and 1 Cor 12:28. A primary text for distinguishing the elder from the minister in the Dort tradition, namely, 1 Tim 5:17, did not function that way with the Reformers. As Te Velde points out, the Reformers took stock of the ministries in the church and then classified them into two or three categories, each category being connected to an office. The two-category view spoke of prophecy and ministry, while the three-category view spoke of doctrine, discipline, and diaconate. Te Velde has also noted that ministers were considered successors to the apostles. While the offices were essentially independent and all office bearers were theoretically equal, in practice there was a certain order, with most of the weight being attached to the office of the minister, less to that of the elder, and even less to that of the deacon.[5]

VARIOUS TRIBUTARIES IN THE DORT TRADITION

When seeking to trace a route from the mouth of the Rhine back to its source, one has many natural waterways to choose from in the Netherlands. The same is true for the offices. The Dort approach argues that the offices in the church can be traced back to Scripture, but within this tradition there are various ways of doing so.

---

5. Te Velde, "Afbakening," 141–43, 157–58. For more information on the views of the Reformers, see Van 't Spijker, *De ambten*, and Boer, "Calvin's View."

Within the Dort tradition, the Heidelberg Catechism gave the Reformed a particular understanding of the offices of the Lord Jesus Christ. As Messiah, that is, the Anointed One, Jesus was the chief Prophet and Teacher, the only High Priest, and the eternal King. Further, this much-loved catechism described the Christian in a similar way: as prophet, priest, and king.[6] At some point in time, the three-fold office of Christ and the three-fold office of the Christian were connected to the three offices in the church. The wellspring of the office of the minister is the office of the prophet, while that of the elder is the king and that of the deacon is the priest. Both H. Bavinck, a professor of systematic theology, and H. Bouwman, an authority on church polity, take this approach.[7] It has also been echoed in North America by authors such as W. Heyns, as well as I. Van Dellen and M. Monsma.[8] Thus, according to this view, the three distinct offices of the new covenant trace their origin back to the old covenant, although these offices have been united in Christ and are also united in each believer.

However, already in Bavinck's day, some authors protested against this arrangement. In an early, seminal study on the work of deacons, P. Biesterveld, J. Van Lonkhuijzen, and R. J. W. Rudolph stated that all three offices spring from the apostolic office.[9] They argued that, in fact, the deacons were instituted first as a separate office. Later on, the remaining official tasks in the church were divided between a teaching and a ruling office. During the 1950s, K. Dijk also challenged the direct and exclusive links laid between the offices of the old and new covenant eras. This challenge was reiterated during the late 1980s by B. Spoelstra in South Africa.[10]

---

6. Bakhuizen van den Brink, *Nederlandse Belijdenisgeschriften*, 168–69.

7. Bavinck, *Gereformeerde Dogmatiek*, 4:424; Bouwman, *Gereformeerd Kerkrecht*, 1:§29.b.

8. Heyns, *Gereformeerde Geloofsleer*, 161; Van Dellen and Monsma, *Church Order Commentary*, 16, 20, 112. To my knowledge, the most recent mention of this approach is Van Dyken, *With All My Heart*, 155–57.

9. Biesterveld et al., *Het diaconaat*, 30–34, 37. It is worth noting that J. van Lonkhuijzen later served as minister in the Christian Reformed Church in North America.

10. Dijk, *Dienst der kerk*, 166, 226–27. It should be noted that Dijk makes an incorrect reference to Bavinck as he provides support for his argument. Spoelstra, *Gereformeerd Kerkreg*, arts. 2&3, A.5.

Not finding much merit in the idea of connecting the three church offices to the three-fold office of Christ, some sought out other explanations. Some explained the origin of the offices as arising from practical needs and based on existing traditions. For instance, L. Berkhof suggested that the office of elder was probably first instituted in the churches of the Jews, perhaps even preceding the diaconate. Furthermore, he posited that at first the teachers were simply elders, but over the course of time, as the apostles fell away, they became a more distinct office. Finally, he found the origin of the diaconate in the seven men chosen in Acts 6.[11] In his writings on church polity, J. Schaver took the same approach, although it is worth noting that he suggested that the office of elder should be linked to the office of elder in the synagogue, something Berkhof did not do.[12] A recent dogmatic textbook in the Dort tradition, written by J. van Genderen and W. H. Velema, comes to similar conclusions.[13] Concerning elders, Van Genderen and Velema posit that nothing is known about the origin of this office. They admit that there is a connection to the elders in the synagogue, but they argue that such elders had no duties with respect to the worship services, as do the elders of the Christian church. Concerning deacons, they note that a direct connection with Acts 6 is uncertain, although they concede that something can be learned from that chapter with respect to office of deacons. Van Genderen and Velema do not discuss the office of the minister in a separate section, suggesting rather that over the course of time this office arose from that of the elder.

MORE STREAMS IN THE DORT TRADITION TODAY

Today, among scholars there is a large variety of positions connected to the Dort tradition. It is not possible, within the scope of this essay, to review them all. As such, what follows is a limited selection. This overview will simply serve to illustrate how diversified the positions have become.

In the Netherlands, there is a debate concerning the extent to which church polity is christological or pneumatological. "Christological" is understood as a system of order that is *office-centered* and structured along lines of positional authority: that is to say, an authority based on

11. Berkhof, *Systematic Theology*, 585–87. Concerning the origin of the deacons in Acts 6, Berkhof does interact with arguments to the contrary.

12. Schaver, *The Polity of the Churches*, 1:24–27, 133, 147–48.

13. van Genderen and Velema, *Beknopte gereformeerde dogmatiek*, 667–71.

calling and appointment. "Pneumatological" is understood as a system of order that is *gift-centered* and structured along lines of personal authority: that is to say, an authority based on charisma[14] and recognition of ability. At this point, an illustration may help to clarify the point. Picture a passenger on a ship that is about to sink. The captain tells the passenger to enter the lifeboat. The passenger may do so because the captain is the one in command; that is positional authority. At the same time, the passenger may do so because he trusts the captain's judgment; that is personal authority.

Some descendants of the Dort tradition feel that this debate has led to an erosion in the functioning of the offices. For example, L. Koffeman has suggested a sharper distinction should be made between the ministers, on the one hand, and the elders and deacons, on the other hand.[15] In his opinion, the office is defined by how it relates to the Word and sacraments. The office of the minister relates directly to Word and sacraments, while the elders and deacons have a more indirect role, as they assist him in fulfilling this calling.

Furthermore, other scholars in the Dort tradition have engaged in hermeneutical and exegetical debates concerning the wellspring of the three offices. J. van Bruggen has argued that the New Testament knows of only one office, namely, that of the elder. In his opinion, deacons are not to be considered office bearers.[16] He also argues that the elders of Jerusalem are not to be equated with today's elders. Moreover, he holds that the office of minister is not essentially, but only functionally, different from that of other elders. In response, A. N. Hendriks argued that the existence of three offices has been a choice made by the church in the course of time.[17] With reference to J. Kamphuis, a contemporary authority on church polity, he also notes that the church has the authority to do this. In short, his response implies there is no *need* to find a direct exegetical basis for the offices. As such, Hendriks felt at liberty to adhere to the three-office approach.

---

14. That is, in the sense of the Greek word for gifts, *charismata*.

15. Koffeman, *Goed recht*, 137–60. It is telling that this recent volume on church polity does not include Bavinck in its bibliography. It may be questioned whether the link to the Dort tradition is still substantial.

16. Van Bruggen, *Ambten*, 65–118, esp. 75–91, 101–6.

17. Hendriks, *Met het oog*, 81–105.

In the early 1990s, M. te Velde took stock of this debate. He observed that, over the years, there has been much criticism of the Reformers' approach to the offices. For example, in 1972, S. G. Huh criticized the exegesis which suggests that the ruling elder should not be connected to the *episkopos* ("overseer"), but only to the *presbyteros* ("presbyter").[18] In 1975, A. van Ginkel argued that in Calvin's Strasbourg, the office of elder was initially created in practice and only subsequently established by theological proof. Following that, in 1982, C. Trimp shifted the focus from three offices to three fields of ministry. In 1984, J. van Bruggen objected to a particular exegetical ground for distinguishing the offices of elders and ministers and indicated that, exegetically speaking, the work of deacons is much broader than currently practiced in the Dort tradition. Te Velde also notes that the exegetical underpinnings for the offices, as well as the functions fulfilled by the office-bearers, have changed. This, he makes clear, is reflected in a revision of the proof texts referenced in the relevant articles in the Belgic Confession, as well as in the revised editions of the liturgical forms used for ordination in the Netherlands. For example, texts referring to the *episkopos* and *presbyteros* were applied also to ruling elders. Moreover, 1 Tim 5:17 was used to support the distinction between ministers and elders. Rom 12 and 1 Cor 12 were somewhat sidelined as scriptural sources, since, it was argued, these texts are about *charismata*, not offices.[19] In addition, Te Velde remarks that, in the Reformed Churches of the Netherlands (liberated), elders have now been granted the right to bestow the blessing. Previously, this was only the prerogative of the minister. Finally, in conclusion, Te Velde has pointed out that the only document which has not (yet) been changed to match this new view is the church order itself.

Thus, Te Velde's analysis identifies three positions currently held in the Dort tradition:

---

18. Huh's dissertation, *Presbyter in Volle Rechten*, investigates the Presybterian debate concerning the offices, particularly between Thornwell and Hodge.

19. It is noteworthy that, with respect to the office of elder, the liturgical form for the ordination of elders and deacons in use in the Canadian Reformed Churches is different from that of the Reformed Churches in the Netherlands (liberated). The Canadian form contains a paragraph on the office of elder in the Old Testament that is not found in the Dutch form. For the original and the later forms used by the Reformed Churches in the Netherlands see *Psalmen* and *Gereformeerd Kerkboek*, 430–39. For the original and later forms used by the Canadian Reformed Churches see the 1972 edition of the *Book of Praise*, 526–38, as well as the 1993 edition of the *Book of Praise*, 619–34.

1. Scripture prescribes a three-office view. The first office is the successor to the apostles, prophets, evangelists, and teachers. The second office is that of leadership. The third office is that of mercy. The first and second offices are distinct, but closely related.

2. Scripture prescribes a two-office view. The first office is that of leadership and teaching, sub-divided into two offices: one focusing primarily on teaching and the other on leading. 1 Tim 5:17 is the key text used to support this distinction. The second office is that of mercy.

3. Scripture has no hard and fast prescriptions for a view of the offices. The church is authorized by God to make arrangements as she feels prudent and wise.

As Te Velde indicates, *in practice* both the first and second positions generally lead to a three-fold approach. Ruling elders, with their daily jobs and lack of training, will function differently from ministers, who are engaged in full-time ministry and, in the Dort tradition, highly trained. However, at least in theory, the second position does place more responsibility on the shoulders of the ruling elders than the first position does.[20]

In sum, the basic question within the Dort tradition has become, do the offices have their wellsprings directly or indirectly in Scripture, or are they the result of the Spirit's guidance in the church, expressed through human prudence? At this point the issue is no longer just exegetical; it has also become hermeneutical.

VAN DAM'S CHANNEL

Having reviewed various tributaries and streams through which the Dort tradition has flowed, we now turn to Van Dam's exposition in *The Elder: Today's Ministry Rooted in All of Scripture*. The subtitle is important. It speaks of a "ministry." Both in the Dort tradition specifically, and in Christendom more generally, a distinction has been made between offices and ministries. However, from the perspective of church polity, nothing should be read into this choice of terms.[21] The expression "rooted in all Scripture," suggests that, on the hermeneutical issue, Van

---

20. Te Velde, "Afbakening," 256–59, 278–82.

21. In fact, in communication via email, Dr. Van Dam informed me that his preference had been for the word "office," but the publisher preferred "ministry."

Dam holds to biblical prescriptions for the office of elder, both ruling and teaching. It has led him to embark on a zealous search in Scripture for data that may be used to define the responsibilities and limits of this ministry. Such a searching zeal is also typical for the Dort tradition. "All" indicates that instruction on the offices is given, not just in the New Testament, but also in the Old Testament. Such an approach is not new to the Dort tradition. Those who saw Christ's three-fold office reflected in the offices of minister, elder, and deacon also drew in data from the Old Testament offices of prophet, priest, and king. However, the specific links that Van Dam makes—from Old Testament priest to today's minister and only from Old Testament elder to today's elder—are different from what is generally found in the Dort tradition. It is this, then, that makes his approach different.

This different approach is connected with Van Dam's conviction that in the New Testament church, in addition to the office of deacon, there are two more offices, the teaching elder and the ruling elder, distinct from each other but sharing an underlying unity. He comes to this conclusion, in part, because "nowhere [in Scripture] is the gift of teaching or exhorting practically or officially linked to that of ruling or governing . . . The gift of ruling belongs to the ruling elder; the gift of teaching belongs to the calling of one who focuses on teaching."[22] However, for Van Dam, the separation between the two offices is not complete. He also writes, "Although I would argue for two distinct offices, it should be noted that because both the ruling elder and teaching elder are called *elders*, their offices do have an underlying unity and purpose that must be acknowledged."[23]

Van Dam has looked for the roots of these two offices in both the Old and New Testaments. The office of the elder, in general, is connected to the Old Testament elder, the *zaqen*, which is an older man, "the bearded head,"[24] while the preachers or teaching elders "are the priests and Levites of today."[25] He holds that "a consideration of the Old Testament background will provide the overall basis for the position that the ruling elder and the teaching elder are two separate offices."[26] Concerning

---

22. Van Dam, *Elder*, 105.
23. Ibid., 106.
24. Ibid., 27.
25. Ibid., 120.
26. Ibid., 108.

the unity between the Old and New Testaments he writes, "If the offices of elder and teacher were clearly distinguished in the old dispensation, then one could expect this to be continued in the new dispensation, with a special teaching office in the Christian congregation. There would have been no need for something this obvious to be specified, and the New Testament should be read with this in mind. It may be asking too much to attempt to discover from only the New Testament whether there were separate teaching and ruling offices."[27]

According to Van Dam, this distinction has several consequences. "First, they [the ministers and elders] each have their specific task, and thus ruling elders normally do not officially bring the Word in public worship. They also do not give the blessing. Second, especially those engaged full-time as the 'priests' and teaching elders of today should be supported monetarily by the gospel. Third, both offices are elder offices and there is to be equality, not hierarchy. Fourth, there is no biblical warrant for a church polity in which the ordained ministry is rejected in favor of only ruling elders who preach and shepherd the church."[28]

Such consequences do not entirely match up with various practices within the Dort tradition. For example, while it is preferable for a minister to lead worship, from the perspective of church polity there is no issue with a ruling elder leading worship, regardless of whether there is a minister present or not. Further, given the discussions in the Netherlands, it is considered exegetically justifiable to have elders give the blessing and to consider the offices of minister and elder to be one in principle and two only in practice. Finally, if the tasks of ministers and ruling elders are so different, to what extent is it justified to have elders supervise and judge issues relating directly to the task of the minister?

Thus, to sum up, there are two noteworthy matters in Van Dam's exegesis. In the first place, the specific correlation he makes between the present-day offices and the Old Testament offices (e.g., connecting minister to priest) is different from that which is typically found in the Dort tradition (e.g., connecting minister to prophet). Secondly, some consequences of his exegesis differ from certain practices in the Dort tradition.

27. Ibid., 111.
28. Ibid., 120.

THE SOURCES OF VAN DAM'S VIEW

At this point, it is helpful to reflect on why Van Dam's exegesis is different from that which is normally found in the Dort tradition. A clue is found when he discusses the distinction between elders and ministers. Here he points his reader to the "Form for Presbyterial Church Government" approved by the Westminster Assembly in 1645,[29] as well as to authorities within the Westminster tradition for further reading on his exegetical approach.[30] In particular, it is interesting that the Form adopted in 1645 makes the same connection that Van Dam makes, namely, between today's pastor and the priests of the Old Testament.[31] At the same time, there are also differences between his position and the Westminster tradition. For example, he rejects the sharp distinction found within the Westminster tradition between the ruling elder and the teaching elder.[32] However, overall, his exegesis is closer to the Westminster tradition than to the Dort tradition.

Taking this a step farther, where might such exegesis lead us? The Westminster tradition of church government differs from that of the Dort tradition in its view of the offices. Dort polity locates its "pivotal position" in the local consistory, which consists of ruling elders and teaching elders, whereas Westminster polity situates its "pivotal position" in the regional presbytery, which consists of all the teaching elders, but not necessarily all the ruling elders, in a particular geographical area.[33] Within the Dort tradition, elders and ministers are substantially

---

29. Ibid., 107 n. 12.

30. See ibid., 105 n. 9, where he points to authorities such as Robert S. Rayburn and Edmund P. Clowney.

31. Under the heading "Pastor," the Form for Presbyterial Church Government states that pastors have the duty, "To read the Scriptures publickly; for the proof of which, 1. That the priests and Levites in the Jewish church were trusted with the publick reading of the word is proved; 2. That the ministers of the gospel have as ample a charge and commission to dispense the word, as well as other ordinances, as the priests and Levites had under the law, proved, Isa. lxvi. 21. Matt. xxiii. 34. where our Saviour entitleth the officers of the New Testament, whom he will send forth, by the same names of the teachers of the Old." See *The Confession of Faith; the Larger Catechism; the Shorter Catechism; the Directory for Publick Worship; the form of Presbyterial church government: with references to the proofs from the Scripture.*

32. Van Dam applies 1 Tim 3:1–7 to both teaching and ruling elders (*Elder*, 115), which the Westminster tradition does not; cf. Miller on 1 Tim 3:1 in Miller, "The New Testament Warrant," 26–34.

33. For example, see *The Practice of the Free Church of Scotland*, which states, "Pivotal position: Presbytery is often described as the radical court of the Church and

similar but functionally distinguished. Thus, the local church is an *ecclesia completa*, even without a minister. However, within the Westminster tradition elders and ministers are substantially distinguished and thus functionally distinguished. Therefore, the local church is only an *ecclesia completa* when a minister is present.[34]

Van Dam has confronted the Dort tradition with some aspects of the exegetical foundation underlying the Westminster tradition. That is a good thing, for both cherish the principle of *sola Scriptura*. However, does the building of Dort polity fit on the exegetical foundation of Westminster polity? Given the practice of the Dort tradition, the answer to date has been, "No." Some may feel that one tradition must be right, and the other wrong. Others may think that there is room for agreeing to disagree, since both the Dort and Westminster traditions are within the boundaries of scriptural prescriptions and the Reformed confessions. Moreover, there are those in the Dort tradition who hold to a three-office view and those in the Westminster tradition who endorse a two-office view.[35] Nevertheless, the fact remains that the buildings are rather different.[36]

Our point is not to dispute the legitimacy or correctness of Van Dam's exegesis. Rather it is to point out the implications of this exegesis for the polity practiced in the Dort tradition. For if the building of Dort does not fit on the foundation of Westminster, and the foundation of Westminster is the more proper one, should the Dort foundation not be re-poured and a new building erected upon it? What would that building look like? Alternatively, the two traditions could continue side by side with their distinctive polities. If the latter option is chosen, Van Dam's exegetical comments are certainly worth noting, but practically

---

the system of Church Government which stems from it is referred to as Presbyterian." That the "radicals" in the polity are different is made clear by the fact that in the Dort tradition excommunication is within the jurisdiction of the consistory, while in the Westminster tradition it is within the jurisdiction of the presbytery. See Hall and Hall, *Paradigms in Polity*, 183, 270. Geographically speaking, the parallel to the presbytery is the classis. Note that in article 76 of the Dort Church Order, the *advice* of the classis is needed to proceed to excommunication, while in the Westminster Assembly Directory for Church Government the classical presbytery "may declare and decern [sic]" that a person is to be excommunicated.

34. E.g., *The Orthodox Presbyterian Church Book of Church Order*, chap. 13, 1, 6.

35. E.g., Knight, "Two Offices"; Clements, *Biblical Church Government*.

36. See note 2 above.

speaking, some of his conclusions cannot operate in a Dort environment. Indeed, some of his comments may even prove to be confusing in a Dort environment.

IMPLICATIONS FOR CHURCH POLITY IN THE DORT TRADITION

Van Dam's work is primarily an exegetical study. However, he does permit himself to draw practical conclusions from the fruit of his labor, and rightly so. We wish to consider some of these conclusions in the light of how church government is practiced in the Dort tradition.

In the first place, if the ministry of reconciliation, the priestly task, is solely for the minister, should elders be allowed to lead public worship services at all? Following the paradigm presented by Van Dam, should not what is true for the sacraments and the blessing also apply to that most central duty of the teaching elder, namely, the public proclamation of the Word? Should this perhaps also extend to the catechism classroom? Van Dam's exegesis creates a point of tension here for the Dort tradition. Indeed, he has used the qualifier "normally" when stating that ruling elders do not officially bring the Word in public worship.[37] However, we wonder if the logic of his paradigm does not imply that "not normally" should read "never."

Secondly, if only the teaching elder is endowed with the ministry of reconciliation, to what extent can the ruling elders exercise authority over the teaching elder on this point? In both the Westminster and Dort traditions, every teaching elder is a ruling elder, but not every ruling elder a teaching elder. Moreover, in the Westminster tradition, not every ruling elder is a member of the presbytery, and thus not every ruling elder is charged with supervising doctrine. Do the exegesis and distinctions presented by Van Dam have consequences, for example, for the examination of a person to be admitted to the office of minister? What will this mean for a practice such as sermon evaluation by a consistory or session?

We raise these questions, not to undermine the legitimacy of Van Dam's exegesis and argumentation, but to point out what the consequences of his convictions might be. More systematic thought will have to be put into this.

---

37. Van Dam, *The Elder*, 120.

CONCLUSION

Ad fontes, back to the sources, is a well-known motto in academic circles. The risk of going back to the source of Scripture, though, is discovering that existing practices require more than just tweaking and fine-tuning. In the Netherlands, the practices of the Dort tradition have been revised due to the work of J. van Bruggen and C. Trimp. As M. te Velde noted in his series of articles, the proof texts in the confessions and the wording of the liturgical forms kept pace with this; however, the church order itself has not.[38]

Van Dam's book confronts the Dort tradition with some exegesis from the Westminster tradition. Having evaluated some of the consequences that flow from his exegesis, we conclude that the one does not truly dovetail with the other. Thus, will the attempt to place the exegetical foundation of Westminster underneath the structure of Dort change the building? Or will the channel that connects the wellspring of Scripture and the lake of church government remain hidden in a fog? Or will the discussion even come to the point where an appeal to freedom of exegesis is used to mask the fact that many choices, even those relating to something as fundamental as the number of offices in the church, are in fact no more than a choice made by the church in human wisdom? If the last scenario materializes, then the discussion is no longer just an exegetical one, but it has become a hermeneutical one. In the early 1990s, Mees te Velde lamented, "As I teach at our university, I frequently notice how difficult it is to explain and apply a church order, in which very fundamental decisions depend on exegesis and arguments which are being fundamentally criticized by authoritative and respected authors in our midst."[39]

Van Dam's book is to be appreciated for exposing the Dort tradition to some Westminster exegesis. Moreover, it is a fine book that opens Scripture in a forthright and thought-provoking manner. Perhaps the resolution of the tension arising through it will lie somewhere in the middle. Maybe those who practice Dort polity in the English-speaking world need to make certain changes, just as the Dutch are now adjusting their polity. The Holy Spirit knows, and he will continue to lead the church in the truth. In that process, Scripture must be the final authority.

---

38. Te Velde, "Afbakening," 258–59.
39. Ibid., 259; translation mine.

BIBLIOGRAPHY

Bakhuizen van den Brink, J. N. *De Nederlandse Belijdenisgeschriften in authentieke teksten met inleiding en tekstvergelijking.* Amsterdam: Ton Bolland, 1976.

Bavinck, H. *Gereformeerde Dogmatiek.* Kampen: Kok, 1911.

Berkhof, L. *Systematic Theology.* 1941. Reprint, Carlisle: Banner of Truth Trust, 1988.

Biesterveld, P., et al. *Het diaconaat.* Hilversum: Witzelf, 1907.

Boer, Jeffrey K. "Calvin's View of the Teaching Elder—Ruling Elder." In *Order in the Offices: Essays Defining the Roles of Church Officers,* edited by Mark R. Brown, 134–54. Duncansville, PA: Classic Presbyterian Government Resources, 1993.

Book of Praise: Anglo-Genevan Psalter. Canadian Reformed Churches. Burlington, ON: The Committee for the Publication of the Anglo-Genevan Psalter, 1972.

Book of Praise: Anglo-Genevan Psalter. Canadian Reformed Churches. Winnipeg: Premier, 1993.

Bouwman, H. *Gereformeerd Kerkrecht.* Kampen: Kok, 1928.

Catholic Church. *Catechism of the Catholic Church.* Liguori, MO: Liguori, 1994.

Clements, Don K. *Biblical Church Government.* Narrows, VA: Metokos, 2005.

Dijk, K. *De dienst der kerk.* Kampen: Kok, 1952.

Gereformeerd Kerkboek. Gereformeerde Kerken in Nederland. Enschede: Boersma, 1975.

Hall, David W., and Joseph H. Hall. *Paradigms in Polity: Classic Readings in Reformed and Presbyterian Church Government.* Grand Rapids: Eerdmans, 1994.

Hendriks, A. N. *Met het oog op de gemeente: Populair-theologische bijdragen.* Kampen: Van den Berg, 1991.

Heyns, W. *Gereformeerde Geloofsleer.* Grand Rapids: Eerdmans Sevensma, 1916.

Huh, Soon-Gil. *Presbyter in Volle Rechten.* Groningen: Vuurbaak, 1972.

Janssen, Roelf C. *By This Our Subscription: Confessional Subscription in the Dutch Reformed Tradition Since 1816.* ThD diss., Theologische Universiteit van de Gereformeerde Kerken in Nederland, 2009. Online: http://igitur-archive.library.uu.nl/theol/2009-0618-200551/Dissertatie_R.C.Janssen.pdf/.

Knight, George W. "Two Offices and Two Orders of Elders." In *Pressing toward the Mark: Essays Commemorating Fifty Years of the Orthodox Presbyterian Church,* edited by Charles G. Dennison and Richard C. Gamble, 23–32. Philadelphia: Committee for the Historian of the Orthodox Presbyterian Church, 1986.

Koffeman, Leo. *Het goed recht van de kerk: een theologische inleiding op het kerkrecht.* Kampen: Kok, 2009.

Miller, Steven F. "The New Testament Warrant of the Minister of the Word." In *Order in the Offices: Essays Defining the Roles of Church Officers,* edited by Mark R. Brown, 6–40. Duncansville, PA: Classic Presbyterian Government Resources, 1993.

Orthodox Presbyterian Church: Book of Church Order. Online: http://www.opc.org/BCO/.

Psalmen: de berijming van 1773 waaraan toegevoegd: enige gezangen, de drie formulieren van enigheid, de drie oude geloofsbelijdenissen, de liturgie, het kort begrip. Gereformeerde Kerken in Nederland. Leeuwarden: Jongbloed, n.d.

Schaver, J. L. *The Polity of the Churches.* Chicago: Church Polity Press, 1947.

Spoelstra, B. *Gereformeerd Kerkreg en Kerkregering.* Pretoria: V&R Drukkery, 1989. Online: http://kerkrecht.nl/main.asp?pagetype=onderdeel&item=10.

Te Velde, Mees. "De afbakening van de ambten." *De Reformatie* 69 (1993) 140–43; 157–60; 176–79; 256–59; 278–82.

The Confession of Faith; the Larger Catechism; the Shorter Catechism; the Directory for Publick Worship; the form of Presbyterial church government: with references to the proofs from the Scripture. Church of Scotland. Edinburgh: William Blackwood & Sons, 1959.

The Practice of the Free Church of Scotland in Her Several Courts. Online: http://www.freechurch.org/images/uploads/presbytery.pdf.

Van 't Spijker, W. *De ambten bij Martin Bucer.* Kampen: Kok, 1987.

Van Bruggen, Jacob. *Ambten in de apostolische kerk: Een exegetisch mozaïek.* Kampen: Kok, 1984.

Van Dam, Cornelis. *The Elder: Today's Ministry Rooted in All of Scripture.* Explorations in Biblical Theology. Phillipsburg, NJ: P&R, 2009.

Van Dellen, Idzerd, and Martin Monsma. *The Church Order Commentary: A Brief Explanation of the Church Order of the Christian Reformed Church.* 1941. Reprint, Grand Rapids: Zondervan, 1951.

Van Dyken, Donald. *With All My Heart: A Guide to the Profession of Faith.* Sunnyside, WA: Line of Promise, 2007.

Van Genderen, J., and W. H. Velema. *Beknopte gereformeerde dogmatiek.* Kampen: Kok, 1992.

13

The Old Testament, Ethics, and Preaching
Letting Confessional Light Dispel a Hermeneutical Shadow

Nelson D. Kloosterman

"The trouble with the Bible," someone has observed, "is that so much of it is Old Testament. And the trouble with the *Old* Testament is just that. It is *old*."[1] Part of the observer's point involves the challenge of using the Old Testament (OT) teaching for New Testament (NT) living. And part of that challenge involves our understanding of the nature, function, and relevance of OT law.

The thesis of this essay is that what has come to overshadow our understanding of the ethical relevance of the OT is the distinction between the moral, civil, and ceremonial laws in the OT. In popular usage, people often employ this distinction in order to establish the claim that only the moral law remains valid today, either for NT believers or for all people, with the consequence that people restrict their search for moral instruction to those so-called moral laws or imperatives. To dispel this shadow, we need the light of another approach, another metaphor or paradigm, this one shining forth most clearly in Article 25 of the Belgic Confession.

DESCRIBING THE SHADOW: THE THREEFOLD DIVISION OF THE LAW

The threefold distinction between moral, civil, and ceremonial laws does not correspond entirely with other common distinctions used to classify laws in the OT. For example, the rabbis often distinguished be-

1. Wright, *Eye for an Eye*, 12.

tween "heavy" and "light" commands according to certain punishments (cf. Matt 23:23–24). Nevertheless, some would argue that the "heavy" commands referred to what later came to be called the "moral law," so that the Bible's own hierarchy of commandments provides warrant for distinguishing more important from less important, enduring principles from temporary prescriptions.[2]

Where and when did this threefold division of the law originate? Many theologians trace it back to the medieval theologian, Thomas Aquinas (1225–1274), who wrote, "We must therefore distinguish three kinds of precept in the Old Law; viz., 'moral' precepts, which are dictated by the natural law; 'ceremonial' precepts, which are determinations of the Divine worship; and 'judicial' precepts, which are determinations of the justice to be maintained among men."[3] Aquinas grounded this distinction in the words of Scripture in Deut 6:1, which mentions the commandments (moral), statutes (ceremonial), and judgments (judicial) of the LORD. He also appealed to Paul's words in Rom 7:12, describing the law as holy (ceremonial), righteous (judicial), and good (moral).

Before Aquinas, however, John of La Rochelle (d. 1245) had defended, against William of Auvergne, the traditional Christian reading of the law in his *Tractatus de praeceptis et legibus*. In this essay, John clarified the law in terms of its three functions or purposes: "*moralia* clarified the law of nature; *iudicialia* repressed evil desire and served as a source for the wicked; *ceremonialia* signified the law of grace."[4]

Long before such medieval discussions,[5] however, Augustine (354–430) had distinguished between the law's moral and symbolical precepts. Earlier still, Tertullian (c.160–220) had distinguished the "primordial law" or "natural law" from the "sacerdotal law" or "Levitical law." Historians have discovered similar distinctions in the writings of Ptolemy the Gnostic (second century) and Justin Martyr (103–165).

So familiar, then, was this threefold division that John Calvin (1509–1564) could call it a "common division" and Philip Melanchthon

---

2. For discussion and literature, see Kaiser, *Toward Old Testament Ethics*, 39–78, esp 44–48.

3. Thomas, *Summa Theologica*, 1a2ae, 90, 4; for more on the view of Aquinas, see Casselli, "Threefold Division," 175–207.

4. Cited in Casselli, "Threefold Division," 198.

5. For an historical overview reaching back to the early church, see Bayes, *Threefold Division of the Law*.

(1497–1560) spoke of "the old and customary divisions."[6] Later, in the seventeenth century, Francis Turretin (1623–1687) observed that the law was "usually distinguished into three species: moral (treating of morals or of perpetual duties towards God and our neighbor); ceremonial (of the ceremonies or rites about the sacred things to be observed under the Old Testament); and civil, constituting the foundation upon which rests the obligation of the others . . ."[7]

Given the historical pedigree of this threefold division, what are contemporary objections against distinguishing between moral, civil, and ceremonial laws? There are exegetical and biblical-theological objections.

Exegetical objections are of two kinds: one linguistic, the other contextual. The linguistic objection insists that this threefold division cannot be grounded in the various terms used in Scripture, despite appeals to threefold descriptions of the law found in Deuteronomy and Romans. Both in the original and in translations, the various terms can be used interchangeably and synonymously. The contextual objection is that this threefold distinction fails to respect the literary, historical, and social contexts of the law both in the canonical Scriptures and in Israel's life situation. Moreover, some laws can be a combination of moral, civil, and ceremonial prescription (e.g., the fourth commandment). Further, most civil and ceremonial laws embody one or more moral principles. Israel herself did not employ such distinctions, but rather viewed the Torah as a unified divine revelation instructing her in the way of living before the Lord. These objections have led one contemporary biblical scholar to conclude that although the threefold division may illuminate certain passages, "it cannot serve as a hermeneutical principle for the interpretation of the Torah as a whole."[8]

Unfortunately, these and similar exegetical observations have been used by some scholars to argue that most OT laws are therefore altogether irrelevant to modern life. Such a view, however, confuses the condition of laws being situationally *specific* with, on that account, laws being situationally *bound*. To help rescue the continuing relevance of OT law, Oliver O'Donovan has employed the helpful distinction between a law's

---

6. Calvin, *Institutes*, 4.20.14; Melanchthon, *Loci Communes 1555*, 83; cf. Bullinger, *Decades*, 2.2; Polyandrum, *Synopsis Purioris Theologiae*, XVII.v.

7. Turretin, *Institutes of Elenctic Theology*, 2.145.

8. Lalleman, *Celebrating the Law*, 46.

claim, which may well be situational and particular, and a law's authority, which derives from God, whose character lends it a universalizable quality.[9] This distinction supplies one useful way whereby we may continue to insist on the relevance of OT law for Christian ethics and for gospel preaching.

In addition to exegetical objections, significant biblical-theological criticisms have been raised against the threefold distinction. Christopher J. H. Wright is one contemporary scholar who specializes in OT ethics and articulates these objections in terms of the tendency to view OT law abstractly. We must remember that OT law was given within a relationship initiated and established by God for and with his redeemed people Israel. OT law was revealed within a history of covenantal divine action and grace. Much theological preoccupation with "the law" tends to distort the ethical value of the OT by ignoring its narrative bedding, its canonical function, and its paradigmatic nature.[10]

Wright explains the importance of these features of OT law. Since we need to read an entire book and a half of the Pentateuch before encountering anything resembling a legal code,[11] it is unfortunate that the Hebrew word *torah* gets translated as "law," when its meaning lies closer to "instruction" or "teaching." The redemptive-historical context of Israel's ethical reflection and action featured God's past gracious activity on her behalf and God's future mission for Israel among and to the nations. "The combination of these two poles of Israel's historical faith, the past and the future, gave immense ethical importance to the present."[12] Canonically, the law served Israel as the foundation for wisdom, which is the creationally suitable and situationally appropriate application of the law. The law also served Israel's prophets as the basis for their exhortations and warnings calling for repentance and holiness. And because these revealed laws were not exhaustive, but selective applications of

---

9. O'Donovan, "Towards an Interpretation," 54–78; this distinction is discussed and adopted by Kaiser, *Toward Old Testament Ethics*, 44–48.

10. In addition to consulting Wright's *An Eye for an Eye*; see also from the same author: *Walking in the Ways of the Lord*; and *Old Testament Ethics for the People of God*.

11. Although "law" is present in Scripture from the beginning as the Word of God, as Psalm 19 teaches.

12. Wright, *Old Testament Ethics*, 35.

moral principles to Israel's life, the law serves a paradigmatic function whereby Israel was taught to live entirely before her Savior and Creator.[13]

Perhaps we might pause a moment to suggest how this analysis of the threefold division of the law affects the matter of OT ethics and preaching. Using the threefold division of the law as a hermeneutical and exegetical tool or grid for understanding OT law can easily lead to ignoring important elements that are essential to lively gospel (i.e., Christ-centered) preaching of the OT law. Among these elements is the social dimension of the law, which included Israel's relationships to the Lord, fellow Israelites, the land of Canaan, and the surrounding nations. To what extent, we may ask, has the threefold division of the law obscured the value of the OT for social ethics, resulting in a corresponding neglect of NT teaching regarding social ethics? Another element easily ignored is the theological dimension of the law, including the frequent appeal to the identity and activity of the Lord within history as the motive for both giving and keeping the law. The Lord is both Redeemer and Creator, and Israel knew her God to be so, and in that sequence! Since the law proceeds from, and reflects, the character of the Lord himself, walking according to the law, living the law as a way of life, would yield a people who looked like their God in the world, a people who indeed fulfilled their calling to be *imago Dei* in a world filled with idols. Since the law—the whole law—was given after the fall in the context of grace and redemption, it pointed forward to the "more" of Jesus Christ, to the blossoming flower of his person and work. The law given to Israel was replete with the shadows of Christ's future work, and belonged to the administration of the covenant of grace from Moses until Christ.

All of this belongs to the Christian preaching of the OT law!

What would happen to both our OT ethics and our preaching if, rather than construing the law in terms of a "no longer valid *versus* still valid" set of categories or paradigm, we replaced these with categories that fit a paradigm of "less to more," or "bud to flower," or "adolescent to adult"?

---

13. This entire matter of the relevance of OT law for NT living has been set forth by Sprinkle, *Biblical Law*. Despite lacking significant interaction with the work of Christopher Wright, this work is probably the clearest and most succinct presentation of various approaches to relating the Mosaic law to Christian living. Chapter 1 is most helpful, with its explanation of the strengths and weaknesses of a number of contemporary approaches, viz., Reformed, classic dispensationalist, Lutheran, Meredith Kline, theonomy (Christian Reconstructionism), and his own principalizing approach.

Consider this analogy. When I was a lad, growing up in western Michigan with seven siblings, my father instructed us always to wear boots or overshoes outdoors when winter required it. Every spring, when the snow melted and warmth arrived, we put the boots away until the following winter and enjoyed being "free from the law" of wearing boots. As the seasons changed, the principle of the law (wear appropriate protective clothing) remained, while the precise wording (form) of the law was no longer relevant to the situation. In addition, modern footwear has been designed to resist exposure to winter weather. More importantly, part of the moral maturity my father wished to cultivate in his son was to "remember the law" by internalizing this principle and applying it year-round to other areas of life, without his having to remind me. The bud of the law of boot-wearing was to blossom into the flower of mature stewardship. The immaturity of childhood would grow up to the maturity of adulthood. Internalizing a law's principle despite a change in the law's form is the principalizing approach defended by a number of ethicists.

The problem with the threefold division of the law, as a hermeneutical, exegetical, and homiletical device, is not that it is wrong, but that it can easily leave us asking the wrong question. On the one hand, it is an appropriate tool and set of categories for adults who think like children but who need to grow up by learning to distinguish between what is permanent and what is passing. Moreover, it is exactly the right tool for setting free these adults who still act and think in a childish, legalistic manner. On the other hand, the threefold division of the law has the potential to leave us celebrating what we don't have to do now that we're adults.[14] And that is a problem.

The deeper problem with the threefold division of the law, however, is that in leading us to ask the wrong question, it can thereby result in distorting our identity in Christ. Returning to our earlier analogy, if, now that I'm an adult, the best description of my new status consists

---

14. This helps explain why the Reformers, and several Reformed confessions, appealed vigorously to this threefold division of the law in response both to the Roman Catholic Church and to the Anabaptists. Our judgment regarding the limitations of the threefold division of the law as moral, civil, and ceremonial comports well with the Westminster Confession of Faith, 19.3–6, with its discussion of the permanent (general equity) and the passing, something very close to the principalizing approach set forth by Joe M. Sprinkle and defended by Douma, *The Ten Commandments*, 355–90.

in the fact that I don't have to wear boots in winter, then I've not yet become the person my father always wanted me to become.

Still another unfortunate consequence is the claim that because the times and seasons of redemption history have changed, NT believers need not "keep" the civil and ceremonial laws. Terms like "abrogation," "abolishing," and "completing" these laws lead Bible readers to suppose these laws have no abiding value for NT living.

For truly Christian preaching of the OT for NT living, then, we need a biblical-theological metaphor that offers more, not less, than the threefold division of the law into moral, civil, and ceremonial laws. We need a metaphor that highlights fulfillment, growth, and maturity in Christ.

SHINING THE LIGHT: BELGIC CONFESSION, ARTICLE 25

This organic metaphor of growth is precisely what we find in the Belgic Confession, Article 25. As we shall see, the central idea of this article involves just as much what remains and continues in Christ as what has "fallen away" with the arrival of a new season in redemption history.

However, before considering Article 25 of the Belgic Confession (1561), take note of the strong resemblance with Article 23 of the Gallican Confession (1559): "We believe that the ordinances of the law came to an end at the advent of Jesus Christ; but, although the ceremonies are no more in use, yet their substance and truth remain in the person of him in whom they are fulfilled. And, moreover, we must seek aid from the law and the prophets for the ruling of our lives, as well as for our confirmation in the promises of the gospel."[15]

Now compare this with Article 25 of the Belgic Confession (we supply the French original first, for later commentary):

> De abrogatione legis ceremonialis, et de convenienta V. et N. Testamenti. Nous croyons que les cérémonies et figures de la Loi ont cessé à la venue de Christ, [Note: Rom 10:4] et toutes ombres ont pris fin, de sorte que l'usage en doit être ôté entre les Chrétiens. [Note: Gal 5:2–4; 3:1; 4:10–11; Col 2:16–17] Toutefois la vérité et la substance nous en demeurent en Jésus-Christ, en qui elles ont leur accomplissement; cependant nous usons encore des témoignages pris de la Loi et des Prophètes pour nous con-

---

15. Schaff, *Creeds*, 3:372–3.

> fimer en l'Évangile, [Note: 2 Pet 1:19] et aussi pour régler notre vie en toute honnêteté, à la gloire de Dieu, suivant sa volonté.
>
> Of the abolishing of the ceremonial law. We believe that the ceremonies and figures of the law ceased at the coming of Christ, and that all the shadows are accomplished; so that the use of them must be abolished among Christians: yet the truth and substance of them remain with us in Jesus Christ, in whom they have their completion. In the mean time we still use the testimonies taken out of the law and the prophets, to confirm us in the doctrine of the gospel, and to regulate our life in all honesty to the glory of God, according to his will.[16]

It is important to observe that the headings above the French language version were supplied by Schaff from the Latin edition of the Belgic Confession. In other words, they were not original.[17] The English text of Article 25 that Schaff provided is based on the Latin version and was authorized by the Reformed Church in America, printed in its *Constitution*.

For purposes of comparison and commentary, here is the most recent English version of Article 25 in use among the Canadian Reformed Churches:

> Art. 25, Christ, the Fulfilment of the Law
>
> We believe that the ceremonies and symbols of the law have ceased with the coming of Christ, and that all shadows have been fulfilled,[1] so that the use of them ought to be abolished among Christians. Yet their truth and substance remain for us in Jesus Christ, in whom they have been fulfilled.[2] In the meantime we still use the testimonies taken from the law and the prophets, both to confirm us in the doctrine of the gospel and to order our life in all honesty, according to God's will and to His glory.[3]
>
> 1. Matt 27:51; Rom 10:4; Heb 9:9–10
> 2. Matt 5:17; Gal 3:24; Col 2:17
> 3. Rom 13:8–10; Rom 15:4; 2 Pet. 1:19; 2 Pet 3:2[18]

We notice first the title or heading above the article. Whereas the Latin version (used by Schaff) spoke of "The abolishing of the ceremonial law," the Canadian Reformed version speaks of "Christ, the Fulfilment of the

---

16. Schaff, *Creeds*, 3:412–13.
17. Ibid., 3:383.
18. *Book of Praise*, 459.

Law." The Latin version of the heading is mistaken: Article 25 says nothing about Christ abolishing *the law*, nor that *this law* ceased or was abrogated or is no longer relevant. Rather, it is *the ceremonies and symbols* of the law that have ceased, and *the shadows* of the law have been fulfilled. Nevertheless, the *truth and substance* of these ceremonies, symbols, and shadows remain today. The latter *pass away*, having been accomplished or fulfilled in Christ; but the former—the truth and substance—*remain* to confirm us in the gospel and to regulate our life to God's glory.

It seems clear, then, that in the Belgic Confession, Article 25, the word "law" refers not to the ceremonial code but to the entire shadow-filled instruction that constituted the Mosaic administration also known as the Old Testament. The content of this instruction was Christ and his work. Therefore, one must be careful with Calvin's contrast between law and gospel. Calvin saw the light of the gospel shining through the law, such that perhaps it is better to speak of the law as the gospel of shadows. In one sense, Christ and his apostles added nothing new to the law and the prophets.[19] From Luke 24:27 and 44, as well as John 5:39, we learn that the law and the prophets spoke of Christ. Paul wrote in Col 2:17 that Christ is the substance (body) of the OT shadows. In his commentary on 2 Tim 3:16, Calvin wrote,

> But here a question arises. In speaking of the Scripture Paul means what we call the Old Testament; how can he say that it can make a man perfect? If that is so, what was added later through the apostles would seem to be superfluous. My answer is that as far as the substance of the Scripture is concerned, nothing has been added. The writings of the apostles contain nothing but a simple and natural explanation of the Law and the prophets along with a clear description of the things expressed in them. Paul was therefore right to celebrate the praises of the Scripture in this way, and since today its teaching is fuller and clearer by the addition of the Gospel [here Calvin must mean the New Testament], we must confidently hope that the usefulness of which Paul speaks will become much more evident to us, if we are willing to make the trial and receive it.[20]

Consider the implications of Calvin's comments. Neither the requirement of faith nor the mode and manner of justification are new

19. Vonk, *Nederlandse Geloofsbelijdenis*, 495.
20. Calvin, *2 Timothy*, 331.

or different in the NT. The contrast between OT and NT consists in that the former had less Word and more ceremonies, while the latter has more Word and fewer ceremonies. We must be very careful, then, when speaking of a contrast between OT and NT, that we do not define the contrast in terms of opposition or hostility, but rather in terms of dimness and brightness.[21] Here, "dim" does not mean pitch black but less bright, less clear, less developed. Since Jesus Christ is the truth (*veritas*) and the substance (*substantia*) of the OT law, we may and must preach OT law gospelishly (i.e., Christ-centeredly) and never legalistically or nomistically.[22]

The biblical-theological metaphor of growth from immaturity to maturity is strongly supported by another key passage often used in the context of this discussion, namely, Matt 5:17–20, especially when we consider the meaning of *plēroō*. The most satisfactory explanation ascribes to the verb *plēroō* the meaning which it has so often in the Gospel of Matthew when it is used in connection with the relation between Christ's person and work and OT Scripture: "to make full, so that what was open is now realized." Most often Jesus is speaking about the fulfilling of what the Lord had said through the prophets (cf. Matt 1:22; 2:15, 17, 23; 4:14; 12:17; 13:35, 48; 21:4; 26:56; 27:9), but this should not be seen in contrast to Scripture as a whole (Matt 26:54). In Luke 24:44 we read about Jesus Christ fulfilling the law of Moses, the prophets, and the psalms (cf. John 15:25; 13:18; 17:12; 19:24, 36–37; Acts 1:16). Supporting this exegesis is the fact that v. 18 speaks of "everything that will come to pass" (*genētai*, which the NKJV renders incorrectly as "till all is *fulfilled*"), pointing to things that must *happen*, things about which the law and prophets already spoke, but which must still be realized.[23] Jesus Christ came to Israel not in order to invalidate God's entire revelation (law) or partial revelation (prophets), but rather to realize that which was still lacking and remained open.

So in Matthew 5:17, the verb *plēroō* means "to fill to the full," and points to the goal of Jesus' redemptive mission as the fulfillment of the

---

21. This constitutes perhaps the fundamental defect of several essays in, if not the entire project titled, *The Law Is Not of Faith: Essays on Works and Grace in the Mosaic Covenant*, These essays are arranged in terms of historical, biblical, and theological studies, with no sustained attention to the implications of these studies for the subject of OT ethics and preaching.

22. For this explanation we have relied on Schilder, *Christelijke Religie*, 82–83.

23. For the connection between happen/be fulfilled, see also Matt 1:22; 21:3; 26:56.

whole of the OT as a declaration of God's will. Jesus filled the OT law and prophets to the full, as the flower is the fullness of the bud, as "redemption matured." This fullness is an organic, not a quantitative, attribute. The term "fulfill" must be filled out (pun intended!) from the progress of the history of redemption, whereupon it comes to mean the bringing to completion in such a way that what was originally intended now receives its definitive form and cast. In view here is redemptive and revelational progress on the basis of continuity. The metaphor of shadow and reality fits here: to "fulfill" means to reveal the full reality of that which in the OT was portrayed in types, shadows, and ceremonies. In the person and work of our Messiah Jesus, the *substance* of OT theocracy obtains its definitive *form*.[24]

What does all this mean, concretely, for OT ethics and preaching? Among other things, this organic metaphor of growth from adolescence to adulthood, from immaturity to maturity, supplies us with a fulsome, whole Bible, and competent answer to "WWJD?" (a popular evangelical ethical formula, "What Would Jesus Do?"). The OT food laws, for example, point us to God's required wholeness, integrity, and holiness, all of them demonstrated by Jesus Christ and accessible only through union with him. The OT debt cancellation laws point to the forgiveness, mercy, graciousness, kindness, and compassion that are both supplied and required by the LORD—again, demonstrated fully by Jesus Christ and imparted to us through faith in him. And the OT warfare laws point us to the church's ongoing battle between the kingdom of God and the kingdom of Satan in the world—a spiritual battle fought with spiritual weapons, offering gracious terms of surrender, using techniques that are humane and respectful, even toward God's enemies. And if you'd like to see someone who has done all this, who has kept all these laws and truly embodies them, then behold Jesus Christ, the True Israel, the Last Adam, the Real Man![25]

Another benefit of this organic metaphor of growth is that it seems preferable to speak of various *aspects* of OT laws rather than various

---

24. In this connection, Matt 3:15 is very relevant: "But Jesus answered and said to him [John the Baptizer], 'Permit it to be so now, for thus it is fitting for us to fulfill [πληρῶσαι] all righteousness.' Then he allowed him." For this understanding of the meaning of πληρόω, cf. Van Bruggen, *Matteüs*, 92–93, and Douma, *The Ten Commandments*, 376–83.

25. These examples and summary are drawn from Lalleman, *Celebrating the Law*, chaps. 4–7.

kinds of OT laws. Although the observance of ceremonies has ceased with the coming of Christ, the truth and substance of those ceremonies continue to confirm us in the gospel and regulate our Christian living. So then, if we continue to use terms like "abolish" and "abrogate," in relation to certain aspects of the unified OT law, we must be clear that *every OT law continues to apply to us somehow*, either directly or typologically.[26]

By way of conclusion, perhaps we might combine several emphases that have surfaced in this essay. The principalizing model should be filled out with O'Donovan's distinction between a law's universalizable authority and a law's particularized claim. This could help us differentiate between the *authority value* of an OT law, whereby that law continues to obligate us for direct obedience, and the *didactic value* of an OT law, whereby its particularized claim value has been transformed into didactic value through the person and work of Jesus Christ.

The point of this essay, then, has been to argue that both the authority value and especially the didactic value of OT law belong equally to NT moral reflection, to OT ethics, and to Christ-centered preaching of OT law. The threefold division of OT law does retain abiding apologetic usefulness, especially in addressing various forms of legalism and antinomianism that often characterize adults who act like children but who need to grow up. Legalists must learn to distinguish the permanent from the passing, so they can internalize a law's principle without being bound by its form, while antinomians must avoid identifying the permanent with the passing, so they can enjoy living the law from the heart.

Since preaching the gospel and discipling believers are far more than apologetics, however, OT ethics and preaching require the added light of the biblical metaphor of fulfillment and growth, so that the law's gracious context and purpose for the people of God might blossom into the flower of joyful obedience that marks children of God who are maturing unto perfection.

---

26. This approach is modeled for us by the Westminster Confession of Faith, 19.3–6, which needs to be understood, interpreted, and applied within the context of WCF 7.5–6. What has been abrogated and abolished is the *form* of the OT Mosaic administration of the covenant of grace, not its *substance*.

BIBLIOGRAPHY

Bayes, Jonathan F. *The Threefold Division of the Law*. Newcastle, UK: The Christian Institute, 2005.

Book of Praise: Anglo-Genevan Psalter. Winnipeg: Premier Printing, 2008.

Bullinger, Heinrich. *The Decades of Henry Bullinger*. 1849–52. Reprint, Grand Rapids: Reformation Heritage, 2004.

Calvin, John. *2 Timothy*. Edited by David W. Torrance and Thomas F. Torrance. Translated by T. A. Smail. Grand Rapids: Eerdmans, 1964.

———. *Institutes of the Christian Religion*. Edited by John T. McNeill. Translated by Ford Lewis Battles. 2 vols. Philadelphia: Westminster, 1960.

Casselli, Stephen J. "The Threefold Division of the Law in the Thought of Aquinas." *WTJ* 61 (1999) 175–207.

Douma, Jochem. *The Ten Commandments: Manual for the Christian Life*. Translated by Nelson D. Kloosterman. Phillipsburg, NJ: P&R, 1996.

Estelle, Bryan D. et al, editors. *The Law Is Not of Faith: Essays on Works and Grace in the Mosaic Covenant*. Phillipsburg, NJ: P&R, 2009.

Kaiser, Walter C., Jr. *Toward Old Testament Ethics*. Grand Rapids: Zondervan, 1983.

Lalleman, Hetty. *Celebrating the Law? Rethinking Old Testament Ethics*. London: Paternoster, 2004.

Melanchthon, Philip. *Melanchthon on Christian Doctrine: Loci Communes 1555*. Translated and edited by Clyde L. Manschreck. 1965. Reprint, Grand Rapids: Baker, 1982.

O'Donovan, Oliver. "Towards an Interpretation of Biblical Ethics." *Tyndale Bulletin* 27 (1976) 54–78.

Polyandrum, Johannem et al. *Synopsis Purioris Theologiae*. Edited by Herman Bavinck. Leiden: Didericum Donner, 1881.

Schaff, Philip. *The Creeds of Christendom with a History and Critical Notes*. Vol. 3, *The Evangelical Protestant Creeds with Translations*. Revised by David S. Schaff. 1931. 6th ed. Reprint, Grand Rapids: Baker, 1983.

Schilder, K. *Christelijke Religie (over de Nederlandse Geloofsbelijdenis)*. 6th ed. Kampen: Copieerinrichting v. d. Berg, 1977.

Sprinkle, Joe M. *Biblical Law and Its Relevance: A Christian Understanding and Ethical Application for Today of the Mosaic Regulations*. Lanham, MD: University Press of America, 2006.

Turretin, Francis. *Institutes of Elenctic Theology*. Translated by George Musgrave Giger. Edited by James T. Dennison Jr. Phillipsburg, NJ: P&R, 1994.

Van Bruggen, J. *Matteüs. Het evangelie voor Israël*. Commentaar op het Nieuwe Testament, 3rd series. Kampen: J. H. Kok, 1990.

Vonk, C. *De Nederlandse Geloofsbelijdenis. Art. 1–21 en 25–26*. De Voorzeide Leer. Barendrecht: Drukkerij "Barendrecht," 1955.

Wright, Christopher J. H. *An Eye for an Eye: The Place of Old Testament Ethics Today*. Downers Grove, IL: InterVarsity, 1983.

———. *Old Testament Ethics for the People of God*. Downers Grove, IL: IVP Academic, 2004.

———. *Walking in the Ways of the Lord: The Ethical Authority of the Old Testament*. Downers Grove, IL: InterVarsity, 1995.

14

Our Missional God

Redemptive-Historical Preaching and the Missio Dei

WILLEM A. VANGEMEREN

WHEN CORNELIS VAN DAM and I were students at Westminster Theological Seminary, more than a few years ago, we benefited from instruction that emphasized redemptive-historical preaching, interpretation, and theology. Edmund Clowney[1] and Richard Gaffin kept our attention by developing an approach suggested by Geerhardus Vos.[2] The publication in 1970 of Sidney Greidanus's dissertation, *Sola Scriptura*, confirmed to us the relevance and difficulty of redemptive-historical preaching.[3]

REDEMPTIVE-HISTORICAL PREACHING

The redemptive-historical approach to Scripture has a rich and variegated history. The term was coined in an Enlightenment context, and it has been used to designate a way of interpreting the Bible that often distinguishes between two types of history: *Geschichte* (the subjective interpretation of events) and *Historie* (the realm of evidence of events). Evangelicals affirm the historical nature of events through a critically realistic interpretation of biblical texts, whereas the practitioners of higher criticism assess the evidence critically with little consideration of divine providence. The former interpreters appreciate the potential

---

1. Clowney, *Preaching and Biblical Theology*.
2. See Gaffin, "Introduction."
3. Greidanus, *Sola Scriptura*.

interpretations of the text, propose models of reconstruction of biblical events, suggest inner- and inter-biblical interpretations, encourage recontextualizations, and study the *Nachleben* of texts. They approach history from a providential perspective and attempt to understand the outworking of God's purposes.[4] Some evangelical scholars have found their home with those of a more critical bent. They affirm certain truths of Scripture, but they also approach the biblical text with a readiness to emphasize its human dimension.[5]

Early in the twentieth century, Geerhardus Vos pioneered an approach to biblical theology that could well be called redemptive historical. He defined biblical theology as "that branch of Exegetical Theology which deals with the process of the self-revelation of God deposited in the Bible."[6] He countered critical views by highlighting the magnificence of God's providence in the working out of his purposes. Redemptive history unfolds progressively, connects verbal revelation with God's work in history, reveals an epochal progressive movement, and advances the knowledge of God over time.

MULTIFACETED INTERPRETATION OF THE OLD TESTAMENT

It is not my intent to provide a theoretical essay on potential refinement of the redemptive-historical approach. My concern in this essay is more with the pastoral practice where hermeneutics, exegesis, theology (biblical and systematic), the Christian community, and the world come together.[7]

One of the strengths of Reformed theology is its concern with connecting the two testaments. Calvin's commentaries reveal a pastoral orientation of applying the text to the context of his time. He may be accused of Judaizing the Old Testament because of his concern with entering into the world of the Old Testament text,[8] but no one can contest

---

4. Yarbrough, "Heilsgeschichte."

5. Sparks, *God's Word in Human Words*. For a defense of the higher critical approach, see Barton, *Nature of Biblical Criticism*.

6. Vos, *Biblical Theology*, 13.

7. I acknowledge with gratitude the comments by Andrew Abernethy (Lecturer in Old Testament, Ridley College), Jason Stanghelle (my teaching assistant), the students of the exegetical class on Isaiah (Fall 2010), and Dr. Robert Smart, the pastor of Christ Church in Normal, IL.

8. Pucket, *John Calvin's Exegesis*, 52–81.

the fact that he was seriously engaged in bridging the two testaments.[9] In his review of Calvin's approach to the two testaments, Sidney Greidanus outlines the main features of Calvin's hermeneutical method and his preaching of Old Testament texts.[10] He observes the nature of Calvin's theocentric interpretation together with his balanced approach to the historical, linguistic, and literary aspects of the text.[11] However, he chides Calvin for rooting himself too much in the text through the theocentric interpretation.[12] Greidanus appreciates that Calvin broke away from medieval moralistic preaching but questions his lack of a unifying focus in preaching the Old Testament.[13] For his part, Greidanus advances arguments in favor of preaching Christ from the Old Testament in a postmodern church context.

Greidanus's emphasis on preaching Christ with relevance in a postmodern context is laudable.[14] He has made a persuasive argument in favor of a focused and balanced approach to preach Christ as the bridge between Old and New. Greidanus rightly approaches the Old Testament as being "open to the future."[15] However, he may have overstated his case when he likens the Old Testament to an incomplete painting and the New Testament to a "complete picture."[16] I agree that, if the relationship between Old and New were that of incomplete and complete, we must see "every part of the Old Testament . . . in relation to Jesus Christ." However, I view both the Old and New Testaments as incomplete pictures. The use of the Old Testament in the New Testament opens up new interpretative possibilities, but the final interpretation lies in the future.

Peter Enns prefers the term "Christotelic" as the designation for a rich interpretation of the Old Testament. In this, Jesus Christ remains connected to the Old Testament "as the driving force behind apostolic

---

9. Ibid., 37–51. For instance, in chapter 3, he speaks of "The 'Jewish Appearance' of Calvin's Exegesis."

10. Greidanus, *Preaching Christ*, 127–51.

11. Ibid., 148–49.

12. Ibid., 148.

13. Ibid., 151.

14. Ibid., 149.

15. Ibid., 46. Bryan Chapell has also significantly contributed to the practical and theological dimensions of "Christ-centered" preaching, see his *Christ-Centered Preaching*.

16. Greidanus, *Preaching Christ*, 47.

hermeneutics."[17] The variety of the Old Testament finds its focus or end in Christ. Enns allows for other foci as well, such as an ecclesiotelic one. He comments, "the apostolic use of the Old Testament does not focus exclusively on the *person* of Christ, but also on the body of Christ, his people, the church . . . the ecclesiotelic dimension of Genesis 12:7 is an *extension* of the Christotelic fulfillment."[18] Enns is correct in his assessment that the forms of apostolic interpretation of the Old Testament certainly are complex. He suggests that we expand the horizon from a single focus so as to include the story of God's people and the hope and expectations of the Old Testament.

The historical-grammatical approach is greatly enriched by a renewed concern for a synoptic vision where the many aspects of exegesis, theology, and praxis come together. Examples are Vanhoozer's reading of Scripture as a drama (*Drama of Doctrine*)[19] and, at the more popular level, Bartholomew and Goheen's *The Drama of Scripture*.[20] One can now speak of the drama of redemption. It unfolds the theological or providential way of God in the affairs of this world and also in Israel. The theocentric dimension of Scripture reveals the cohesiveness of the God-story (gospel). Many writers, actors, acts, and scenes unfold the *mission of God* (the *missio Dei*).

THE *MISSIO DEI*

Use of the Christological lens in teaching and preaching the Old Testament, together with Calvin's theocentric focus, opens up even more connections between Old and New. The missional interpretation is inclusive of both of these lenses because of its Trinitarian concern. God's plan embraces the redemption of the whole of creation, and each person of the Trinity is involved in this plan. Christopher Wright's work ties Old and New together under the umbrella of the mission of God. He speaks of a "messianic centering" and the "missional thrust."[21] He nuances "missional" as a reading of the Bible that sees God's mission from beginning to end. He, too, approaches the Bible from the perspective of

---

17. Enns, *Inspiration and Incarnation*, 154.
18. Ibid., 154–55.
19. Vanhoozer, *The Drama of Doctrine*.
20. Bartholomew and Goheen, *The Drama of Scripture*. The main plots are the Kingdom of God and the Salvation of Creation.
21. Wright, *Mission*, 29.

a grand narrative, but pays attention to the participants in the mission and to the stage of mission: the God of mission, the people of mission, and the arena of mission.[22]

Wright's hermeneutical interest is matched by his concern for contextualization of the gospel. He argues that the Old Testament generates and responds to "fundamental worldview questions"[23] that encourage an exploration of the Bible by allowing readers to discern "the major features of the (biblical) landscape" and "also other less well-trodden paths and less scenic scholarly tourist attractions" that reveal "surprising and fruitful connections with the main panorama."[24] Wright employs the analogy of using a map on a journey, the Bible being like a map in that it provides "a hermeneutical framework."[25] The perspectives given by the "missional hermeneutic"[26] are such that they open up more avenues, roads, and paths for exploration. While maps do not represent every geographic feature in the landscape, they do provide a reliable way of planning a journey. The "missional hermeneutic" opens up ways of engaging the Bible for viewing reality from several vantage points: God, people, and world.

A road map may be useful for the main roads, but it does not provide sufficient detail for hiking. However, a "web" image is more open-ended; it opens the possibility of first becoming lost, but then discovering details and connections, and enjoying a sense of wonder and amazement. Similarly, when readers of the Old Testament may *get lost in the text*, they discover markers, intersections, and connections in the text. From what they have discovered, they are encouraged to move deeper into unexplored areas. As they enter the text more freely and frequently, they learn to "indwell" the text and grow more confident of reading texts in association. The interpretive process creates nodes of insight that in turn create webs of connectivity. Vanhoozer calls this form of connectivity "synoptic vision." He writes, "By imagination I mean the power of synoptic vision—the ability to synthesize heterogeneous elements into a unity. The imagination is a cognitive faculty by which we see as a whole what those without imagination see only as unrelated parts... Where

22. Ibid., 27.
23. Ibid., 55.
24. Ibid., 69.
25. Ibid.
26. Ibid.

reason analyzes, breaking things (and texts) up into their constituent parts, imagination synthesizes, making connections between things that appear unrelated."[27]

An understanding of the biblical text evidently results from indwelling the text and synoptic vision. To this end, the study of God's Word may need to undergo a change so that the two hemispheres of the brain are brought into connection with each other. Imagining involves an ability to connect things synoptically. Like any skill, it can be nourished or impoverished. New research into brain psychology has demonstrated how Western culture may inhibit the imaginative faculty of the mind. The psychiatrist Ian McGilchrist makes a strong plea for the importance of connectivity between the left and the right hemispheres of the brain. He laments that Western civilization has encouraged a "virtual world" by a scientific approach to reality. Such a world is characterized by a more sequential, rational, logical, and mathematical approach to problem solving, through the dominance of the left-brain hemisphere. He writes that the virtual world is a culture created and perpetuated way of life that is "self-consistent, but self-contained, ultimately disconnected from the Other, making it powerful, but ultimately only able to operate on, and to know, itself."[28] In such a world the brain has lost its imaginative ability but loves texts and encourages reading biblical texts in such a way that "lacks metaphorical subtlety and is highly conventional."[29]

McGilchrist argues that it is, rather, the right brain, uniquely endowed with the gift of seeing the world from many different perspectives, that should be or actually is the master. It forms connections between the information gained and processed by the left hemisphere of the brain, which is only the emissary or vizier. It creates a "world of individual, changing, evolving, interconnected, implicit, incarnate living beings within the context of the lived world, but in the nature of things never fully graspable, always imperfectly known—and to this world it exists in a relationship of care."[30] The lived world opens up individuals to art, in search of beauty, awe and wonder, and pathos.[31] He observes that the present situation is the opposite of how it should be: "At present our

---

27. Vanhoozer, "Lost in Interpretation," 121.
28. McGilchrist, *The Master and His Emissary*, 93.
29. Ibid., 441.
30. Ibid., 174.
31. Ibid., 238–45.

domain—our civilization—finds itself in the hands of the vizier, who, however gifted, is effectively an ambitious regional bureaucrat with his own interests at heart. Meanwhile the Master, the one whose wisdom gave the people peace and security, is led away in chains. The Master is betrayed by his emissary."[32]

The synoptic vision connects the two hemispheres of the brain in interpretation. The left provides the data and the right integrates the data. Rather than limiting oneself to certain avenues and bridges, the person with synoptic vision is open to exploring many avenues and crossing many bridges. In the process of interpretation, the interpreter discovers intersections that he returns to again and again. These intersections create a web of providential patterning.

PROVIDENTIAL PATTERNING OR FIGURATION

The church fathers, Calvin, and modern interpreters have been struck by the magnificence of God's providential patterning in Scripture. There are manifold associations or resonances within the various parts of a book, across books and divisions of the Old Testament, and between the Old and the New Testaments. These intertextual resonances in turn create patterns and figurations within the mind. The testimony of the Spirit enforces a sense of wonder in God's providential working out of his plan of redemption. Figuration results from the recognition of the patterns of God's providence. Though spoken in time, every text of Scripture is meant to be heard across cultural and temporal limitations. Christopher Seitz observes, "Figural interpretation has assumed there is a surplus of intended meaning in every divine revelation. This assumption has a basic theological grounding, involving a doctrine of providence and sovereignty. God remains the custodian of the word he speaks and can by the Holy Spirit effect things through a word delivered once upon a time, heeded or unheeded, at yet a later time."[33]

For example, the *Commentary of the New on the Old* magnificently illustrates the many ways the New Testament authors contextualized the Old Testament texts. The connections between Old and New are much more complex, as is the message of the Old Testament. A paradigm shift in hermeneutics is taking place that requires a much more carefully nu-

---

32. Ibid., 14.
33. Seitz, *Figured Out*, 32.

anced approach to the canonical connections within the Old as well as with the New.[34] Good results can be had by textual isolation, but better results by a careful analysis of texts in synthetic relations to other texts.

Biblical interpretation is not the only field which is experiencing a paradigm shift that involves the right hemisphere of the brain. Fractal geometry is also undergoing a similar development. For example, Benoit Mandelbrot was occupied with the problem of measuring irregular shapes. Euclidian geometry was of limited use in this as it can only be used to measure straight lines and predictable angles, which most of the world does not consist of. Mandelbrot came up with a new concept of doing geometry that he called fractal geometry. Mathematicians shunned him because fractal designs cannot be measured in Euclidean geometry. Mandelbrot demonstrated both the existence of fractal designs in nature and the method of measuring them mathematically. Slowly, scientists began to accept the paradigm shift and to apply the fractal itineration to other disciplines, such as technology, medicine, astronomy, ecology, and nature. Such is the way of paradigm shifts. They are hard to come by, but in time they reveal the order of nature.[35]

Similarly, the variety of the Old Testament cannot be restricted by one approach or another. Typology is a way of connecting texts, of discovering potential connections, and of reading texts in relationship to each other.[36] Connections give a sense of cohesiveness.[37] Francis Young's study of patristic typology unfolds the importance of the Fathers' sense of narrative cohesiveness. More recently, John Dawson[38] has proffered the term figural to describe the Fathers' extensions beyond the literal sense. The church fathers and John Calvin saw connections that set them on paths of interpretation that created a holistic reading. Calvin has been accused of uncritically accepting "allegorical" interpretations.[39] However, James Barr,[40] Francis Young, and Dawson have demonstrated the problems inherent in our modern understanding of allegorical in-

---

34. Seitz, *Prophecy and Hermeneutics*.
35. Mandelbrot, *Fractal Geometry*.
36. See Treier, "Typology."
37. Young, *Biblical Exegesis*, 162. Also see particularly her essay, "Typology," concerning how intertextuality suggests typological connectives.
38. Dawson, *Christian Figural Reading*.
39. See Greidanus, *Preaching Christ*, 149–50.
40. See Barr, *Old and New*, 103–48.

terpretations. The Fathers were proposing extended meanings of biblical texts.[41] Their intent was not to be dismissive of Scripture. In our enthusiasm for a straightforward meaning of the text, we have often separated the children from the Fathers, the moderns from the premoderns.[42]

In order to better illustrate the point we have been developing, a brief exegesis of Isa 48:16b will illustrate how we might become lost in the text, only to discover the textual possibilities within an increasingly larger scope of passages. This approach is multifaceted and encourages a multidisciplinary, multidimensional, and synoptic view of the text. It is a reading of the text that synoptically involves both hemispheres of the brain. In the process of discovery, we may experience what Kevin Vanhoozer calls indwelling the text. As he writes, "By learning imaginatively to follow and indwell the biblical texts, we see through them to reality as it really is 'in Christ.'"[43] The Old Testament gives rise to a multitude of expectations that cohere in the mission of God in Jesus Christ (2 Cor 1:20). These still structure our expectations: the Messiah,[44] the new creation, the New Jerusalem, the temple of God,[45] the new people of God, and the glory of God in creation and in redemption.

A TEST CASE: ISAIAH 48:16B

Employing a synoptic view of this verse, we shall consider one aspect of Isaiah's contribution to a missional perspective by focusing on the enigmatic "missionary" whose voice is heard in Isa 48:16b: "And now the Sovereign LORD has sent me, with his Spirit."[46]

---

41. See the study by Peter Martens titled "Origen the Allegorist and the Typology/Allegory Distinction."

42. See my presentation entitled "Retrospective and Prospective Considerations for Entering the Textual World of the Psalms: Literary Analysis" at the 2009 Meeting of the Evangelical Theological Society. On that occasion I said, "Metaphors, poetic analysis, and linguistic facts create a web of connections. In turn, these connections connect the Old with the New and beyond to reconnect the 'fathers' with their 'children' through the history of interpretation of the Psalms. The synoptic vision is theological at its very center. We discover God's providence and wisdom in the textual witnesses. We experience his transformative and renewing power to recreate us in the image of his Son. We respond to him with awe and a renewed commitment to live wisely and with renewed perspectives on his purposes in the world."

43. Vanhoozer, "Lost in Interpretation," 122.

44. See Rose, "Messianic Expectations."

45. See Beale, *Temple and Church's Mission*.

46. Scripture quotations in this article are taken from the New International Version (NIV).

The issue of this unknown missionary is usually treated as one of *identification*. The rich figural and associative possibilities within the text may become lost in an all too ready desire to solve this puzzle created by the text. The ambiguity of the text illustrates how problematic, and at the same time highly suggestive, this task can be. Synoptic vision produces a thick interpretation of Isaiah, bringing the mission and persona of the servant to the foreground while pushing the actual identification to the background, thus enabling readers in all ages to participate in the mission of the servant.

Scholars have identified many potential persons who might be identified as the voice speaking in this text. Paul Wegner summarizes the main candidates: Isaiah, Deutero-Isaiah, Trito-Isaiah, the Servant, the Messiah, and Cyrus.[47] Persuaded by the logic of the structural connections between vv. 12–15 and v. 16, he concludes that Cyrus is the object in v. 15 and the subject in v. 16b. Both sections begin with an invitation to listen, and both provide evidence of God's use of Cyrus in history.

Wegner's reading has the advantage of simplicity. He connects the two temporal references, "from the first . . . and now" (v. 16), with God's self-identification, "I am he; I am the first and I am the last" (v. 12). The merism in v. 12 is unlike the expressions in v. 16 ("the first announcement . . . And now"). Wegner's structural connection of the two meristic expressions is most interesting. He connects "I am the first and I am the last" with "From the first announcement . . . And now" in such a manner that "I am the first" connects with "(F)rom the first announcement" and "I am the last" with "(A)nd now." He takes both expressions to be meristic for God's sovereign control over human affairs, and more particularly his use of Cyrus as the agent of redemption. Wegner understands "and now" to signify that God's raising up of Cyrus completes his plan. Wegner concludes, "This passage begins with God describing the deliverance that he will bring about through Cyrus and then appears to end by proclaiming in Cyrus's own words that God has sent him to do a job. In the context there are two people mentioned, God and Cyrus—it seems unlikely that the reader is to assume someone outside of the context."

However, if v. 16b begins a new thought, the temporal dimension becomes secondary. We agree with Wegner that God is sovereign in working out his purposes, including the past ("from the first announce-

---

47. See Wegner, "Isaiah 48:16."

ment") and the present ("[a]nd now"). There is, however, another way of understanding the syntax of *we'atta*. Goldingay takes "And now" to be disjunctive, "But now."[48] The thought of v. 16 is broken up by the introduction of an enigmatic agent of redemption. Yahweh had spoken to Israel in the past through Moses, but now he is speaking through his servant, reminding them of the past revelation with its openness to the future (48:17-19). This message has two aspects: (a) Israel had rejected God's revelation with its inherent promises of peace and righteousness (48:17-19) and (b) Israel has a new opportunity to witness God's goodness in the demise of Babylon and the Second Exodus (48:20-21). Moreover, all who do not respond will not enter his peace (v. 22).

Connections within Isaiah 40–48

Proclamation of Redemption: Isaiah 40:6

The enigmatic speaker in 48:16b has its parallel with the first person speaker in 40:6: "A voice says, 'Cry out.' And I said, 'What shall I cry?' 'All men are like grass, and all their glory is like the flowers of the field.'" The mission of the speaker undergoes a transformation as his proclamation shifts from oracles of judgment to proclamation of redemption. The exilic community would see the fulfillment of the proclamation of judgment ("all men are like grass"). The proclamation of redemption begins with the good news that Yahweh is coming to vindicate his people (40:9-10) and to reveal his glory (40:3-5). The message of judgment is thoroughly transformed by the message of comfort.[49] Isaiah's mission was to open the audience up to God's coming to vindicate his people and to the new act of his redemption. Yahweh, the God of the exile, is the liberator of his people out of Babylon. The God of the exodus from Egypt is the Redeemer of his people out of Babylon.

A Global Mission of the Spirit (Justice, Meekness, Faithfulness): 42:1-4

The Spirit-filled enigmatic speaker in 48:16b also resonates with the Spirit-endowed servant in 42:1. The mission of the servant of the Lord is to bring the light of Yahweh's *torah* of justice to the nations (42:1-4, 6-7) and to the covenant community (42:6-7). The character and suc-

---

48. Goldingay and Payne, *Isaiah 40–55*, 2:143.
49. Childs, *Isaiah*, 300.

cess of the servant's mission comes to the foreground. He is humble and caring (vv. 2–3), perseveres in faithfulness (vv. 3–4), administers justice to the ends of the world (vv. 3–4), and instructs the nations in the way of God's kingdom (v. 4). He is an agent of righteousness. He delivers Israel out of exile into a covenant relationship with Yahweh (vv. 6–7) and brings the light of the new era to the nations (vv. 7–12).

The Failure of the Servant: 42:19

The introduction of the enigmatic speaker in 48:16b also finds a resonance in the messenger introduced in 42:19. There the servant of the Lord is a frail messenger: "Who is blind but my servant, and deaf like the messenger I send? Who is blind like the one committed to me, blind like the servant of the Lord?" In the course of the argument, it becomes clearer that the servant of the Lord is rebellious, deserves judgment, and is incapacitated. Chapter 48 closes the argument of chapters 40–48 with a series of renewed appeals to respond to God's promise to bring the exile to an end and to deliver "captive Israel."

Israel's God

The prophetic ministry in chapters 40–48 is intended to respond to the complaints and superstitions of Israel and to impress them with God's overwhelming power and plan of redemption. The final chapter of this section, chapter 48, calls for a response with the repeated call "listen" (vv. 1, 12, 14, 16). The words of the enigmatic messenger (48:16b) are somehow connected with Yahweh's mission. A closer look at the three titles given to God in Isa 48:16–17 further illustrates this connection.

Sovereign Lord—The compound title "sovereign Lord" connects the various parts of Isaiah. In chapters 40–48, the title only occurs in 48:16b, where its use is of singular importance, and in 40:10, "See, the Sovereign Lord comes with power, and his arm rules for him. See, his reward is with him, and his recompense accompanies him." The resonance between the two uses may link the mission of the enigmatic servant with the prophetic proclamation of the coming of the Sovereign Lord to deliver Zion.

The Redeemer, the Holy One of Israel—In Isa 48:17a the messenger presents Israel with their God. Yahweh is Israel's "Redeemer, the Holy One of Israel." This word Redeemer also occurs in 41:14, 43:3, 14–15, and

47:4, thus tying chapters 40–48 together. Its first occurrence in Isaiah is in 41:14, "'Do not be afraid, O worm Jacob, O little Israel, for I myself will help you,' declares the LORD, *your Redeemer, the Holy One of Israel*" (emphasis mine). Moreover, the opening and closing chapters, namely Isa 40–41 and Isa 48, outline the thematic developments of the entire section. Yahweh has planned everything, including Israel's exile (40:1–3; 48:9–11), the raising up of agents of redemption (Cyrus, 41:1–4, 25; 48:14–15; Israel, 41:8–13; the enigmatic messenger, 48:16b), the demise of Babylon (41:11–16; 48:14–15), the New Exodus (41:4; 48:12, 20), and the provision of water in the wilderness (41:18–20; 48:21).

"I am the LORD your God, who teaches you"—Further, God's self-identification in Isa 48: 17b is reminiscent of the opening of the Ten Commandments, *"I am the LORD your God . . ."* (Exod 20:2). Not only is he Israel's Redeemer from Egypt and the Holy One of Israel, he is also Israel's teacher: "I am the LORD your God, who teaches you what is best for you, who directs you in the way you should go" (48:17). Even when the servant's mission of instruction (42:4) may fail, Yahweh's mission will never fail. He remains the source of the royal and global instruction into the way of justice and righteousness (see 51:4–6; cf. Gen 18:19). The New Exodus is to be distinguished from the first Exodus. The mission of the first Exodus failed because of unbelief (Ps 95:10–11; cf. Heb 4:3). Yahweh's people were cut off from the covenantal blessings: "If only you had paid attention to my commands, your peace would have been like a river, your righteousness like the waves of the sea. Your descendants would have been like the sand, your children like its numberless grains; their name would never be cut off nor destroyed from before me" (48:17–19). Yet, the enigmatic speaker opens up a new and even greater future.[50] Yahweh remains committed to his promises, even though the covenant had been ruptured by Israel's rebelliousness.

Resonances in Chapters 49–66

We have observed the many connections within chapters 40–48, as well as the bookends linking the beginning and the end. Isaiah 48:16b also creates a series of resonances with the following chapters in Isaiah. For

---

50. See Goldingay and Payne, *Isaiah 40–55*, II:147. He comments concerning v. 19b, "these verbs in the final colon leave the future more open."

the purposes of this study, we shall be very selective, but hopefully also suggestive of many more avenues of exploration.

The connection between the enigmatic voice of the commissioned servant (v. 16b), the messenger formula with a restatement of Israel's past and potential future (vv. 17–19), and the command to leave Babylon suggests that the servant is a Moses-like persona. Like Moses, the servant is endowed with the Spirit of God, commissioned,[51] and comes in the name of "the sovereign LORD."[52] We shall explore these resonances separately.

SOVEREIGN LORD

The compound name occurs 26 times in Isaiah, in order to assure God's people that Yahweh speaks, plans, executes, and works out his redemption.[53] The name is closely connected with the mission of the prophet, or servant, who speaks as a divine messenger in the name of the LORD, such as in 30:15, "This is what the Sovereign LORD, the Holy One of Israel, says: 'In repentance and rest is your salvation, in quietness and trust is your strength, but you would have none of it.'" In chapters 49–66 the compound name reassures Israel that the message of the servant is reliable (49:11). Below we will have opportunity to return to this particular title and consider how it is used in 50:4, 5, 7, 9, and in 61:1, but first we need to pay attention to the manner in which the servant refers to himself.

THE FIRST PERSON SINGULAR ("I/ME")

The change from the third person description of the servant in chapters 40–48 to the first person in 48:16b continues in chapters 49, 50, and 61.[54] The first person narrative awakens the curiosity of the reader to the question of the identity and mission of the enigmatic speaker of 48:16b. It is probable that the oracle reminded Israel of her lost heritage (48:17–19) and the exhortation to leave Babylon (48:20) that came from his mouth.[55] His mission appears to be a continuation of that of

51. The Targum adds the gloss "the prophet says." Cf. Goldingay and Payne, *Isaiah 40–55*, 2:143.

52. See especially 61:1.

53. See 7:7; 25:8; 28:16; 30:15; 40:10; 48:16b; 49:22; 50:4, 5, 7, 9; 51:21; 52:4; 56:8; 61:1, 11; 65:13, 15.

54. See Childs, *Isaiah*, 382, where he reads Isa 40–55 as a "prophetic narrative."

55. See Blenkinsopp, *Isaiah 40–55*, 295. There he observes that the lament is closely connected to the third part of the book.

the prophet.[56] In chapters 49–50, he is further identified as a faithful and suffering servant. Since Israel has been unresponsive to his ministry, the Lord calls him "Israel" (49:3).[57] Even though he is suffering shame and his ministry is ineffective (49:4), the beginning of a new future for the nation Israel and for the nations lies in *the new Israel* (49:6–8).[58] He continues the mission of the servant (42:1–9) and lives up to Yahweh's expectations even to the point of suffering. The Lord promises to vindicate him, assure his people of their Comforter, and bring his justice and instruction in the global and royal way of life to Israel and to the nations (49:6; also see 42:1 and 51:4).

The autobiographical voice in 50:4–9 creates a definitive resonance with 48:16b by the fourfold use of the title "Lord Yahweh" (Sovereign Lord) and by the first person narrative. The servant's autobiographical description reveals character, commitment, and perseverance. The faithful servant submits himself to Yahweh's instruction and commits himself to bringing divine consolation[59] to the very people who resist his ministry (50:4). The servant, like Moses, perseveres in his mission, even when he must suffer disgrace and abuse from the very people to whom he is ministering (50:6–7).[60] He is confident of Yahweh's help (50:7–9) and confident that the opposition will come to an end.[61] While Moses had repeatedly called on Israel to fear the Lord (Deut 5:29), the Lord challenges the community to listen to his servant and to trust in the Lord or, if not, suffer the consequences (50:10–11). In chapter 51, we find a new community of faithful servants who have responded to the

---

56. Calvin, *Isaiah*, 8:483–84, and Blenkinsopp, *Isaiah 40–55*, 294, identify him with a prophet.

57. I accept Child's reading of Isaiah 49:3, i.e., "And he said to me, 'You are my servant, you are Israel, in whom I will be glorified.'" Childs, *Isaiah*, 378.

58. The Lord had offered Moses to be the new beginning of the nation but had demanded that Israel be terminated. Isaiah does not speak of termination or supersessionism. The ministry of the servant is to function as Israel should have and at the same time to bring Israel back. Moreover, his ministry extends to the nations as well.

59. The meaning of the verb translated in the NIV as "sustains" is uncertain. It only occurs here. In Aramaic, it has the meaning of "help." There is no paucity of suggestions. The word "weary" (40:30–31) is closely connected with waiting for comfort and renewal by God's word (ch. 40).

60. The theme of the suffering servant is continued in 52:13—53:12. It goes beyond the purposes of this chapter to enter this important section.

61. The Apostle Paul applies the servant's confidence to himself and to all suffering saints in Rom 8:34–39.

paradigmatic ministry of the servant. They listen to the LORD, "you who pursue righteousness and who seek the LORD" (51:1), and his *torah* is internalized by them (v. 7). They are children of Abraham (51:2–3) who will enjoy the Garden of Eden (v. 3) and rejoice at seeing the everlasting salvation of the LORD in a renewed creation (vv. 4–8).

THE SPIRIT

The nature or purpose of the association of the Spirit with the servant is not stated in 48:16b, but may be understood in connection with other texts.[62] A resonance is suggested by the mention of the Spirit in 42:1–4, 59:21, and in 61:1. The servant is endowed with the Spirit and is commissioned to bring the *torah* of justice to the nations (42:1–4). He is called to bring freedom to the prisoners and to be "a covenant for the people and be a light for the Gentiles" (42:6).

The autobiographical voice is also heard in 59:21 and 61:1–3. The LORD promises to continue the ministry of his servant from generation to generation by giving his word and the Spirit to the servants of the LORD: "'As for me, this is my covenant with them,' says the LORD. 'My Spirit, who is on you, and my words that I have put in your mouth will not depart from your mouth, or from the mouths of your children, or from the mouths of their descendants from this time on and forever,' says the LORD" (59:21). We shall consider 61:1–3 below.

The Identity of the Servant

In the history of the church, 48:16b has been interpreted as a Trinitarian formula: the Father sent, the Son went, and the Spirit ministered to and empowered the Son in his mission.[63] Though true, Isaiah did not have a Trinitarian understanding. So from whom does the enigmatic voice come? I agree with Childs that the autobiographical note of 48:16b anticipates a further development in the description of the servant as well of as his mission.[64] The servant is a "persona," whose identity is second-

---

62. See W. A. VanGemeren and Andrew Abernethy, "The Spirit and the Future: A Canonical Approach." In *Presence, Power, and Promise: The Role of the Spirit of God in the Old Testament*, ed. David G. Firth and Paul D. Wegner (Nottingham: InterVarsity, forthcoming).

63. For a limited discussion, see Wegner. Notice that his article is entitled "Isaiah 48:16: A Trinitarian Enigma?"

64. Childs, *Isaiah*, 377.

ary to his mission and whose mission is further developed as the drama of the book unfolds. The identification must be sufficiently fluid so as keep together the mission, role, character, proclamation, and audience of the servant.[65] Efforts to prematurely identify the servant with the Lord Jesus impose a hermeneutic foreign to Isaiah and connects the dots too quickly into a focused picture rather than a web.[66] Examples of a focused approach are given by Oswalt and Motyer. Oswalt perceives two specific predictions in Isaiah 40–55: the prediction of Cyrus' mission and the prediction of the mission of Jesus Christ.[67] Motyer connects the Davidic agent in chapters 1–39 with the servant in chapters 40–55, and with the Divine Warrior in chapters 56–66.[68] We have seen in the many connections within Isa 40–55, as well as in Isa 61, that the prophet presents us with an agent whose divine mission will be accomplished. The particular identity is secondary to the qualities of obedience, loyalty, perseverance, compassion, gentleness, and meekness, as well as the breadth of his concern (Jews and Gentiles), and the time of his concern (until the kingdom of God are established in justice and righteousness).

When we focus on mission rather than identity the reading of Isa 61:1–3 suggests new possibilities:

> *The Spirit of the Sovereign* LORD *is on me*, because the LORD has anointed me to preach good news to the poor. He has sent me to bind up the brokenhearted, to proclaim freedom for the captives and release from darkness for the prisoners, to proclaim the year of the LORD's favor and the day of vengeance of our God, to comfort all who mourn, and provide for those who grieve in Zion— to bestow on them a crown of beauty instead of ashes, the oil of gladness instead of mourning, and a garment of praise instead of a spirit of despair. They will be called oaks of righteousness, a planting of the LORD for the display of his splendor (italics mine).

The opening words (in italics) connect with 48:16b: the ministry of the Spirit, the usage of the divine name (Sovereign LORD), and the autobiographical language ("on me"). The description of the servant is intentionally iconic and includes a network of textual connections.[69] The

---

65. Childs, *Isaiah*, 385.
66. See Oswalt, *Isaiah*, 289. So also Young, *Isaiah*, 3:259.
67. Oswalt, *Isaiah*, 289 n. 21.
68. Motyer, *Isaiah*, 29.
69. Williamson, *Variations on a Theme*, 188, speaks of a figure with "a composite character."

mission of the Spirit-filled servant (see 42:1) comes full circle in 61:1–3. The prophet draws various parts of his message together and gives a holistic presentation of the mission of the servant. His ministry is evidently continuous with the message and ministry of the prophet and of the various descriptions of the servant of the Lord. The proclamation of the good news includes many aspects: presence of divine vindication (40:10), divine favor (49:8), freedom and justice (42:1–4, 6–7), and reversal of fortunes—from shame to glory, grief to joy, despair to praise. Blenkinsopp comments on the similarities between these verses and the message of Isa 40–55: "The wording of the account of investiture and mission is also reminiscent of language dealing with the same phenomena in chapters 40–55."[70]

It is tempting to view this text as a prediction of Jesus' ministry. After all, the Lord Jesus spoke on this text and contextualized it in his ministry (Luke 4:18–19). A closer study of Luke 4:18–19 within the context of Luke 4 and of Luke-Acts reveals that Luke contextualized the quotation from Isa 61 by intentionally including other texts from Isaiah so as to help his readers understand that Jesus' ministry conformed to Isaiah's figuration. It was not a prediction in the narrow sense, but a typological fulfillment in the fuller sense. David W. Pao and Eckhard J. Schnabel perceive Luke's use of the quotation as a means of connecting the ministry of Jesus with the apostles: "the theological significance of this passage is not limited to Luke's gospel. . . . Thus the ministry of Jesus is again connected with the ministry of the apostles in a setting containing a lengthy Isaianic quotation."[71]

Our Lord fulfilled Isaiah's expectations, but so did pre-exilic, exilic, and post-exilic servants of the Lord, such as the prophets and leaders (e.g., Ezra, Nehemiah).[72] The Lord Jesus perceived of his mission in Isaianic terms, and the Apostle Paul did much the same.[73] Further, the apostles exhort Christians to continue the mission outlined by Isaiah and lived out by the Lord Jesus and his apostles.[74] We are not denying

70. Blenkinsopp, *Isaiah*, 3:221.
71. Pao and Schnabel, "Luke," 290.
72. McConville, "Ezra-Nehemiah."
73. See Wright's discussion of "Paul's Adoption of the Servant Mission," in *Mission* 519–22.
74. See particularly Moyise and Menken, *Isaiah in the New Testament*, and Beale and Carson, *Commentary*.

the uniqueness of the Lord Jesus or the unique efficacy of his ministry. Isaiah's vision of the mission of the servant can only be fully fulfilled by the Lord Jesus. However, Isaiah's vision intentionally includes all who pursue God, are loyal to him, serve him with obedience, and readily present themselves as an offering for others. The mission is worth it and is not yet finished. We may share in what Paul calls "the fellowship of sharing in his (Jesus') sufferings" (Phil 3:10).

CONCLUSION

What is the pastor to do with a complex text whose story line continues from chapter to chapter, from book to book, and from one testament to another? The focal approach is tempting but in the end defeats the purpose of providing a good example of interpretation so as to lead God's people to the springs of living water. They may find the main road, but when the road becomes rougher, as secondary and tertiary roads often do, they may become discouraged rather than lose themselves in the text. The pastor who has gotten lost for a while in the text may develop a greater sensitivity to its unfolding plot. The web approach to the text allows for intersections and nodes. The web approach has natural synergy with the missional approach because it leaves the reader open to the freedom of God in working out his plan. The web approach creates a multidimensional topography. When combined with a missional approach, the textual web comes to life in conjunction with theocentric, Christotelic, ecclesiotelic, and eschatological foci. The interpreter may use a map to discover the main roads or themes, but at a certain point he may have to leave these roads for an examination of the panoramic view. Pastors, teachers, and theologians will do well to study the new landscape of the text, to shun generalizations and principles, and to immerse themselves in the text.

It has been our purpose to start a journey in the text and to leave it unfinished. The linguistic, literary, and canonical features of 48:16b suggest many associations within the Isaianic corpus. We have suggested that the exploration keeps one from defining words or concepts prematurely. Interpretation brings together science and art, the left and the right hemispheres of the brain, and in this process the interpreter loses himself in the biblical text.

The interpreters who indwell the text welcome a variety of potential interpretations as they search for meaning and learn to discern the grand scheme of God's plan of redemption. In so doing, they readily give themselves to serve the Lord Jesus, hunger and thirst for a world of justice and righteousness, and persevere in their suffering for the kingdom. They return again and again to understand the Scriptures of both Old and New, and define their lives by God's mission while longing for the coming of the Lord Jesus to bring in an eternity of time in which the Triune Godhead will comfort all who have longed for redemption. The servants of the Lord who indwell Scripture by the Spirit of God incarnate the character of the servant of the Lord in their imitation of the great Servant, the Lord Jesus Christ; of Moses; of the prophets and sages of Israel; of the apostles; of the Fathers; and of the faithful ministers of the church.

BIBLIOGRAPHY

Barr, James. *Old and New in Interpretation: A Study of the Two Testaments.* The Curry Lectures 1964. New York: Harper & Row, 1966.

Bartholomew, Craig G., and Michael W. Goheen. *The Drama of Scripture: Finding Our Place in the Biblical Story.* Grand Rapids: Baker Academic, 2004.

Barton, John. *The Nature of Biblical Criticism.* Louisville: Westminster John Knox, 2007.

Beale, G. K. *The Temple and the Church's Mission: A Biblical Theology of the Dwelling Place of God.* New Studies in Biblical Theology 17. Downers Grove, IL: IVP Academic, 2004.

Beale, G. K., and D. A. Carson, editors. *The Commentary on the New Testament Use of the Old Testament.* Grand Rapids: Baker Academic, 2007.

Blenkinsopp, Joseph. *Isaiah 40–55.* AB 19A. New York: Doubleday, 2002.

Calvin, John. *Commentary on the Book of the Prophet Isaiah.* Translated by William Pringle. Grand Rapids: Baker, 1984.

Chapell, Bryan. *Christ-Centered Preaching: Redeeming the Expository Sermon.* Grand Rapids: Baker Academic, 2005.

Childs, Brevard S. *Isaiah.* OTL. Louisville: Westminster John Knox, 2001.

Clowney, E. P. *Preaching and Biblical Theology.* Philipsburg, NJ: P&R, 2002.

Dawson, John David. *Christian Figural Reading and the Fashioning of Identity.* Berkeley: University of California Press, 2002.

Enns, Peter. *Inspiration and Incarnation: Evangelicals and the Problem of the Old Testament.* Grand Rapids: Baker Academic, 2005.

Gaffin, Richard B., Jr. "Introduction." In *Redemptive History and Biblical Interpretation: The Shorter Writings of Geerhardus Vos,* edited by Richard B. Gaffin Jr., ix–xxiii. Philipsburg: P. & R., 1980.

Goldingay, John, and David Payne. *A Critical and Exegetical Commentary on Isaiah 40–55.* London: T. & T. Clark, 2006.

Greidanus, Sidney. *Preaching Christ from the Old Testament.* Grand Rapids: Eerdmans, 1999.

———. *Sola Scriptura: Problems and Principles in Preaching Historical Texts.* Kampen: Kok, 1970.

Mandelbrot, Benoit B. *The Fractal Geometry of Nature.* New York: Freeman, 1977.

Martens, Peter. "Origen the Allegorist and the Typology/Allegory Distinction." Online: www.pitts.emory.edu/hmpec/secdocs/Martens_Origen_SBL_04.pdf.

McConville, J. G. "Ezra-Nehemiah and the Fulfillment of Prophecy." *VT* 36 (1986) 205–24.

McGilchrist, Iain. *The Master and His Emissary: The Divided Brain and the Making of the Western World.* New Haven: Yale University Press, 2009.

Motyer, J. Alec. *Isaiah.* TOTC 20. Downers Grove, IL: InterVarsity, 1999.

Moyise, Steve, and Maarten J. J. Menken, editors. *Isaiah in the New Testament.* New Testament and the Scriptures of Israel. Lodnon: T. & T. Clark, 2005.

Oswalt, John. *The Book of Isaiah: Chapters 40–66.* NICOT. Grand Rapids: Eerdmans, 1998.

Pao, David W., and Eckhard J. Schnabel. *Luke.* In *Commentary on the New Testament Use of the Old Testament,* edited by G. K. Beale and D. A. Carson, 251–414. Grand Rapids: Baker Academic, 2007.

Pucket, David L. *John Calvin's Exegesis of the Old Testament.* Columbia Series in Reformed Theology. Louisville: Westminster John Knox, 1995.

Rose, Wolter. "Messianic Expectations in the Old Testament." *Die Skriftig* 35 (2001) 275–88.
Seitz, Christopher R. *Figured Out: Typology and Providence in Christian Scripture.* Louisville: Westminster John Knox, 2001.
———. *Prophecy and Hermeneutics: Toward a New Introduction to the Prophets.* Studies in Theological Interpretation. Grand Rapids: Baker Academic, 2007.
Sparks, Kenton L. *God's Word in Human Words: An Evangelical Appropriation of Critical Biblical Scholarship.* Grand Rapids: Baker Academic, 2008.
Treier, Daniel J. "Typology." In *Dictionary for Theological Interpretation of the Bible,* edited by Kevin J. Vanhoozer, et al., 823–27. Grand Rapids: Baker Academic, 2005.
VanGemeren, W. A., and Andrew Abernethy. "The Spirit and the Future: A Canonical Approach." In *Presence, Power, and Promise: The Role of the Spirit of God in the Old Testament,* edited by David G. Firth and Paul D. Wegner. Nottingham, UK: InterVarsity, forthcoming.
Vanhoozer, Kevin J. "Lost in Interpretation: Truth, Scripture, and Hermeneutics." In *Whatever Happened to Truth?,* edited by Andreas Köstenberger, 93–130. Wheaton, IL: Crossway, 2005.
———. *The Drama of Doctrine: A Canonical-Linguistic Approach to Christian Theology.* Louisville: Westminster John Knox, 2005.
Vos, Geerhardus. *Biblical Theology: Old and New Testaments.* Grand Rapids: Eerdmans, 1948.
Wegner, Paul. "Isaiah 48:16: A Trinitarian Enigma?" In *Spirit and the Missio Dei.* David G. Firth and Paul D. Wegner. Downers Grove, IL: InterVarsity, forthcoming.
Williamson, Hugh G. M. *Variations on a Theme: King, Messiah, and Servant in the Book of Isaiah.* Carlisle, UK: Paternoster, 1998.
Wright, Christopher J. H. *The Mission of God: Unlocking the Bible's Grand Narrative.* Downers Grove, IL: IVP Academic, 2006.
Yarbrough, Robert. "Heilsgeschichte." In *Evangelical Dictionary of Theology,* edited by Walter A. Elwell, 547–48. 2nd ed. Baker Reference Library. Grand Rapids: Baker, 2001.
Young, E. J. *The Book of Isaiah: The English Text, with Introduction, Exposition, and Notes.* Grand Rapids: Eerdmans, 1972.
Young, Frances M. "Typology." In *Crossing the Boundaries: Essays in Biblical Interpretation in Honour of Michael D. Goulder,* edited by Stanley E. Porter et al., 29–48. Biblical Interpretation Series 8. Leiden: Brill, 1994.
———. *Biblical Exegesis and the Formation of Christian Culture.* Cambridge: Cambridge University Press, 1997.

15

Foreign Mission by the Local Church

ARJAN DE VISSER

INTRODUCTION

IN 2008, I HAD the privilege of accompanying Cornelis Van Dam on a trip to Khartoum, Sudan, where we both presented lectures at a ministerial conference.[1] Among the many good memories that I cherish from that trip, I specifically remember being impressed by the remarkable energy and enthusiasm of my older colleague, as well as his effectiveness in teaching ministers and evangelists of different cultural backgrounds.

During his three decades of service as a theological professor, Dr. Van Dam has made many teaching trips to countries in various parts of the world. Clearly, the proclamation of the gospel to all nations is a matter that is close to his heart. With this in mind, it seems appropriate to devote some attention in this book to mission work. The topic that I would like to discuss is the approach of the Canadian Reformed Churches (CanRC) to foreign mission work, more specifically, the *organizational model* that supports the foreign mission work of the CanRC. I will first describe this approach, then explain its historical background, and, finally, evaluate its effectiveness.

---

1. Van Dam, "Pastors' Conference," 217–9.

MISSION BY THE LOCAL CHURCH

The approach to foreign missions by the CanRC may be summarized with the slogan, "Foreign mission by the local church." This means that, within the CanRC, international mission projects are initiated and supervised by local churches. For example, missionaries working in Port Moresby, Papua New Guinea, are sent out and supervised by the church at Toronto, Ontario. Likewise, missionaries in north-eastern Brazil are sent out and supervised by the churches at Hamilton, Ontario, and Surrey, British Columbia.

These churches, called "sending churches," take on a huge responsibility. Their mandate includes not only *sending out* missionaries but also *supervising* their work, which involves evaluating reports, giving guidance where needed, and approving important decisions. Unlike other church federations in North America, the CanRC do not have a synodically appointed board for foreign missions. All mission boards are local, appointed by church councils of the various sending churches. There is no foreign missions office, no international missions director, no advisory board, and no website. Although the CanRC do organize some projects federationally, for example, training for the ministry, the decision to leave the organization of foreign mission work in the hands of local churches was a conscious one.

As indicated, this is a unique approach. Most Reformed and Presbyterian churches in North America have taken the approach of establishing a board of foreign missions and maintaining a foreign missions office that is staffed by an executive director and a number of assistants.[2] Given the complexity of international mission work, this seems to be a sensible approach. The question comes up: why did the CanRC decide not to organize their international mission work at a national level? To understand this we need to turn to the history of the churches.

MIDDELBURG 1896

The Canadian Reformed Churches were established in the 1950s by immigrants from the Netherlands. The founding generation came to

---

2. A few examples: the Orthodox Presbyterian Church has a Committee on Foreign Missions with a general secretary and other staff working at their headquarters in Willow Grove, Pennsylvania. The Associate Reformed Presbyterian Church has a board of foreign mission, called World Witness, with an executive director and several other people working in an office in Greenville, South Carolina.

Canada with their memories and experiences of how foreign mission was carried out by the Reformed Churches in the Netherlands. They were familiar with the basic principles of Reformed mission, and they had some knowledge of how these principles had been implemented on mission fields in the Dutch East Indies, now called Indonesia.

To a large extent, the Reformed approach to foreign mission had been determined by decisions taken by the General Synod of Middelburg in 1896. This synod was one of the first synods after the Union of 1892 in which the Secession churches and the Doleantie churches merged to form the Reformed Churches in the Netherlands. The new church federation needed to find direction with respect to foreign missions. The Secession churches had used a *centralized* approach: their mission projects in the East Indies were supervised by a committee that represented all the churches.[3] The Doleantie churches had only come into existence ten years earlier, and, thus, they did not really have an established tradition in foreign mission work. However, they emphasized the significance of the local church, which, as a consequence, led them to prefer a *decentralized* approach.

The Synod of Middelburg 1896 received two reports regarding the matter of foreign mission work: a majority report and a minority report. The majority report proposed a centralized approach by recommending that the synod should appoint a committee that would direct foreign mission projects for the churches. The minority report preferred a decentralized approach, proposing that missionaries should be sent out by local churches. After lengthy discussions, Synod Middelburg rejected both reports and appointed a committee that was mandated to draft a new proposal. This outcome may be ascribed to the influence of Dr. Abraham Kuyper who addressed the synod for three hours and effectively torpedoed both reports![4]

Since Dr. Kuyper was very influential at the Synod of 1896, it is important to take a closer look at his views. It should be mentioned that he worked together closely with his colleague, Dr. F. L. Rutgers, who taught church polity at the Free University in Amsterdam. Rutgers had the reputation of being an expert on the theology of the seventeenth-century theologian Gisbertus Voetius. It is thus no coincidence that there are remarkable similarities between the approach of Voetius and

---

3. Boersema, "'1892' en de zending," 147–62.
4. Boersema, "Een halve eeuw zending," 61.

the final report that was accepted by the Synod of Middelburg.⁵ To mention just one example, Voetius had stated that missionaries should be sent out by churches, not by mission societies.⁶ Kuyper, speaking at the end of a century that had seen tremendous activity by mission societies (e.g., William Carey's society), also emphasized that missionaries should be sent out by churches, just like Paul and Barnabas had been sent out by the church at Antioch (Acts 13:1–4).

Interestingly, there are differences between Voetius and Kuyper as well. Voetius was of the opinion that there is nothing wrong with missionaries being sent out by classes,⁷ regional synods, or national synods.⁸ He referred to 2 Cor 8:19 and 23, where the apostle Paul mentions that Titus and other mission helpers had been chosen and sent out by the *churches* (plural). Kuyper, however, maintained that a missionary should be sent out by a local *church* (singular). This difference is to be explained, to a large extent, within the context of Kuyper's view of the church. He argued that the local church is fully church: not a branch of a national church but a complete church of Christ in its own right. Based on this principle, he said that office bearers, including missionaries, should be ordained by local churches and do their work under the supervision of the church council that gave them their mandate.

In Kuyper's view, this does not mean that local churches should work in isolation. He recognized that local churches may lack the necessary expertise. Already at a mission conference held in Amsterdam in 1890, Kuyper had stated, "The authority and calling to do mission lies with every local church. Since individual churches are lacking in manpower and resources it is necessary that churches cooperate for this purpose. This cooperation should be organized not by way of a separate organization but through the regular ecclesiastical structures, and be subject to decisions made by the churches in their Synod."⁹

---

5. Especially Voetius's *De Plantatione Ecclesiarum*, translated into Dutch by Rev. D. Pol and published as *Gijsbertus Voetius' Tractaat over de planting en de planters van kerken*. Groningen: Bouwman & Venema, 1910.

6. Voetius, *Tractaat*, 40–41.

7. Here classes is the plural of classis, a regional assembly of delegates from various local churches.

8. Voetius, *Tractaat*, 41–42.

9. Kuyper, "Referaat," 176; translation mine.

At the Synod of 1896, Kuyper defended this approach with renewed vigor.[10] He explained that centralization cannot be good because the authority does not lie with deputies but with the local church. However, that does not mean that local churches should not engage in cooperation and consultation. They have the authority to take decisions, but they are also called to consult with the other churches in the federation and work within a certain framework. Thus, Kuyper believed that national deputies are needed as well. He wanted the general synod to appoint a committee of mission deputies that would serve local churches with advice and support in matters such as selecting new mission fields and the division of tasks between sending churches. He also suggested that regional synods should appoint committees of deputies to serve sending churches with guidance and advice in practical decisions. The mandate and authority of such deputies should be regulated in a kind of church order for mission work or, as it came to be known, a "mission order."

Thus, the direction that Kuyper proposed may be summarized as follows. First, foreign mission is the mandate of the church, not of a society. Second, missionaries should be sent out and supervised by local churches, not by major assemblies. Third, the churches together, via their broader assemblies, should formulate a set of guidelines to which sending churches should bind themselves. Fourth, the synod should appoint mission deputies to help the sending churches with advice and to facilitate consultation and cooperation.

The Synod of 1896 approved Kuyper's proposals. Local churches were encouraged to consider becoming sending churches. At the same time, the synod appointed a committee of deputies for foreign mission work. The suggestion to draft a mission order was followed up as well. In 1902, the churches adopted a mission order that contained regulations about various aspects of mission work, such as the training and examination of candidate missionaries, the financial support of sending churches, the use of native evangelists on the mission field, and the installation of office bearers on the mission field.[11]

---

10. Boersema, "Een halve eeuw," 61.

11. This mission order was revised and expanded in subsequent years. The 1939 version is available at www.kerkrecht.nl/main.asp?pagetype=onderdeel&item=120&subitem=3565.

KAMPEN 1951

The decisions of the Synod of Middelburg opened the door for the Reformed Churches in the Netherlands to engage in mission projects with renewed zeal and vigor. During the first half of the twentieth century, many missionaries, mission teachers, medical doctors, and nurses were sent out to Java and other islands in the East Indies. The churches at home received reports about remarkable blessings on the mission field.

As the work on the mission field expanded and flourished, something else expanded as well, namely, the role and the power of the committee of mission deputies. J. A. Boersema observes that mission deputies often usurped power, sidelining the sending churches in the process.[12] D. Griffioen agrees that there was growing centralization, but, interestingly, he suggests that Kuyper himself may have facilitated this development since it was he who often emphasized the need to have people with expertise serving on sending committees.[13]

After the Liberation of 1944, the newly established Reformed Churches (Liberated) made a new start in many ways. The churches had to find new mission fields and reorganize the structures for doing foreign mission work. Due to the painful memories of the heavy-handed approach of the Synod of 1943–1944, there was a strong backlash against anything that smelled like hierarchy. In 1949, Rev. K. Doornbos published a pamphlet entitled "Mission according to Reformed Principles"[14] in which he criticized the powerful position of mission deputies. He emphasized the role of the local church as sending church.

Soon after this, the Synod of Kampen 1951 was convened. Rev. Doornbos was one of the delegates. He found Rev. G. Visee and others on his side, as those who desired to take action against perceived remnants of hierarchy in the church. The Synod of Kampen took drastic decisions with respect to foreign missions. Article 52 of the Church Order, the article stipulating that the foreign mission work of the churches was regulated by a mission order, was deleted. As a result, the mission order, which had served the churches since 1902, was declared obsolete. In addition to this, Synod decided to discontinue the committee of mission deputies. From that point on there would be no general regulations for

12. Boersema, "Een halve eeuw," 62.
13. Griffioen, "De structuren van de zending," 49.
14. Doornbos, K. *Zending naar gereformeerde beginselen*. Groningen: De Jager, 1949.

foreign mission work, and it was considered inappropriate to discuss matters concerning foreign mission work at major assemblies. The responsibility for international mission work was to be carried, solely and completely, by the local churches.

The decisions of Kampen 1951 were hailed as a victory over hierarchy. The expectation was that local churches would take up the calling to send missionaries to all corners of the world. It was expected that mission projects would be enthusiastically supported by the members in the pew, and that mission projects would flourish under the blessing of the Lord.

Others were more cautious. Dr. K. Schilder, reflecting on the decisions of General Synod 1951, stated, "Mission deputies, as a top-down functioning institution, are no more; we understand this and we agree with the rationale for doing this—and thus with the decision as well. Time will tell, however, whether there may not be a need arising from the grass roots level to appoint general advisory committees. There is so much in common that needs to be thought through."[15]

In the following years, it became clear that by deleting the mission order and discontinuing the committee of mission deputies, Synod Kampen 1951 had created two significant problems. First, with the removal of the mission order, mission work was no longer regulated. Potentially, this could lead to confusion and even conflict, with various sending churches following different approaches. Second, with the discontinuation of the mission deputies, there was no longer an address where local mission boards could go for advice and expertise.

In following years and decades, it became clear that Synod Kampen 1951 had been too drastic in its zeal to reform the supporting structures for foreign mission. Prof. J. Kamphuis claimed that Kampen 1951 had "inflicted wounds,"[16] and he supported proposals to reinstate a mission order.[17] Using stronger terminology, C. J. Haak referred to the decisions of that synod as a "black page"[18] in the history of mission work. Along the same lines, D. Griffioen judged that Kampen 1951 had thrown out

15. Schilder, "Jaaroverzicht 1951/52," 168; translation mine.

16. Kamphuis, "Jaaroverzicht 1974," 237. The original says, "Wanneer zullen de wonden door de general synode van Kampen-1951 in éénmaal en onverhoeds geslagen, eindelijk geheeld zijn?"

17. Kamphuis, "Jaaroverzicht 1975," 225–26.

18. Haak, "Vaste beloften," 255 n. 32.

the baby with the bath water—the bath water being hierarchy, the baby being expertise in international mission work.[19]

During the 1970s and 1980s, the Reformed Churches (Liberated) started to move away from the extreme position taken by Kampen 1951. Committees were established in which representatives of the various sending churches could meet to discuss matters of common concern.[20] This was followed by the decision of Synod 1981 to establish an institute for the training of missionaries.[21] During the 1990s, the pendulum swung back even farther as general synods once again decided to appoint national mission deputies.

CARMAN 1958

Having followed this excursion into Dutch mission history, it is now time to turn our attention to the Canadian Reformed Churches. Soon after the first wave of Reformed (Liberated) immigrants had settled in Canada and the first congregations had been established in the early 1950s, foreign mission appeared as an item on the agenda of classical meetings. There was a widespread conviction that the CanRC should take on a foreign mission project, perhaps in cooperation with the Dutch churches, but definitely a project for which they would take full responsibility. The expectation was that the first general synod, to be held in 1954, would take decisions in this regard. In preparation, Classis East 1952 sent a proposal to general synod that the CanRC should establish their own mission project. They asked synod to make necessary decisions to that end.

Soon afterwards, however, the spirit of Kampen 1951 found its way into the Canadian churches. In his book *Inheritance Preserved*, Rev. W. W. J. VanOene describes the developments.[22] In the eastern classis, as well as the western classis, the conviction grew that foreign mission matters should not be discussed at classis meetings or synods. Classis East, the classis that had originally submitted a proposal to synod, sent a follow-up letter to synod in which they distanced themselves from their

19. Griffioen, *De structuren van de zending*, 50.

20. For example, Commissie van Overleg (CvO), 1958 and College van Samenwerking (CvS), early 1970s.

21. Gereformeerde Missiologische Opleiding (GMO), the forerunner of the Institute for Intercultural Reformed Theological Training (IRTT).

22. VanOene, *Inheritance Preserved*, 206–17.

earlier proposal. The rationale given was that "mission work should be taken up by the local church."[23]

By the time the first general synod of the CanRC was held in 1954, it was clear that the churches had accepted the principle that foreign mission work was the responsibility of the local churches. The synod took note of letters submitted regarding the matter of foreign missions but decided to receive these letters "for information" only.[24] Since that time, mission work has seldom been discussed at classis meetings and synods of the CanRC.

This does not mean that the mission mandate was ignored or neglected. On the contrary! Meetings were organized and representatives of various local churches discussed the possibilities of starting up a foreign mission project. An important meeting was held in Carman, Manitoba, in 1958.[25] At this conference, delegates from Ontario and from the western provinces discussed how foreign mission should be initiated. Although the meeting had no power to make decisions, it succeeded in setting the direction with respect to three important issues: (1) Dutch New Guinea (present day West Papua) was going to be the mission field, (2) the church at Toronto was going to be the sending church, and (3) all the other churches were going to support Toronto. A major achievement was the compilation of a draft Agreement of Cooperation that outlined the mandate of the sending church and the support expected from the cooperating churches.

As the CanRC grew in numbers, more mission fields were added and more congregations took up the task of being a sending church. The basic organizational model, however, remained the same. Missionaries were sent out by sending churches in Canada (Toronto, Surrey, Hamilton, etc.) with each sending church being supported by a cluster of churches in its region. Beyond these clusters of cooperating churches, nothing has ever emerged at a federational level. The churches have never appointed national mission deputies. There is no foreign mission office. Whether or not sending churches consult with each other is left to the discretion

23. *Acta Homewood-Carmen*, art. 93.
24. *Acta Homewood-Carmen*, art. 90.
25. A report of this meeting found its way into the Acts of Synod, Homewood-Carman 1958, but it was explicitly noted that the report was not part of the Acts of Synod. See "Kort Verslag van de zendingsvergaderingen gehouden te Carman, Manitoba, door de afgevaardigden naar de synode van Homewood-Carman 1958" in *Acta Homewood-Carman*, 227–30.

of those churches.[26] Clearly, the approach of the CanRC mirrors the approach of the Dutch churches after Kampen 1951.

EN ROUTE TO CARMAN-WEST 2013

In 1960, the first missionary of the CanRC, Rev. H. Knigge, left the shores of Canada to travel to (Dutch) New Guinea, eventually settling down in one of the most remote places in the world, a village called Butiptiri. More than fifty years have passed, and many other missionaries have followed the example of Rev. Knigge. The work has been richly blessed. The gospel has been preached in towns and villages in West Papua, Papua New Guinea, Brazil, and other places in the world. People have come to faith in Christ, churches have been planted, and young church federations formed. Young men from among the native populations have been trained for the ministry. There is much to appreciate; there are many things for which we should be thankful.

After fifty years of mission work, the question as to whether the approach of foreign mission done by the local church still serves the churches well needs to be raised. Since Synod Carman 1958, foreign mission work has seldom been an item on the agenda of major assemblies of the CanRC. Is this a positive thing? In my view, the CanRC would do well to move away from a rigid approach of foreign mission done *strictly* by the local church. While local sending churches have an important role to play, it would be beneficial if their work could somehow be embedded in the ecclesiastical structures. The fundamental question is probably whether there are biblical or theological reasons to cling to the approach of foreign mission done by the local church only. The more practical question is which approach is more beneficial for the mission work as such.

First of all, from a biblical perspective, the argument for foreign mission by the local church is not as strong as it seems. Indeed, in Acts 13:1–4 we have the example of the local church at Antioch that was involved in sending out Paul and Barnabas on their missionary journey. However, as noted before, in 2 Cor 8:19 the Apostle Paul refers to a brother who was "chosen by the churches" (plural) to accompany him on his missionary journey. In fact, there is not much that can be gleaned

---

26. The churches of Hamilton and Surrey have developed a kind of partnership since they both have missionaries in north-eastern Brazil.

from the Scriptures in terms of the practical organization of mission work.

Secondly, from a historical perspective, the prevalent approach appears to be a combination of local initiative and federational involvement. We have already noted the opinion of Voetius, that major assemblies can play a role in organizing mission work. The old Dutch mission at Java and other islands in East India was overseen by major assemblies in the Netherlands. Some classes were very active in this regard; for example, Classis Amsterdam and Classis Walcheren.[27] The mission in the Dutch colonies was often discussed at major assemblies.[28] Similarly, the churches of the 1834 Secession organized their mission work as a federation, and appointed mission deputies to oversee the work.

Thirdly, from the perspective of church polity, there can be no real objections against placing mission work on the agenda of major assemblies. The CanRC have a standing committee for the Book of Praise and a board of governors for the Theological Seminary. Why would it be wrong to have a committee for foreign missions? As we noted earlier, the Reformed Churches in the Netherlands adopted a mission order in 1902. This order left room for the involvement of local churches as sending churches. At the same time, the churches together, via their broader assemblies, were involved in matters such as allocating new mission fields to sending churches, providing guidelines for the training of missionaries, and providing guidelines for the training of indigenous preachers of the gospel.

This brings us, finally, to the more practical question. What organizational model will best support the foreign mission projects of the CanRC? Even though Dr. Abraham Kuyper was a strong supporter of the principle of the local church as sending church, he was also a firm believer in the need for cooperation and consultation. Kuyper observed that it is a tall order for a local church to be responsible for a mission project in a foreign country. Local churches often lack resources, manpower, and expertise. For this reason, Kuyper felt that the churches in general should help the local sending church by adopting a set of regulations for

---

27. See Joosse, *Scoone dingen*, 582ff.

28. See for example the summary of discussions regarding foreign mission work as held at the Regional Synod of Holland-North: *Archief voor de geschiedenis der oude Hollandsche zending. Vol. 1: Aanteekeningen uit de Acta der Provinciale Synoden van Noord-Holland.* Utrecht: C. Van Bentum, 1884.

mission work, namely, a mission order, and by appointing a committee of mission deputies that would serve the churches with advice.

The arguments given by Kuyper still stand today. If anything, it could be argued that doing mission work has become more complex than before. In Kuyper's days, Reformed missionaries worked in a colonial setting under the umbrella of the Dutch government. That context is gone. Former colonies have become independent, the former Third World has become the developing world, and the world has become more interconnected. Leaders of indigenous churches tend to be more confident and "streetwise" in terms of financial issues. Mission boards in Canada are often confronted with requests for financial support for certain projects on, or connected to, the mission field. It is not easy to make responsible decisions on these things.

In addition, a new situation for the sending church in Canada arises as soon as churches are instituted on the mission field and as soon as those churches start to organize themselves as a federation. Instead of just having to deal with the missionary or the mission team, the sending church now has to get used to dealing with a new partner on the mission field: the young mission church and its federation. Again, it is easy to make mistakes in maintaining this partner relationship. It is no surprise that "problems in partnerships" is a frequently discussed topic in missiological literature.

Another change since the days of Kuyper is that in many countries the gospel has already been preached in some way, yet often in a skewed version. As Reformed missionaries preach the gospel in villages and townships in South America, Africa, and Melanesia, they are often confronted with a bewildering mix of pagan, Christian, and secularized beliefs among their target groups. As a result, there is a need for solid theological instruction. Yet, what is the best way to do this? Missionaries have different opinions. Some believe in a top-down approach: train elite leaders as quickly as possible and the effect will trickle down. Others believe in a bottom-up approach: build strong congregations and the future leaders will emerge. One missionary may feel that a full-scale seminary should be established on the mission field while another may feel that short courses are more beneficial. How is a local mission board in Canada going to work through all the relevant issues and be able to give direction to its missionaries on the field?

These things are not mentioned in order to say anything negative about the work of members of mission boards of sending churches. On the contrary, the hard work that is being done voluntarily is greatly appreciated. Some members of mission boards build up wisdom and expertise as they continue to serve! At the same time, it should be recognized that local mission boards are doing their work in relative isolation, without the benefit of organized consultation, and without being able to draw from the expertise that is available elsewhere in the federation and in ecumenical organizations such as North American Presbyterian and Reformed Council (NAPARC) and the International Conference of Reformed Churches (ICRC).

In conclusion, then, I believe that the CanRC are still too much in the Kampen 1951 mode, and I suggest that the churches could learn from the wisdom in the Middelburg 1896 approach. A prudent way forward would be for a general synod to appoint mission deputies with a mainly advisory mandate. In other words, while mission deputies should be mandated to serve the churches, particularly sending churches, with advice, information, and expertise, the mandate should also make clear that this body should not develop into a centralized board of mission. The task of sending out missionaries should remain the prerogative of local churches. At the same time, there is no doubt in my mind that our sending churches would benefit in significant ways from the services of synodically appointed mission deputies.

In closing, we note that the next general synod of the Canadian Reformed Churches is scheduled to be held in 2013 in Carman, Manitoba. We are reminded of the mission meeting of 1958 that was held in the same place. May the matter of foreign missions be a significant item on the agenda of Carman-West 2013!

BIBLIOGRAPHY

Acta van de Synod Homewood-Carman 1958 der Canadian Reformed Churches. Smithville, ON: Canadian Reformed Publishing House, n.d.

Boersema, J. A. "'1892' en de zending." In *Vereniging in wederkeer: Opstellen over de Vereniging van 1892*, edited by D. Deddens and M. te Velde, 147–62. Barneveld: De Vuurbaak, 1992.

———. "Een halve eeuw zending van de Gereformeerde Kerken (Vrijgemaakt) tegen de achtergrond van Middelburg 1896." In *ZGKN100: Een bundel opstellen over de Zending van de Gereformeerde Kerken in Nederland ter gelegenheid van de honderdjarige herdenking van de Synode van Middelburg 1896*, edited by P. N. Holtrop, 57–76. Kampen: Stichting WZOK, 1996.

Doornbos, K. *Zending naar gereformeerde beginselen*. Groningen: De Jager, 1949.

Griffioen, D. "De structuren van de zending." In *Met vereende kerken: De 'zendingssynode' van Middelburg 1896 na 100 jaar herdacht*, edited by C. J. Haak et al., 45–57. Zwolle: Gereformeerde Missiologische Opleiding, 1996.

Haak, C. J. "Vaste beloften, ook voor allen die verre zijn. Zendingsgeschiedenis vanaf de Vrijmaking." In *Vrijmaking—Wederkeer: Vijftig jaar Vrijmaking in beeld gebracht 1944-1994*, edited by D. Deddens and M. te Velde, 247–75. Barneveld: De Vuurbaak, 1994.

Joosse, L. J. *Scoone dingen sijn swaere dingen: een onderzoek naar de motieven en activiteiten in de Nederlanden tot verbreiding van de gereformeerde religie gedurende de eerste helft van de zeventiende eeuw.* Leiden: Groen, 1992.

Kamphuis, J. "Jaaroverzicht 1974." In *Handboek ten dienste van de Gereformeerde Kerken in Nederland 1975*, 228–42. Goes: Oosterbaan & Le Cointre, 1975.

Kamphuis, J. "Jaaroverzicht 1975." In *Handboek ten dienste van de Gereformeerde Kerken in Nederland 1976*, 220–38. Goes: Oosterbaan & Le Cointre, 1976.

Kuyper, A. "Referaat van Dr A. Kuyper over 'zending.'" In *ZGKN100: Een bundel opstellen over de Zending van de Gereformeerde kerken in Nederland ter gelegenheid van de honderdjarige herdenking van de Synode van Middelburg 1896*, edited by P. N. Holtrop, 174–7. Kampen: Stichting WZOK, 1996.

Schilder, K. "Jaaroverzicht 1951/52." In *Handboek ten dienste van de Gereformeerde Kerken in Nederland 1952*, 129–91. Goes: Oosterbaan & Le Cointre, 1952.

Van Dam, C. "A Pastors' Conference in Sudan." *Clarion* 57 (2008) 217–9.

VanOene, W. W. J. *Inheritance Preserved: The Canadian Reformed Churches and Free Reformed Churches of Australia in Historical Perspective.* Revised edition. Winnipeg: Premier, 1991.

Voetius, Gijsbertus. *Tractaat over de planting en de planters van kerken*. Translated by D. Pol. Groningen: Bouwman & Venema, 1910.

Bibliography

Publications by Cornelis Van Dam[1]

BOOKS AND BOOKLETS

La teología de la liberación, trans. R. Cerni. Rijswijk: FELiRe, 1978. [Translation of "The Theology of Liberation," *Clarion* 25.13 (1976) 214–15, 224; 25.14 (1976) 234–35].

Los Testigos de Jehová desenmascarados, trans. H. Casanova. Rijswijk: FELiRe, 1979. [Translation of "Jehovah's Witnesses." In *Test the Spirits*, ed. G. Van Dooren, 13–32. Winnipeg: Premier, 1979].

"The Urim and Thummim. A Study of an Old Testament Means of Revelation." 2 vols. ThD dissertation. Kampen: Uitgeverij Van den Berg, 1986.

Divorce and Remarriage in the Light of Old Testament Principles and Their Application in the New Testament. Winnipeg: Premier, 1996.

The Urim and Thummim. A Means of Revelation in Ancient Israel. Winona Lake: Eisenbrauns, 1997.

Fathers and Mothers at Home and at School. Reformed Guardian, New Series 8. Kelmscott: n.p., 2000.

Perspectives on Worship, Law and Faith: The Old Testament Speaks Today. Kelmscott: Pro Ecclesia, 2000.

The Elder: Today's Ministry Rooted in All of Scripture. Explorations in Biblical Theology. Phillipsburg: P&R, 2009.

God and Government: A Biblical Perspective on the Role of the State. ARPA Canada, 2009.

EDITORIAL WORK

The Challenge of Church Union. Speeches and Discussions on Reformed Identity and Ecumenicity, ed. C. Van Dam. The Burlington Reformed Study Centre 1. Winnipeg: Premier, 1993.

The Liberation: Causes and Consequences. The Struggle in the Reformed Churches in the Netherlands in the 1940s, ed. C. Van Dam. Winnipeg: Premier, 1995.

Tinkering with Creation? The Promise and Perils of Genetic Engineering, ed. C. Van Dam. The Burlington Reformed Study Centre 4. Winnipeg: Premier, 2002.

De Jong, Jack. *Treasures New and Old: Exploring the Riches of Scripture*, ed. C. Van Dam. Winnipeg: Premier, 2004.

Work and Leisure in the Life of a Christian, eds. C. Van Dam and Kristen Kottelenberg-Alkema. The Burlington Reformed Study Centre 5. Winnipeg: Premier, 2004.

Gootjes, Nicolaas H. *Teaching and Preaching the Word: Studies in Dogmatics and Homiletics*, ed. C. Van Dam. Winnipeg: Premier, 2010.

Editor of *Clarion* from Jan 1998 to June 2000; coeditor from 1986 to 1997, and from 2005 to the present.

---

1. All entries in each section are in chronological order.

ARTICLES

"The Office of David: A Preliminary Look at David as *Nagid*." *Koinonia* 1.1 (1978) 5–19.

"Jehovah's Witnesses." In *Test the Spirits*, ed. G. Van Dooren, 13–32. Winnipeg: Premier, 1979.

"Roman Catholicism." In *Test the Spirits*, ed. G. Van Dooren, 103–20. Winnipeg: Premier, 1979.

"Wisdom, Knowledge, and Teaching." In *Thinking Christianly About Education: A Reader for Use at the Canadian Reformed Teachers College, Hamilton, Ontario*, ed. T. M. P. van der Ven, 110–17. Hamilton: n.p., 1987. [Reprinted in *Canadian Reformed Teachers' Association Magazine* 15.2 (1985).]

"The Elder in the Gate: Some Aspects of the Judicial Task of Elders in the Old Testament and its Relevance for Today." *Diakonia* 1.4 (1988) 11–16.

"The Diaconal Task: Some Old Testament Roots and Their Continuing Significance." *Diakonia* 2.2 (1988) 30–36. [Reprinted in *Deacons Go Visiting!* ed. W. Huizinga. The Reformed Guardian, New Series 16. Kelmscott: n.p., 2003.]

"The Meaning of בִּשְׁגָגָה." In *Unity in Diversity*, ed. R. Faber, 13–24. Hamilton: The Senate of the Theological College of the Canadian Reformed Churches, 1989.

"The Elder as Preserver and Nurturer of Life in the Covenant." In *Proceedings of the International Conference of Reformed Churches June, 19–28, 1989*, 277–98. Winnipeg: Premier, 1989.

"The New Revised Standard Version: Some First Impressions." *Christian Renewal* 9.5 (1990) 12, 17; also appeared in *Clarion* 40.3 (1991) 55–56.

"How Shall We Read Genesis 1?" *Mid-America Journal of Theology* 6 (1990) 19–32.

"The Origin and Character of Sacrifice in Scripture." *Mid-America Journal of Theology* 7 (1991) 3–16.

"The Incense Offering in Its Biblical Context." *Mid-America Journal of Theology* 7 (1991) 179–84.

"The Burnt Offering in Its Biblical Context." *Mid-America Journal of Theology* 7 (1991) 195–206.

"Pascal Centrum in Canada onderzoekt de relatie tussen geloof en wetenschap." *Nederlands Dagblad*, 2 March 1991.

"Reformed Theology in Canada." *Acta Theologica* 12 (1992) 28–32.

"Duidelijke Taal. De boodschap van de hemelen volgens Psalm 19:5a." In *Een Sprekend Begin. Opstellen aangeboden aan Prof. Drs. H. M. Ohmann*, ed. R. ter Beek et al, 86–93. Kampen: Uitgeverij Van den Berg, 1993.

"When Brothers Dwell in Unity [Ps 133]." In *The Challenge of Church Union: Speeches and Discussions on Reformed Identity and Ecumenicity*, ed. C. Van Dam, 201–12. Burlington Reformed Study Centre 1. Winnipeg: Premier, 1993. Originally published in *Clarion* 41.19 (1992) 399–402.

"Creation and Evolution in the Classroom." *Canadian Reformed Teachers' Association Magazine* 24.3 (1994) 4–10.

"Divorce and Remarriage: A Closer Look at Some Exegetical Arguments for an Indissoluble Marriage Bond and Some Consequences." *Koinonia* 17.1 (1996) 1–27.

"Education in the Word in an Age of the Picture." In *Bible Instruction and Curriculum: Proceedings of the Bible History Conference August, 1996*, 69–85. Hamilton: CARE, 1997. Originally published in *Clarion* 37.25 (1988) 524–25; 38.1 (1989) 8–9; 38.2 (1989) 31–32.

"God with Us: The Gospel of the Holy of Holies." *Koinonia* 18.2 (1999) 2–14.

"Reformed or Evangelical?" In *The Challenge of Being Reformed Today*, ed. J. Mulder, 102-7. Burlington Reformed Study Centre 3. Winnipeg: Premier, 1999.
"Behind the Curtain: The Gospel of the Holy of Holies." *Modern Reformation* 10.1 (2001) 8-12.
"A Check of the Accuracy of Kurelek's Painting of Hebrew Scripture." Unpublished manuscript submitted to the Niagara Falls Art Gallery at their request. 2001. (Based on Kurelek's paintings as published in William Kurelek, *The Passion of Christ according to Saint Matthew*. Niagara Art Gallery and Museum: Niagara Falls, ON, 1975).
"Saying Farewell to Dr. De Jong." In *Treasures New and Old: Exploring the Riches of Scripture*, ed. C. Van Dam, vii-xi. Winnipeg: Premier, 2004.
"Response to Dr. Gideon Strauss." In *Work and Leisure in the Life of a Christian*, eds. C. Van Dam and Kristen Kottelenberg-Alkema, 55-58. The Burlington Reformed Study Centre 5. Winnipeg: Premier, 2004.
"Words Spoken at the Memorial Service of Dr. Jelle Faber." In *In Memory of Dr. Jelle Faber*, 52-54. Hamilton: n.p., 2005.
"Theological College Evening 2005 of the Canadian Reformed Churches." *The Outlook* 55.10 (Nov 2005) 22-23.
"This is My Father's World." *Christian Legal Journal* (Spring 2010) 17-19.

CONTRIBUTIONS TO REFERENCE WORKS

"Urim and Thummim." In *The International Standard Bible Encyclopedia*, edited by G. W. Bromiley, 4:957-59. Rev. ed. Grand Rapids: Eerdmans, 1988.
"Urim and Thummim." In *Evangelical Dictionary of Biblical Theology*, edited by W. Ellwell, 794. Grand Rapids: Baker, 1996.
"Elder." In *Evangelical Dictionary of Biblical Theology*, edited by W. Ellwell, 197-99. Grand Rapids: Baker, 1996.
Various articles in *The New International Dictionary of Old Testament Theology and Exegesis*, ed. W. Van Gemeren. 5 vols. Grand Rapids: Zondervan, 1997.
אָבַד "perish, be destroyed" (1.223-25)
אֲגוֹרָה "payment" (1.254-55)
אוּרִים; תֻּמִּים "Urim; Thummim" (1.329-31)
אֵיד "disaster" (1.371)
אָרָה "pluck (grapes)" (1.498-99)
בָּדַד "alone, separate" (1.600-2)
בָּדַל "separate" (1.603-5)
בָּלַק "devastate" (1.669)
בָּעַט "kick, disdain" (1.681)
גּוֹרָל "lot" (1.840-42)
דּוּד "cooking pot" (1.924-25)
דּוּךְ "pound (in mortars)" (1.929)
דְּמָה "ruin" (1.971-72)
דָּמַם "perish" (1.974)
דָּקַק "crush" (1.982-83)
הָגָה "separate" (1.1008-9)
הָוָה "become; stay" (1.1017-18)
הָלַם "beat, strike" (1.1040-41)

הָרַס "demolish" (1.1061)
חָבַט "beat from" (2.5–6)
חָבַל "treat badly" (2.11–12)
חָלַק "divide" (2.161–63;
חָלַק "destroy" (2.163–64)
חְתָא "be destroyed" (2.320–21)
חָתַר "break through" (2.330–31)
טָחַן "grind" (2.361)
טָרַף "tear in pieces" (2.386–87)
כָּתַשׁ "grind down" (2.745–46)
כָּתַת "beat fine" (2.746–47)
מָחָה "wipe out; destroy" (2.913–14)
מָחַץ "beat to pieces" (2.920)
מָלַח "be torn in pieces" (2.946–47)
מָלַק "pinch" (2.969)
מַרְחֶשֶׁת "baking or frying pan with lid" (2.1104)
מִשְׁפָּח "breach of law" (2.1116)
מַשְׂרֵת "baking or frying pan" (2.1118)
נְבָא "be whipped" (3.101–2)
נָכָה "strike" (3.102–5)
נָסַח "tear down, away" (3.113)
נָסַע "tear out, start out" (3.117–19)
נָצָה "fall in ruins" (3.137–38)
נָתַס "break up" (3.212)
נָתַץ "tear down, demolish" (3.212–13)
נָתַק "tear away" (3.213–14)
סִיר "(cooking) pot" (3.245–46)
סְלָא "paid (with gold)" (3.258)
פָּאָה "dash to pieces" (3.571)
פִּיד "ruin" (3.614)
פָּרוּר "cooking pot" (3.680–81)
פָּרַץ "break through" (3.691–94)
פָּרַק "pull away, tear" (3.694–95)
צָדָה "be devastated" (3.743)
צָעַן "break down" (3.826)
קוּץ "tear apart" (3.906–7)
קָטַף "pick, pluck" (3.912–13)
קַלַּחַת "pot" (3.925)
קָרַע "tear up" (3.993)
רָעַע "break in pieces" (3.1158–59)
רָצַץ "crush, smash up" (3.1191–93)
שָׂכַר "hire" (3.1244–46)
שָׁדַד "devastate" (4.48–49)
שׁוּף "crush" (4.66–68)
שָׁחַק "grind down" (4.82)
שָׁחַת "spoil" (4.92–93)
תַּבְלִית "annihilation" (4.273)

coauthored:
דָּכָה "crush" (1.946–47)
חָמַס "do violence to" (2.177–80)
כָּלָה "complete" (2.641–43)
מָרַח "spread (fig) on boil" (2.1103–4)
פּוּרִים "festival of Purim" (3.590–91)

"Golden Calf." In *Dictionary of the Old Testament: Pentateuch*, edited by T. Desmond Alexander and David W. Baker, 368–71. Downers Grove: InterVarsity Press, 2003.
"Priestly Clothing." In *Dictionary of the Old Testament: Pentateuch*, edited by T. Desmond Alexander and David W. Baker, 643–46. Downers Grove: InterVarsity Press, 2003.
"Rod, Staff." In *Dictionary of the Old Testament: Pentateuch*, edited by T. Desmond Alexander and David W. Baker, 693–94. Downers Grove: InterVarsity Press, 2003.
"Divination, Magic." In *Dictionary of the Old Testament: Prophets*, edited by Daniel G. Reid. Downers Grove: InterVarsity Press, forthcoming.

CONTRIBUTIONS TO SYNOD REPORTS FOR THE CANADIAN REFORMED CHURCHES

Hosea study and other sections in *The Report of the Bible Translation Committee to Synod Toronto, 1974*.
Major contributions to *Report to General Synod Abbotsford, 1995: NASB, NIV, or NKJV: Which Version Now?*
    Notes on Translation Policy and Technique, 64–98.
    NASB, NIV, and NKJV in the Light of Past Submissions on the RSV, 107–26.
    Notes on Style, 133–43.
    Hosea and Zechariah 12, 196–234.
Major contribution to "Why Do the Canadian Reformed Churches have Their Own Seminary?" in *Committee Report to General Synod Chatham 2004 of the Theological Education Sub-Committee of The Committee for the Promotion of Ecclesiastical Unity*, 221–36.

ARTICLES IN *CLARION*

1969

"Why is There a Westminster Theological Seminary?" 18.7 (1969) 2–3.
"Westminster Seminary Organized and Tested." 18.8 (1969) 2–3.
"Westminster Grows." 18.9 (1969) 2–3.

1972

"The Jesus People." 21.15 (1972) 1–4.

1973

"Of Speaking a New Language: Some Thoughts on the Church's Language in This World." 22.1 (1973) 3–4.
"Singing a New Song: Some Further Thoughts on the Church's Language in This World." 22.6 (1973) 2–4.

1974

"Studying the R.S.V." 23.7 (1974) 8; 23.8 (1974) 10; 23.9 (1974) 4; 23.10 (1974) 3.
"News from the Committee on the R.S.V." 23.23 (1974) 5.

1975

"A School of Sons and Daughters." 24.9 (1975) 2.

1976

"The Theology of Liberation." 25.13 (1976) 214–5, 224; 25.14 (1976) 234–5; reprinted in *Lux Mundi* 2.2 (1983) 5–7; 3.1 (1984) 9–11.
"The Struggle around Israel." 25.16 (1976) 272–73; 25.17 (1976) 284–85; 25.18 (1976) 304–5.

1978

"When Will He Come?" 27.1 (1978) 11.
"The Beginning of Birth-pangs." 27.2 (1978) 33–34.
"The Covenant Service of Love for the Joy and Freedom of God's Children: Some Principles for Diaconal Service." 27.11 (1978) 234–36; 27.12 (1978) 258–59; 27.13 (1978) 282–83.

1981

"The Genesis Flood Account: Revelation of God's Faithfulness." 30.19 (1981) 352–54; 30.20 (1981) 375–78.

1984

"In Memoriam: Prof. H. J. Schilder (1916–1984)." 33.12 (1984) 266–67.

1986

"Pentecost Fulfilled." 35.9 (1986) 187–88.
"Mission Work among the Jews?" 35.19 (1986) 384.
"'The People Who Walked in Darkness . . .': Galilee in the History of Revelation." 35.24 (1986) 482–83; 35.25 (1986) 512–13.
"The King Has Come! 'We Have Seen His Star in the East.'" 35.25 (1986) 508–10.

1987

"The Old Testament and Archaeology: A Silver Priestly Blessing." 36.3 (1987) 50.
"Our 'Tropical' Arctic." 36.4 (1987) 74.
"The Old Testament and Archaeology: Ur of the Chaldeans." 36.8 (1987) 166.
"In Memoriam—Dr. Cornelius Van Til, 1895–1987." 36.11 (1987) 248–49.
"We Pray for the Mission among Jews." 36.13 (1987) 286–87.
"The Old Testament and Archaeology: Abram, Sarai, and Surrogate Motherhood." 36.18 (1987) 384–85.
"Is Unborn Life Human?" 36.19 (1987) 406–7.
"The Task of Government Today: Some Introductory Remarks." 36.22 (1987) 478–79; 36.23 (1987) 502–3; 36.24 (1987) 528–30.

1988

"The Christian Heritage Party: A Newcomer on the Federal Scene." 37.2 (1988) 36–37.
"The Christian Heritage Party and Our Response." 37.3 (1988) 58–62; Response to letter to the editor 37.13 (1988) 276.
"Language and Corruption." 37.5 (1988) 100–101.
"Language and Redemption." 37.6 (1988) 124–26.
"Church and Politics: Some Historical Notes." 37.13 (1988) 274–75.
"Church and Politics: Can We Co-operate with Others?" 37.14 (1988) 304–5.
"Congratulations, Rev. J. Visscher." 37.15/16 (1988) 322.
"The First Verse." 37.24 (1988) 486–87.
"Is There a Time Gap between Genesis 1:1 and 1:2?" 37.25 (1988) 516–17.
"Education in the Word in an Age of the Picture." 37.25 (1988) 524–25.

1989

"Is There a Time Gap between Genesis 1:1 and 1:2?" 38.1 (1989) 4–5.
"Education in the Word in an Age of the Picture." 38.1 (1989) 8–9; 38.2 (1989) 31–32.
"Bible and Science: Some Basic Factors." 38.3 (1989) 54–55.
"The First Day." 38.4 (1989) 74–75.
"What Did the Days of the 'Creation Week' Consist Of?" 38.5 (1989) 94–95.
"Report of the Committee for Contact with the OPC." 38.6 (1989) 121–25.
"The OPC and the PCA: Questions and Answers: A Written Interview with the Rev. J. P. Galbraith." 38.6 (1989) 131–32.
"A Written Interview with the Rev. J. J. Peterson." 38.6 (1989) 132–33; Response to a letter to the editor 38.9 (1989), 204.
"Science, Scripture and the Age of the Earth." 38.7 (1989) 146–47.
"The Report of the Committee on Bible Translations." 38.8 (1989) 173.
"TV at Fifty: Cause for Celebration or Concern?" 38.22 (1989) 462–63.
"The Elder as Preserver and Nurturer of Life in the Covenant: What the Bible Says." 38.22 (1989) 467–69; reprinted in *Lux Mundi* 8.3 (1989) 9–12.
"The Elder as Preserver and Nurturer of Life in the Covenant: Two Questions." 38.23 (1989) 487–90; reprinted in *Lux Mundi* 8.4 (1989) 4–9.
"Family Singing." 38.24 (1989) 510–11.

1990

"Unworthy Slaves." 39.1 (1990) 13–14.
"Mid-America Reformed Seminary." 39.3 (1990) 55.
"Why? More Reactions." 39.21 (1990) 442–43; Response to letters to the editor 40.1 (1991) 14.
"The Sixth Meeting of the Christian Reformed Alliance." 39.25 (1990) 547–50.

1991

"A Schilder Symposium." 40.6 (1991) 136.
"Which Church Order?" 40.8 (1991) 178–79.
"The Inauguration and Dedication of the Pascal Centre." 40.10 (1991) 231–32.
"Genealogy and Chronology." 40.13 (1991) 296–97.
"Reformed or Evangelical?" 40.22 (1991) 470–71.
"Getting Dressed for the Job." 40.23 (1991) 498–99.

"The Christian Reformed Alliance Becomes the Alliance of Reformed Churches." 40.25 (1991) 549–53 [with J. Mulder].

1992

"How Does God Reveal Himself in His Works and Word?" 41.8 (1992) 154–56; 41.9 (1992) 179–81; 41.10 (1992), 201–2.

"Reaching Out to Each Other." 41.11 (1992) 227–28.

"Educating Our Children within the Communion of Saints—Whose Task is it?" 41.13 (1992) 275–76; 41.14 (1992) 299–301; Response to a letter to the editor. 41.22 (1992) 480–81.

"When Brothers Dwell in Unity." 41.19 (1992) 399–402.

1993

"The Alliance of Reformed Churches Met." 42.1 (1993) 10–12; 42.2 (1993) 35–37 [with J. Mulder].

"Stirring the Ecumenical Waters." 42.4 (1993) 84–86. An interview with John Van Dyk, reprinted from *Christian Renewal*, 11.9 (1993) 4–5.

"The Destruction Continues." 42.14 (1993) 306–7.

"Had a Good Holiday?" 42.17 (1993) 355–56.

"To Stay or to Leave?" 42.18 (1993) 374–75.

"Reformed Work in the Ukraine." 42.23 (1993) 493–94.

"A Living Faith?" 42.24 (1993) 510–11.

1994

"Alliance of Reformed Churches, November 16–18, 1993." 43.1 (1994) 4–7 [with R. Aasman].

"The Independent Christian Reformed Churches and the Canadian Reformed Churches." 43.20 (1994) 467–69; 43.21 (1994) 493–95.

"OPC and Canadian Reformed—What Now?" 43.25 (1994) 601–3.

1995

"Annual Meeting of the Alliance of Reformed Churches, 1994." 44.1 (1995) 12–14 [with R. Aasman and P. Feenstra].

"Angels Everywhere." 44.5 (1995) 106.

"OPC and Canadian Reformed—A Response to Criticism." 44.5 (1995) 117–19; Response to letter to the editor 44.9 (1995) 213.

"Church Membership and Baptism—Response to Questions." 44.9 (1995) 213.

"Watch Your Language!" 44.10 (1995) 226.

"Questions About a Decision." 44.13 (1995) 298.

"In Memoriam: Rev. G. Van Dooren." 44.18 (1995) 404–5.

"Suffering in Sudan." 44.21 (1995) 478.

"'The World Passes Away and its Lusts, But . . .'" 44.25 (1995) 573–74.

1996

"A Burning Issue." 45.3 (1996) 50–51; Response to a letter to the editor 45.19 (1996) 425.

"Look Up!!" 45.8 (1996) 170.

"Reaping the Fruit of Gambling." 45.11 (1996) 242–43.

"Which Bible Translation?" 45.17 (1996) 375–77; 45.19 (1996) 419–21.

1997

"Is Evolution Compatible with Scripture?" 46.6 (1997) 122–23; reprinted in *Lux Mundi* 16.4 (1997) 16–17.
"Wanted: More Christian Vision in Politics." 46.10 (1997) 214–15.
"The Light of the Gospel in Mexico." 46.14 (1997) 316–19; 46.15 (1997) 339–40.
"The Need for the Right Focus." 46.17 (1997) 362.
"God with Us: The Gospel of the Holy of Holies." 46.20 (1997) 437–40; reprinted in *Una Sancta* 45 (1998) 91–95; reprinted in *Lux Mundi* 17.3 (1998) 6–10.
"Congratulations Rev. J. Visscher." 46.21 (1997) 471.
"The Need for the Reformed Faith." 46.22 (1997) 476–77; reprinted in *Lux Mundi* 17.4 (1998) 3–5.

1998

"Christian Home Culture." 47.1 (1998) 2–3.
"Zion, the City of the Living God." 47.3 (1998) 58–60; 47.4 (1998) 81–83.
"News from Mexico: Fiftieth Anniversary Celebration." 47.6 (1998) 139.
"Having the Mind of Christ." 47.7 (1998) 154–55.
"The OPC Report at Synod Fergus." 47.9 (1998) 212–13.
"Israel's 50th Anniversary." 47.10 (1998) 230–31.
"The Appropriation of Salvation. Where Are We At? A Summary of the Discussion." 47.13 (1998) 306–7.
"News from Mexico: Juan Calvino Seminary Update." 47.13 (1998) 317.
"News from Mexico: Ongoing Challenges and Opportunities." 47.15 (1998) 364.
"The Work Research Foundation." 47.17 (1998) 402–3.
"The Miracle of the Written Word and a New Acquisition." 47.20 (1998) 470–71; reprinted in *Lux Mundi* 18.1 (1999) 13–14.
"Is Peace with Church Divisions Really Better?" 47.21 (1998) 507.
"News from Mexico: New Developments in Mexico." 47.22 (1998) 532.

1999

"The Future of Canadian Reformed Schools." 48.3 (1999) 50–51.
"Reflections on a Decision." 48.4 (1999) 74–76.
"The Light of the Gospel in the Land of the Mayas." 48.6 (1999) 130–35.
"The Light of the Gospel in the Land of the Virgin of Guadalupe." 48.7 (1999) 149–52.
"The Future of Reformed Education." 48.11 (1999) 246–47.
"Greetings from Australia!" 48.18 (1999) 414–15.
"The Reformed Churches of New Zealand." 48.19 (1999) 450–52.
"An Update—Supporting the Reformed Faith in Mexico." 48.24 (1999) 564.

2000

"'To You O Lord I Lift up My Soul.' A Prayer for the New Year." 49.1 (2000) 2–3.
"Hope for the Family—Closing Reflections." 49.6 (2000) 129.
"The Glory of Christ Crucified and Resurrected." 49.8 (2000) 170–71.
"Creation and Confession." 49.10 (2000) 218–20.

"What is Worship? Some Biblical Principles of Public Worship." 49.11 (2000) 245–46; 49.12 (2000) 266–68; 49.13 (2000) 289–92.

"Changes in *Clarion's* Editorial Committee." 49.14 (2000) 312.

2001

"The Privilege and Challenge of Educating the Lord's Special Children." 50.16 (2001) 384–85; 50.17 (2001) 406–8.

"The Nurturing Rains." 50.19 (2001) 456–57.

2002

"Opportunities for the Reformed Faith in Latin America." 51.8 (2002) 185–86.

2003

"Spreading the Reformed Faith in Latin America." 52.10 (2003) 234–35.

"Elders Seeing God." 52.22 (2003) 513–16.

"Reading Genesis One." 52.23 (2003) 537–39.

2004

"Saying Farewell to Dr. J. De Jong." 53.6 (2004) 134–36.

"Welcome Dr. A. J. De Visser." 53.7 (2004) 164.

"The Demise of Partners in Reformed Education." 53.11 (2004) 263–64.

"In Memoriam—Dr. Jelle Faber (1924–2004)." 53.22 (2004) 538–39; reprinted in *Lux Mundi* 23.3–4 (2004) 61–62.

2005

"A Biblical View of Marriage." 54.1 (2005) 7–9.

"The Weakening of the Institution of Marriage." 54.2 (2005) 31–33.

"Same-Sex Marriage." 54.3 (2005) 54–57.

"In Memoriam—Dr. Karel Deddens." 54.6 (2005) 139–40.

"Our Sister Churches in South Africa." 54.17 (2005) 399–401; 54.18 (2005) 432–33; 54.19 (2005) 455–57.

"Why do We Believe the Bible?" 54.24 (2005) 578–80.

2006

"Kingdom Citizens in Secular Canada." 55.1 (2006) 2–3.

"Under the Blessing Hands." 55.10 (2006) 234–35.

"Sing a New Song!" 55.16 (2006) 378–80.

"Defending Christian Freedom: Our Civic Responsibility." 55.16 (2006) 382–85; 55.17 (2006) 406–8; 55.18 (2006) 429–32.

"Theological Education and Church Unity." 55.22 (2006) 526–27.

2007

"Christians and Muslims: Across the Divide." 56.2 (2007) 26–28.

"Male and Female He Created Them." 56.6 (2007) 126–28; reprinted in *The Messenger* 54.6 (2007) 5–6.

"Cause for Celebration? 25 Years of the Charter of Rights and Freedoms." 56.12 (2007) 286–88.
"Has Mid-America Reformed Seminary Changed its Course?" 56.16 (2007) 390–93.
"Further Discussion—A Response to the Faculty of Mid-America Reformed Seminary." 56.21 (2007) 526–27.
"Why Work?" 56.18 (2007) 442–44.
"To Bury or to Burn?" 56.22 (2007) 542–44.

2008

"Saving Planet Earth." 57.3 (2008) 50–52; translated and reprinted in *Kompas* 17.10 (2008) 14–16.
"Reflections on a Conference." 57.5 (2008) 104–5; 57.6 (2008) 133–35.
"No Apologies!" 57.9 (2008) 210–211; Response to a letter to the editor 57.12 (2008) 308.
"A Pastor's Conference in Sudan." 57.9 (2008) 217–19.
"A Growing Darkness?" 57.16 (2008) 402–4.
"Elders—A Treasure to Cherish." 57.22 (2008) 550–52.
"The Preacher as Priest." 57.23 (2008) 590–93.

2009

"All or nothing?" 58.2 (2009) 30–32; Response to a letter to the editor 58.7 (2009) 167.
"Is Genesis 1 Real History." 58.7 (2009) 158–60.
"The Church and Public Policy." 58.12 (2009) 274–76.
"What's a Good Holiday?" 58.15 (2009) 350–52; reprinted in *Una Sancta* 56.21/22 (2009) 438–40.
"'Sunday Best.'" 58.18 (2009) 430–32; reprinted in *Faith in Focus* 37.2 (2010) 9–11.
"Remembrance Day: A Prophetic Voice in a City Park." 58.23 (2009) 558–60.

2010

"The Future of Theological Education." 59.7 (2010) 170–72; 59.8 (2010) 198–201.
"What is Human Dignity?" 59.13 (2010) 330–32.

COLLEGE CORNER COLUMN IN *CLARION*

1988–1993

"Great is His Faithfulness." 37.15/16 (1988) 325.
"Blessings from Above." 38.16/17 (1989) 347.
"A Visitor from South Africa." 39.5 (1990) 97, 99.
"A New Doctor of Theology for the College." 39.10 (1990) 220–21.
"Much Appreciated Gifts." 39.12 (1990) 260.
"A Special Issue." 39.17 (1990) 346.
"The Library." 39.17 (1990) 355–57.
"Principal's Report, 1990." 39.20 (1990) 425–26.
"Gifts for the Library." 39.25 (1990) 558.
"An Update from Our Theological College." 40.12 (1991) 277–78.
"Notes of Appreciation." 40.17 (1991) 372.
"Principal's Report." 40.20 (1991) 433–35.
"Donations Gratefully Received." 41.1 (1992) 10.

"An Update from Our Theological College." 41.10 (1992) 207–8.
"Principal's Report, 1992." 41.19 (1992) 403–6.
"Many Reasons for Gratitude." 41.23 (1992) 498–99.
"Another School Year Draws to a Close." 42.12 (1993) 271–72.
"Principal's Report, 1993." 42.19 (1993) 401–3.

2002–2005

"A New Season Has Started!" 51.22 (2002) 527–28.
"Theological College Update." 52.2 (2003) 35–36.
"Another School Year Draws to a Close." 52.12 (2003) 287–88.
"Principal's Report, 2003." 52.21 (2003) 493–95.
"Events at the Theological College." 52.25 (2003) 594–95.
"The Winter Semester at the Theological College." 53.9 (2004) 219–20.
"News from the Theological College." 53.14 (2004) 337–39.
"Principal's Report, 2004." 53.21 (2004) 519–21.
"Principal's Report." 54.23 (2005) 560–62.
"First Semester Events." 54.2 (2005) 36–37.
"The Work at the Theological College." 54.14 (2005) 328–30.

PRESS REVIEW COLUMN IN *CLARION*

1988

"RES Harare, 1988 and the GKN." 37.21 (1988) 426.

1989

"The Realignment of Some Orthodox Presbyterian Congregations." 38.1 (1989) 7.
"Operation Rescue: A Biblical Strategy?" 38.2 (1989) 36–37.
"Disastrous Times for Children." 38.5 (1989) 103.
"The Reformed Cause in Britain and Zaire." 38.7 (1989) 150.
"Publications from the Valley." 38.9 (1989) 199.
"The Reformed Church in the United States." 38.10 (1989) 225–26.
"The Menace of the New Age." 38.12 (1989) 255–57.
"The Christian Reformed Synod, 1989." 38.20 (1989) 423–24.
"Recent Ecclesiastical Assemblies." 38.21 (1989) 447–48.

1990

"Russian Christians in An Age of Glasnost." 39.1 (1990) 6–7.
"Opportunities and Threats in Eastern Europe and Russia." 39.3 (1990) 56–57.
"Reformed Christians in Romania." 39.4 (1990) 78.
"A Debate on the Health of the Christian Reformed Church." 39.5 (1990) 100.
"The Middle East Reformed Fellowship." 39.8 (1990) 172.
"Events in South Africa and the Reformed Confession." 39.9 (1990) 191.
"The Christian Reformed Alliance." 39.10 (1990) 219–20.
"Once Again, the Christian Reformed Alliance." 39.11 (1990) 237.
"The Leeuwarden Synod." 39.12 (1990) 259.
"Synod, Statistics, and Questions." 39.15/16 (1990) 326–27; Response to letters to the editor 39.20 (1990) 433.

"Leeuwarden III: Relations with Churches Abroad." 39.17 (1990) 358–59.
"Leeuwarden IV: New Sister Churches." 39.18 (1990) 373–74.
"Aftermath of CRC Decision about Women in Office." 39.19 (1990) 399–400.
"News from the FRC, OPC and the RCUS." 39.20 (1990) 427.
"Who Would Have Expected This?" 39.21 (1990) 448.
"Find Each Other in the Unity of the True Faith." 39.23 (1990) 494.
"New Religious Freedom in Russia." 39.24 (1990) 517–18.
"Schilder Remembered." 39.25 (1990) 572–73.

1991

"The Reformed Cause in Japan and Romania." 40.4 (1991) 85.
"The Reformed Faith in France." 40.5 (1991) 107–8.
"Is Theistic Evolution An Option?" 40.7 (1991) 160.
"The OPC and the International Conference of Reformed Churches." 40.9 (1991) 205–6.
"Christians Can Watch Very Little Television." 40.11 (1991) 253–54.
"Dutch Initiatives in Brazil and the U.S.A." 40.13 (1991) 298–99.
"Developments in the Christian Reformed Church." 40.17 (1991) 371–72; 40.18 (1991) 391.
"A Confessional Conference." 40.21 (1991) 453–54.
"A Response to N. Kloosterman." 40.25 (1991) 556.
"Leaving the Christian Reformed Church." 40.23 (1991) 495–96; 40.24 (1991) 514–15.

1992

"Encouraging Ecclesiastical Developments in Great Britain." 41.3 (1992) 55–56.
"The Orthodox Presbyterian Church: Struggle and Challenge." 41.4 (1992) 77.
"Opportunities in Russia." 41.5 (1992) 99–100.
"Reformed Believers in the Ukraine." 41.6 (1992) 121–22.
"MERF and Egypt." 41.8 (1992) 158–59.
"Fencing the Lord's Table." 41.9 (1992) 182–83.
"Canadian Developments Among Independent Reformed Churches." 41.11 (1992) 229–30.
"No to Ordination, but Yes to an Open Pulpit." 41.14 (1992) 301–2.
"Assembly Notes." 41.15/16 (1992) 328–29.
"What's happened to reading?" 41.18 (1992) 388.
"Notes on the OPC." 41.21 (1992) 450–51.
"The 'Liberation' from and the Struggle in the CRC Continues." 41.23 (1992) 497–98.
"Disciplining Our Children." 41.25 (1992) 545–46.

1993

"Opportunities for the Reformed Faith in Eastern Europe." 42.11 (1993) 253–54.
"Synod Ommen, 1993." 42.15/16 (1993) 332–33.
"The CRC Synod and the Concerned." 42.18 (1993) 379–80.
"Assembly Notes—Free Reformed Synod." 42.20 (1993) 422–23; Response to a letter to the editor 43.3 (1994) 69.
"Ommen Decides in Favour of Women Voting." 42.22 (1993) 465–66.
"Reformed Young People at Home in the World." 42.24 (1993) 514.

1994

"The Retirement of Professor H. M. Ohmann." 43.2 (1994) 37–38.
"NDP Seeks to Muzzle Pro-Life." 43.3 (1994) 64–65.
"Improving Our Experience of Worship." 43.4 (1994) 92–93.
"Get a Life: Throw Out Your Television." 43.6 (1994) 139–40.
"Developments in the Ukraine." 43.9 (1994) 208–9.
"The Issue of Smoking." 43.10 (1994) 236–37.
"Free Reformed Synod in South Africa." 43.11 (1994) 259.
"CRC Synod Says No to Women Ordination." 43.15/16 (1994) 367.
"Assembly News." 43.20 (1994) 470–72.
"Independent Churches Organize Ontario Fellowship." 43.21 (1994) 498.
"Reformed Work in the Ukraine and Russia." 43.25 (1994) 599–600.

1995

"Persecution of God's Children." 44.4 (1995) 93.
"News Miscellany." 44.6 (1995) 140–41.
"Building Seminaries in the Ukraine, Zaire and Korea." 44.11 (1995) 263.
"Roman Coliseum Financed with Temple Treasures." 44.12 (1995) 289–90.
"Expelled from the Reformed Church of America." 44.14 (1995) 328–29.
"The Divided CRC Synod, 1995." 44.14 (1995) 329–30.
"'Prehistoric' Pines Discovered." 44.15/16 (1995) 354.
"Who Remembers the Armenians?" 44.15/16 (1995) 355.
"Selective Gleanings from Ecclesiastical Assemblies." 44.18 (1995) 413–14.
"Christelijke Gereformeerde Synod Meets in Holland." 44.24 (1995) 562.

1996

"Christelijke Gereformeerde Synod Meets in Holland." 45.1 (1996) 8.
"Conservative Action in the Christian Reformed Church." 45.3 (1996) 59.
"Reformed Work in the Ukraine." 45.4 (1996) 83–84.
"Ecclesiastical News Briefs." 45.6 (1996) 130–31.
"Persecution Past and Present." 45.7 (1996) 153.
"News from Our Dutch Sister Churches." 45.12 (1996) 277.
"Synod News from the Dutch Sister Churches." 45.14 (1996) 324.
"The 1996 General Assembly of the OPC." 45.15/16 (1996) 345.
"Synod 1996 of the Christian Reformed Church." 45.15/16 (1996) 346.
"More Decisions from the Synod at Berkel and Rodenrijs." 45.17 (1996) 370–71.

REVIEWS IN *CLARION*

1973–1980

Cheeseman, J. et al. *The Grace of God in the Gospel.* 22.13 (1973) 5, 9.
Davis, John J. *Contemporary Counterfeits.* 23.22 (1974) 17.
Whitcomb, J. C. *The World that Perished.* 23.23 (1974) 13.
Kidner, Derek, *Psalms 1–72.* 24.25 (1975) 24.

1981–1990

Blok, M. J. C. *Ecclesiastes, 15 Outlines.* 37.24 (1988) 500.
Van Dyke, Harry. *Groen van Prinsterer's Lectures on Unbelief and Revolution.* 38.20 (1989) 419–20.
Vanwoudenberg, E. *A Matter of Choice.* 39.2 (1990) 38–39.
Berghoeff, Gerald, and Lester DeKoster. *The Great Divide: Christianity or Evolution?* 39.7 (1990) 150.
Chapell, Bryan. *Standing Your Ground: Messages From Daniel.* 39.7 (1990) 150.
Lok, P. *The Minor Prophets.* 39.8 (1990) 173.
Hoogsteen, Ted. *God Meant it for Good: The Covenant and the Church Today.* 39.18 (1990) 382.
Bijl, C. *As Rich as Job.* 39.18 (1990) 382.

1991–2000

El Camarada Jesus. Liberation Theology, Reality or Fiction? Video recording. 40.6 (1991) 141.
Van Essen, J. L., and H. D. Morton. *Guillaume Groen van Prinsterer: Selected Studies.* 41.3 (1992) 61.
Warfield, B. B. *The Saviour of the World.* 41.5 (1992) 105.
Meeter, H. Henry. *The Basic Ideas of Calvinism*, revised by Paul A. Marshall. 41.8 (1992) 166–67.
Moody, Stuart Alexander. *The Life of John Duncan.* 41.14 (1992) 307.
Overduin, Jan. *Favourite Dutch Hymns and Psalms.* Audio recording. 41.20 (1992) 434.
Deddens, K. *Enduring Joy: Five Outlines on Philippians.* 41.22 (1992) 481.
Calvin, John. *Sermons on 2 Samuel.* 42.2 (1993) 39–40.
Gairdner, William D. *The War Against the Family.* 42.23 (1993) 499–500.
Miller, J. Graham. *Calvin's Wisdom.* 43.3 (1994) 70.
Calvin, John. *Daniel 1-6.* 43.7 (1994) 167.
Van Rongen, G. *"True" and "False." How do we read Article 29 of the Belgic Confession?* 43.14 (1994); Response to a letter to the editor 43.21 (1994).
Calvin, John. *Sermons on Job.* 43.18 (1994) 420.
Helder, Margaret J. *Completing the Picture: A Handbook on Museums and Interpretive Centres Dealing with Fossils.* 43.17 (1994) 396.
Robertson, O. Palmer. *The Final Word: A Biblical Response to the Case for Tongues and Prophecy Today.* 43.21 (1994) 506.
Kelley, Michael. *The Burden of God: Studies in Wisdom and Civilization from the Book of Ecclesiastes.* 43.22 (1994) 528.
Calvin, John. *Ezekiel 1-12.* 43.25 (1994) 628.
Gootjes, N. H. *Both in Life and Death: Biblical Notions in Connection with Today's Tendency Towards Euthanasia.* 44.2 (1995) 39.
Van Rongen, G. *The Liberation of the Forties.* 44.10 (1995) 238.
Vos, Geerhardus. *Grace and Glory.* 44.12 (1995) 289.
Distributed by Reformed Believers United. *Directory of Independent and Alliance Congregations.* 44.15/16 (1995) 363.
Kloosterman, Nelson D. *Useful Study Aids on 1 Peter.* 44.15/16 (1995) 363.
Beeke, Joel R. *Holiness.* 44.15/16 (1995) 363.
Calhoun, David B. *Princeton Seminary.* 44.17 (1995) 388.
Calvin, John. *Sermons on Galatians.* 45.3 (1996) 62.

Weeks, Noel. *Gateway to the Old Testament.* 45.19 (1996) 42.
Zuidhof, A. *The Molten Sea on Computer.* (software) 45:24 (1996) 545.
Calvin, John. *Sermons on Galatians.* 46.19 (1997) 424.
Calvin, John. *Sermons on Election and Reprobation.* 46.4 (1997) 87.
Calvin, John. *Sermons on Psalm 119.* 46.4 (1997) 88.
Calhoun, David B. *Princeton Seminary, Vol. 2: The Majestic Testimony 1869–1929.* 46.9 (1997) 203.
de Jong, P. *Job's Perseverance.* 46.2 (1997) 38.
Gootjes, N. H., et al. *Watching Movies No? Yes? How?* 46.2 (1997) 39.
Selles, L. *1 Corinthians in Twenty-one Outlines.* 46.2 (1997) 39.
Zorn, Raymond O. *Christ Triumphant: Biblical Perspectives on His Church and Kingdom.* 47.7 (1998) 170.
Kelly, Douglas F. *Creation and Change.* 47.18 (1998) 435; reprinted in *Lux Mundi* 18.3 (1999) 15–16.
Rendle-Short, John. *Green Eye in the Storm.* 47.18 (1998) 436; reprinted in *Lux Mundi* 18.3 (1999) 16–17.
Proceedings of the International Conference of Reformed Churches. 47.9 (1998) 221.
Martin, Robert P. *A Guide to the Puritans.* 47.9 (1998) 221.
Brentall, John M., ed. *Just a Talker: Sayings of John ("Rabbi") Duncan.* 47.9 (1998) 221.
Horne, George. *Commentary on the Psalms.* 47.9 (1998) 222.
Stam, Clarence. *Celebrating Salvation.* 47.11 (1998) 266.
De Jong, D. *Praktisch perspectief. Zes vervolg-preken over Prediker.* 47.18 (1998) 437.
Ortlund, Raymond C. *Whoredom. God's Unfaithful Wife in Biblical Theology.* 47.18 (1998) 437.
Panflute and Organ. Audio recording. 48.24 (1999) 566.
Unto the Hills. A Collection of Psalms and Sacred Songs. Audio recording. 49.3 (2000) 65.
Van Rongen, G. *The Church: Its Unity in Confession and History.* 49.14 (2000) 320.
Boersema, John. *Political-Economic Activity to the Honour of God.* 49.20 (2000) 448.
Selles, L. *2 Corinthians in Fifteen Outlines.* 49.19 (2000) 426.
Van den Berg, C. *The Acts of the Apostles Vol. One.* 49.19 (2000) 426.
Van Wijk, P. C. *You . . . God's Child.* 49.19 (2000) 426.
Van Wijk, P. C. *You . . . His Guest.* 49.19 (2000) 426.
Bremmer, R. H. *Johannes G. Sikkel: A Pioneer in Social Reform.* 49.19 (2000) 426.
Green, William Henry. *Conflict and Triumph: The Argument of the Book of Job Unfolded.* 49.20 (2000) 449.

2001–2010

Oosterhoff, F. *Ideas have a History: Perspectives on the Western Search for Truth.* 50.17 (2001) 410–11.
Byl, John. *God and Cosmos: A Christian View of Time, Space and the Universe.* 51.18 (2002) 432–43.
Agema, D. G. J. *1 & 2 Timothy: A Study Guide.* 52.25 (2003) 608.
Bos, C. G. *Believe and Confess.* Vol. 1 52.25 (2003) 608.
Feenstra, Peter G. *You Only: A Popular Commentary and Study Guide on the Prophecy of Amos.* 54.18 (2005) 435.
Leishman, Rory. *Against Judicial Activism. The Decline of Freedom and Democracy in Canada.* 55.18 (2006) 439–42.

Pearcey, Nancy R. *Total Truth: Liberating Christianity from its Cultural Captivity (Study Guide Edition)*. 56.1 (2007) 15.
Kostenberger, Andreas, ed. *Whatever Happened to Truth?* 56.4 (2007) 88.
Farah, Joseph. *Stop the Presses! The Inside Story of the New Media Revolution.* 57.9 (2008) 223.
Farrow, Douglas. *Nation of Bastards: Essays on the End of Marriage.* 57.11 (2008) 284.
Shaidle, Kathy, and Peter Vere. *The Tyranny of Nice: How Canada Crushes Freedom in the Name of Human Rights.* 58.8 (2009) 193.
Pol, Andrew Jacob. *A Noble Task: The Work of Elders in the Canadian Reformed Churches.* 59.18 (2010) 473–74.

Scripture Index

OLD TESTAMENT

Genesis
1–2	142–43, 145–48
15:6	110–11
22	110–11

Exodus
19	28–31
20:4–6	13–25
20:22—23:33	1–3
21:6	3
21:12–14	10
21:23–25	8
21:29–30	9
22:8–9	3
22:10	4
24	31–34
32:32	127–28
34	35–38

Leviticus
20:1–5	20–21

Numbers
5:11–31	5

Deuteronomy
13	21–22
17:2–5	22

1 Samuel
15:2	15–16

2 Samuel
3:8	15

Psalms
1	48–53
57	57–74
69	128

Isaiah
40–48	208–10
40:6	208
42:1–4	208–9
42:19	209
48:16	206–8, 213–14
49–66	210–13

Jeremiah
2–3	78–79
2:27	79–81
3:4	91–82
3:19	82–86

Lamentations
4:22	16–18

Daniel
5	90–100
12	128

~

NEW TESTAMENT

Matthew
5:17–20	194–95

Luke
10:20   129

Acts
13:1–4   229

Romans
4   103

2 Corinthians
8:19   229

Philippians
4:3   128–29

Hebrews
12:24   129

James
2   103
2:24   110, 112

Revelation
5   117–33

Subject Index

Abraham, 110–13
adiaphora, 158
adoption, 84
adultery, 9, 85
affections, 44
allegory, 205–6
angel, 35
anger. *See* wrath.
Antiochus IV Epiphanes, 90–91
apologetics, 196
apostasy, 22–24
Aqedah, 111
Aquinas. *See* Thomas Aquinas.
Aramaic, 90, 92–93, 99
Aristotle, 142
Asherah, 79
astrology, 96–99
Athanasius, 42–43, 49, 53
Augsburg Interim, 153–59
Augustine, 43, 47–48, 50–51, 140, 143, 186
Augustus, Emperor, 122
authority, ecclesial, 173, 181, 188, 196, 223–24

Baal, 79
Babylon, 86, 94, 96, 98, 141, 211
Basil of Caesarea, 42, 46, 50, 52
Bavinck, Herman, 135–50
Belgic Confession, 111, 175, 191–94
Belshazzar, 91–93, 95–100
bishop, 170
blessing, 178, 181
blood, 32–33, 72–73, 125
body, 44–45
Book of Life, 117, 127–29, 132–33

book of the covenant, 1
brain, 203–4
Bullinger, Heinrich, 153, 155, 160, 162–66

Calvin, John, 140, 152–67, 171, 186, 193, 199–200
   Idelette (wife), 152, 165–67
Canadian Reformed Churches, 220–21, 227
Chaldeans, 97
Charles V, Emperor, 153–55
children, 13, 23–24
Christ, 86, 156–57, 161–62, 172, 190
   as priest, 124
   as the Lamb, 117, 123, 132–33
   fulfillment of the law, 189, 192–96, 201
   in the Psalms, 46–51, 54–55, 128
church fathers, 41–55, 205
church, local, 180, 221, 223–24, 226
church polity
   Dort, 169–70, 171–76, 180–82
   Reformed, 171
   Roman Catholic, 170
   two- or three-office view, 176, 180
   Westminster, 169–70, 179–80, 182
church, sending, 221, 229
commandment, second, 13, 18, 25
compassion, 82
concordism, 145
Consensus Tigurinus, 153–56, 159–64

Subject Index

Copernicus, Nicolaus, 143
courts, 3
covenant, 27–39, 83, 86
   conditions within, 28–29
   meal, 34
creatio ex nihilo, 138
creation, 135–50
   days of, 142–44, 147–48
   first and second, 142
   purpose of, 137–38
Cyrus the Great, 95–96, 207

Daniel, book of, 90–91, 100
Darius the Mede, 91, 100
Darwin, Charles, 145, 148–49
Darwin, George Howard, 143
deacon, 170, 172–74
demons, 129
desires, 44
divorce, 81
Doleantie, 222

earth, age of, 144–45
ecumenism, 154, 157, 167
elder, 1, 11, 34, 77, 169, 173–75, 177
'elohim, 3, 6, 62
ephod, 122
ethics, 185, 195
evidence, legal, 4
evolution, 148–49
exegesis, prosopological, 50–51
exile, 86

faith, 108–10, 112
family, 21, 24
Farel, Gillaume, 153
father, 78–81
final judgment, 127, 131
final testament, 130
flood, 148

geocentrism, 143
geology, 144–45
geometry, 205

Geschichte, 198
God the Father, 82–88
golden calf, 35–37, 127
Gregory of Nyssa, 42, 44, 52

Heidelberg Catechism, 111, 115, 172
Hellenism, 105–6
Hilary of Poitiers, 43, 48–49
Historie, 198
holiness, 30, 107
Holy Spirit, 213
husband, 81, 83, 85

idolatry, 20–22, 24–25, 36, 78, 79, 81
image of God, 149, 189
imprecatory psalm, 58
inheritance, 83–84, 130
instruction, 210

James, letter of
   authorship, 104
   date, 105–6
   relation to Paul, 103, 105–6, 114
Jeremiah, 78
Jerusalem, 78, 86, 129, 132
John of la Rochelle, 186
Judaism, 108
judge, 62, 77–78
judgments, 132–33
justice, 58, 63, 74, 94, 98, 208–9
justification, 103–4, 107–8, 110–12, 114, 157

kingdom of priests, 27–29
Kuyper, Abraham, 222–23, 230

law
   Old Testament, 185–96
   threefold division of, 185–88
lawlessness, 63
lex talionis, 7, 8, 10
Liberation of 1944, 225

Libra (constellation), 96–99
Lord, name of, 35
Lord's Supper, 153–55, 158–60, 162–66
Luther, Martin, 103, 114–15, 160

marriage, 81
materialism, 138–39
Melanchthon, Philip, 186
mene, 92–96
Michael, 128
microcosmos, 45
miktam, 61
minister of the Word, 174–75, 216
mission
    board of, 221
    deputies, 224–25, 231
    order, 224–25, 230–31
    work, 30, 201–2, 206, 200
Molech, 20–21, 23
Moses, 37–38, 127–28
murder, 10
music, 43–45

Nabonidus, 98, 100
Nebuchadnezzar, 91, 97
New Perspective on Paul, 108

oath, 4–6, 32
Oecumenius, 129–30
offerings. *See* sacrifices.
office bearer. *See* elder, deacon, minister of the Word.

pantheism, 138–39
parents, 13, 23–24
parsin, 92–96
pastor. *See* minister of the Word.
preaching, 181, 185, 189, 195–96, 200
    redemptive-historical, 198–99
priest, 30, 169, 170, 177
Psalms, the, 41–55
Ptolemy, 142

punishment, 13, 14, 18
reason, 44
redemption, 210
restitution, 7–11
retribution, 19, 24
righteousness, 107

sacrifice, 32–33, 87, 124, 131
sanctification, 104, 107, 110, 113–15
Schilder, Klaas, 226
Schmalkaldic League, 155
science. *See* Scripture and science.
scriptio continua, 92
Scripture
    and science, 145–47
    clarity of, 108
    inspiration of, 50
scroll, 118–19, 121–23, 131
seal, 118, 120–23, 125, 129, 131
Secession, 222
Septuagint, 57–74
servant of the Lord, 207, 213–14
Sinai, 27
singing, 43–45
soul, 44, 54–55
sprinkling, 34
stele, 61
Strasbourg, 171, 175
superscription, 59
synagogue, 173
synergism, 157

tekel, 92–96
Theodoret of Cyrus, 43, 53
Thomas Aquinas, 186
torah, 105, 187–88, 208
transubstantiation. *See* Lord's Supper.
Trinity, 137, 213
Turretin, Francis, 187
typology, 44

Van Dam, Cornelis, xi-xvi, 42, 57, 77, 90, 102–3, 117, 135–36, 152, 198, 220
vengeance, 73
violence, 64
Viret, Pierre, 152
virtue, 43–46, 52–53, 55
Voetius, Gisbertus, 222–23, 230

wife, 81, 83
works, pre- and post-conversion, 109–10, 114
worldview, 138–40, 202
worship, 157–58, 162
wrath, 65, 70–71, 82

Zanchius, Jerome, 140
Zion. *See* Jerusalem.
Zürich, 153, 160, 162

www.ingramcontent.com/pod-product-compliance
Lightning Source LLC
Chambersburg PA
CBHW071245230426
43668CB00011B/1599